REDRAWING **DUBLIN**

REDRAWING DUBLIN

Paul Kearns | Motti Ruimy

Gandon Editions Kinsale

REDRAWING DUBLIN by Paul Kearns + Motti Ruimy

Published by Gandon Editions Kinsale, the specialist producer and publisher of books on Irish art + architecture.

ISBN 978 0948037 801

illustrations	all photography, graphics, maps and conceptual imagery are the original artwork of Paul Kearns and Motti Ruimy
	– base maps courtesy of Dublin City Council
	– statistics courtesy of the Central Statistics Offfice
	– additional illus courtesy of the architects whose projects are featured on pp68-69 and pp265-277, and to HKR for pp224, 234
production	produced by Gandon Editions Kinsale (John O'Regan, Nicola Dearey, Gunther Berkus)
printing	Nicholson & Bass, Belfast
distribution	distributed by Gandon and its overseas agents

GANDON EDITIONS, Oysterhaven, Kinsale, Co Cork
T +353 (0)21-4770830 / F +353 (0)21-4770755 / E gandon@eircom.net
W www.gandon-editions.com / W www.gandon.co

Gandon Editions is grant-aided by The Arts Council / An Chomhairle Ealaíon

This is the 353rd book on Irish art + architecture produced by Gandon Editions. Visit our website, or see our colour catalogue for information on 200+ titles in print.

GANDON
www.gandon.co

The authors

MOTTI RUIMY was born in Petah Tikva, Israel, in 1975. He studied architecture at Bezalel Academy of Art & Design, Jerusalem, graduating in 2007. He had previously studied fine art at Bezalel Academy, graduating in 2000. He moved to Dublin in 2000, and has since lived between Dublin, Tel Aviv and Jerusalem. He worked for Scott Tallon Walker Architects in Dublin from 2008 to 2010, and is currently working with Amos Brandeis – Architecture, Urban & Regional Planning in Hod HaSharon, Israel.

PAUL KEARNS was born in Ballyfermot, Dublin, in 1966. He graduated from University College Dublin with a BA in Economics and Geography in 1988 and a Masters in Urban Planning in 1990. He worked in the European Commission in Brussels and with Dun Laoghaire Rathdown County Council before joining Dublin City Council Planning Department in 1997. Between 2002 and 2004 he worked in Jerusalem as a freelance Israeli-Palestinian correspondent for the *Sunday Tribune*. He is currently working as a Senior Planner with Dublin City Council.

Acknowledgements

The authors would like to thank the following: Bertie Ahern, Sevit Aka, Mayan Amir, Ido Bar-El, Amos Brandeis, Liam Carroll, Eoin Collins, Jamie Cudden, Ciaran Cuffe, Bernadette Dawson, Nicola Dearey, Angela Delaney, Yvonne Farrell, Dick Gleeson, Zvi Golstein, John Graby, Ali Grehan, Nili Renana Harag, Philip Jackson, Olesh Kaye, Carol Kearns, Stella Kearns, Paul Keogh, Jim Keoghan, Kineret Levy, Frank McDonald, John Martin, Alan Mee, Paul O'Connell, Dr Sandra O'Connell, John O'Regan, Ayala Ronel, Kieran Rose, Sharon Rotbard, Etti Ruimy, Tali Sagi, Ruti Sela, Michael Stubbs, Dr Ronald Tallon, Leonardo Fionn Tavernaro, Nahom Tevet, John Tierney, Michael Wall, Mick Wallace, Natalie Weadick, Ruth Zrihen

Contents

Detailed Contents

Sponsors

Gandon Editions and the authors gratefully acknowledge the support of the following institutions, companies and individuals who made the publication of this book possible.

The Arts Council / An Chomhairle Ealaíon
The British Council (Open Cities Programme)
CB Richard Ellis
The Convention Centre Dublin
Henry A Crosbie Property
Stewart Harrington
Davy Hickey Properties

Department of Environment, Heritage
   and Local Government
   (Government Policy on Architecture,
   2009-2015)
The Digital Hub
Dublin City Business Association
Dublin City BID
Dublin City Council
ILAC Shopping Centre
Linders of Smithfield
MCO Projects
Kieran Rose

The Royal Institute of the Architects of Ireland
Senator Fergal Quinn
Scott Tallon Walker Architects
Stephen's Green Shopping Centre
Sudway & Company, Chartered Surveyors
Temple Bar Cultural Trust
Urban Capital
Wallace Group
+ additional anonymous sponsors

To our parents, William and (the late) Bridget Kearns, Yacob and Yehoudit Ruimy,
for all their years of support and encouragement.

Foreword

Our motivations to 'write' this book were many and varied. REDRAWING DUBLIN has been driven and inspired as much by a fascination and love of cities as it has by the very personal and many exciting city experiences. Being an architect and an urban planner, perhaps our combined 'academic' background in geography, economics and fine art proved irresistible and fertile ground to be inspired to take on an entire city and tell its story. Whichever came first, a passion for city-living or training in city-making, whatever drove us to tell the story of Dublin, this is our story of this city.

REDRAWING DUBLIN is our fourth collaborative visual urban project. In *Urban Urinal* (2002) and *Vortex* (2002) we explored, through the medium of photography and temporary installations, the nature of 'hidden' but disappearing social spaces in Dublin city. In *Wall* (2005) we journeyed and documented, over an eighteen-month period, the impact of the Israeli separation barrier on the urban landscape of Jerusalem, Bethlehem and Qalkiliya.

In REDRAWING DUBLIN we endeavour to deconstruct the urban psyche of an entire city. Our storytelling is the culmination of a four-year journey, a journey of local experiences and distant travelling. It's born from an intimate knowledge of how Dublin city works and an acute observation of where and when it doesn't, offering parcelled recipes for how it should. Most of all, in a collection of playful images and thoughtful, sometimes provocative essays, we call it as it is.

PAUL KEARNS AND MOTTI RUIMY
November 2010

---

opposite – LOLLIPOP DUBLIN is a playful pictorial representation of overlapping identities and influences, both urban and rural, that have shaped Dublin city. This is a suburban city in transition between a Georgian, British or Anglo-Irish and decidedly recent urban past, and a possible future post-European international cosmopolitan city with a thoroughly metropolitan future. Dublin, located at the geographical epicentre of these islands, is at the crossroads of its urban history, looking back and looking forward. All the flavours are there.

Introduction

REDRAWING DUBLIN is a story of a city. It is a celebration and affirmation of a city and the people who live there. It is design-driven to creatively inform and stimulate. REDRAWING DUBLIN is about city-making. It draws possibilities, draws thinking and draws space. It is both a visual essay and an act of 'action urbanism'.

REDRAWING DUBLIN captures a snapshot of Dublin today, reveals glimpses of recent memory and imagines alternative possible futures. This is an urban and suburban journey that walks the streets of Dublin, explores local neighbourhoods and maps the wider city metropolitan region. It opens the door to existing buildings and buildings that never happened, investigates abandoned spaces and the people who inhabited them, aborted skylines and the language that tried to make them happen.

Why Dublin? Because the authors, Motti Ruimy and Paul Kearns, an architect and an urban planner, currently live and work there. It could, however, be the story of any city. The questions posed, the imagery employed, and the subject matter dissected, with few exceptions, are common to most cities. Cities that are obviously visibly different often mask remarkably similar but invisible tensions. Cities are full of hidden facts, surprising statistics, unspoken truths and delightful private experiences.

All cities are full of hidden facts, surprising statistics, unspoken truths and delightful private experiences. This book leans substantially on personal experiences, blending them with visual imagery, photography and imaginary places. It borrows and recycles to so that it can inform, entertain and hopefully provoke a meaningful debate about the future of Dublin.

Popularising ideas, information and imagery is critically important in democratising access to this city debate, a debate that has, perhaps, for too long been the preserve of a small group of professionals or experts in the field of urbanism. Architects, planners and urban designers are no different from everybody else. They, like everybody else, come to any subject with unspoken prejudices and assumptions, vision and hopes. This is not a criticism, but simply an observation, a truism of any human endeavour. The future of this city, the complexity of the challenges and opportunities it faces, are too important and too exciting to be left to the professionals in architecture, urban design and planning to theorise or strategise behind closed doors. There is an urgent need now more than ever to broaden the discussion about the future direction of Dublin city and the future of the people who choose either to live there, who might wish to come or who may wish to leave.

In this discussion and debate, REDRAWING DUBLIN unapologetically promotes real urbanism, celebrates diversity and champions city-living. The book has a passion for facts and honesty.

The ability to see things afresh, to debunk your own as well as others' assumptions, to challenge previously strongly held notions is important in city-making. Confounding oneself is an important and creative exercise, and arguably a more important one than trading in new learned facts or urban linguistic jargon.

The book explores the city's urban psyche and identity, prods and probes suburban assumptions and urban prejudices. It challenges policy-makers and citizens to confront Dublin's urban contradictions, to see and tell it as it is, not as it is imagined or often believed to be. This is a story that asks uncomfortable questions but offers hopeful solutions. A strong theme in the book is the inherent tensions between urban and suburban Dublin. Where does the city begin and end? Is Dublin really a Georgian city or a city of two-storey housing? What is the difference between the city centre and the inner city, and why is it desirable to live in one but not the other?

At its simplest, the book endeavours to paint an honest picture of a city. Envisioning and creative picturing is a simple and powerful tool. Delightful or provocative imagery has the capacity to stretch the imagination and broaden understanding. Visualisation also demystifies the language employed by architects and planners, a language often invoked to mystify or obscure a subject for others. Great ideas can usually be described or pictured simply. Nonsense, on the other hand, can be, and very often is, indescribably difficult to understand but can be shamelessly and beautifully articulated.

Insightful language, received wisdoms and fashionable academic theory are often necessary, sometimes interesting and occasionally fun. They are, however, no substitute for the enquiring and curious mind that paves the way and opens the door to the diversity, energy and contradictions of the personal experience of living in the city.

REDRAWING DUBLIN believes that anyone who actually lives in a city is an 'urbanist'. Those who live at its heart are very often the most acute observers of the simple things that make their city, their neighbourhood and their street work or not. It may seem innocuous, indeed obvious, to some, yet curiously will prove provocative or challenging for others, but we believe to be a true 'urbanist' – loosely defined as 'having a real affection for and an understanding of urbanism' – one actually must experience a sustained period of urban living.

Finally, one doesn't have to know Dublin particularly well to enjoy this book. One doesn't even have to have visited the city. The story of REDRAWING DUBLIN is universal, its urban images everyday.

PAUL KEARNS AND MOTTI RUIMY
November 2010

What is a city eclipse? Have you ever seen one? What is an exurb county and who lives there? Where are the Dub-urbs? How does gentrivilification affect urban regeneration? Where is the Arc of Disadvantage and why is it so important to Dublin's future? What is nano-apartment architecture? Are you a touring urbanist or an urban tourist? What is the planning eruv? Is eruv urb legal? What are the seven deadly risks to regeneration? How do you recognise the phoney urbanist? Is Dublin a tidal city or a living city? Are you loco green or urban clever? Who travels where in Metrobusland? Where is Metropolia and who lives in Celtic Tiger Metropolitan? How can you act-in the city to improve your neighbourhood? Is Dublin a SUPERCITY? Would you walk the Guinness draft? Do you live near the geography of cool? What is post-zonism? Do you understand your street DNA? What are urban blind spots and why are they so invisible?

Is BUILDN DUBLIN an anagram or an insight? Can the OPW become open parks working? Can Dublin become a human entrepot? Does Dublin have an urban stroll? Who is a sub-urbanist? And does it matter? Why texting 'splash' can clean your city? What's the state of Dublin's North West Bank? Do you metro walk? What is the regeneration paradox? Are you ready to take the '10 minutes away' test? How big is Planet Dublin? How many times a week do you take a SparTrek journey? Where is the geography of the Historical Archipelago and the Georgian Islands? Are you an urbino? Urban In Name Only.? Have you seen inside the urban urinal? Why it's difficult to sit down in bumparks? Is this a toy town of Noddy corners? Who are the moral guardians of the aborted skylines? Are you a groupie of the SuperGrouper? Perhaps you are a member? Where is the ledge city? Do you live in the Arc of Low Expectation?

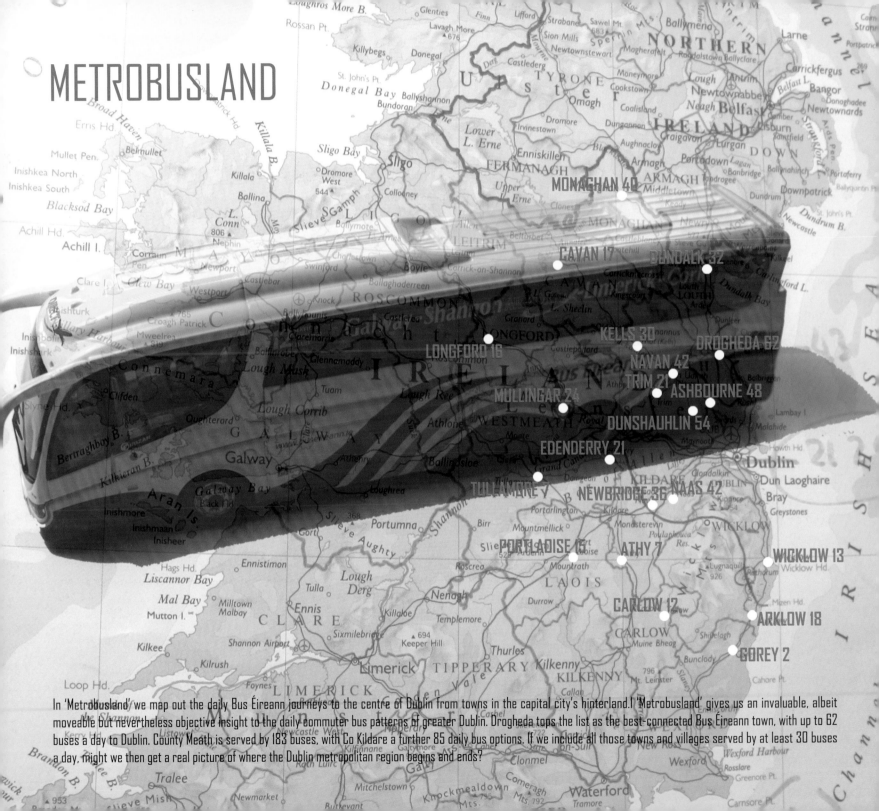

METROBUSLAND

MONAGHAN 40

CAVAN 17 DUNDALK 32

KELLS 30 DROGHEDA 62

LONGFORD 18 NAVAN 42

TRIM 21 ASHBOURNE 48

MULLINGAR 24 DUNSHAUHLIN 54

EDENDERRY 21

TULLAMORE 7 NEWBRIDGE 36 NAAS 42

PORTLAOISE 15 ATHY 7 WICKLOW 13

CARLOW 12 ARKLOW 18

GOREY 2

In 'Metrobusland' we map out the daily Bus Éireann journeys to the centre of Dublin from towns in the capital city's hinterland. 'Metrobusland' gives us an invaluable, albeit moveable but nevertheless objective insight to the daily commuter bus patterns of greater Dublin. Drogheda tops the list as the best-connected Bus Éireann town, with up to 62 buses a day to Dublin. County Meath is served by 183 buses, with Co Kildare a further 85 daily bus options. If we include all those towns and villages served by at least 30 buses a day, might we then get a real picture of where the Dublin metropolitan region begins and ends?

Beyond the Pale

In search of Metropolitan Dublin

It's a superficially simple question but a notoriously difficult and challenging one to answer for any city. Where does your city really begin and end? Where are its borders? How many people actually live there? In endeavouring to determine the extent of the Dublin metropolitan region we do not seek to map out or unearth some artificial administrative, historic or municipal boundary. We instead try to discover that real but elusive boundary where the 'real city' begins to fizzle away, to spatially scatter, where competing images of green fields bleed into single-storey factories, out-of-town shopping centres and spanking new office parks, all connected and disconnected by an ever-changing, bewildering and exciting network of motorways and flyovers. It's confusing, it's mutating. It is, however, in the case of Dublin, home to hundreds of thousands of people. Urbanists have fashionably termed it 'edge city' or the 'exurbs'. The 'exurbs' theoretically exist on the fringes of the suburbs; in reality they spatially blend together and are often physically and socially indistinguishable. To exclude the 'exurbs' or edge city from any definition of 'the city' invariably presents an incomplete picture, an artificial understanding of the realities of both the local suburban geography and the regional urban economy.

In ROUTE 66 we took the 1 hour 35 minute Dublin Bus journey westwards from the centre of Dublin city to the commuter town of Maynooth in the 'exurb' county of Kildare. From the front row on the upper deck of route 66 it is possible to capture perfectly the seemingly seamless urban-suburban 'exurb' landscape. This is a metropolitan landscape that extends from College Green to the green fields of Kildare and beyond. Defining the exact boundary of that metropolitan landscape is in many ways academically subjective and geographically meaningless, yet nevertheless is politically critically important. What gets measured gets valued. Define your metropolitan boundary and you define the parameters for calculating everything from its population and its density to its wealth and potential tax base or subsidy.

So where or what is Metropolitan Dublin? Who actually lives there? Where does it begin and end? In our search we have somewhat dispensed with conventional academic analysis in the hope of discovering unexplored geographies and as yet undiscovered worlds. An initial Google search of the term 'Metropolitan Dublin' led to a spatial cul-de-sac. The first three Google hits included a pub, a club and the Catholic archdiocese of Dublin. Interestingly, the latter, the Catholic archdiocese of Dublin, excludes the eastern fringes of Meath just across the Dublin border, but extends as far south as Co Wexford.

If Metropolitan Dublin is difficult to locate, perhaps the Dublin Regional Authority (DRA)[1], its somewhat politically toothless cousin, will throw some light as to where the Dublin urban area really extends. The DRA comprises the four municipal authorities of Dublin – Dublin City Council, Fingal County Council, Dun Laoghaire-Rathdown County Council and South Dublin County Council. The headquarters or administrative capital of the DRA has been 'decentralised' to Swords off the M50 Motorway, a convenient and, perhaps, fitting location for the predominantly suburban car-dependent citizens of the DRA.

Somehow the DRA doesn't quite fit the picture or tell the whole story. The three surrounding counties of Wicklow, Meath and Kildare are all intrinsically and functionally connected to Metropolitan Dublin. A significant number of residents from these counties commute daily to Dublin city. These three commuter counties have their own administrative authority: this is the half-doughnut-shaped and functionally disconnected Mid-East Regional Authority or MERA. The capital of metropolitan MERA is located, relative to the rest of the citizens of MERA, in the very inaccessible Wicklow town. To confuse matters more, the Regional Planning Guidelines for the Greater Dublin Area, 2004-2016 comprise all the Dublin local authorities of the DRA and the three surrounding counties of MERA. Might this be the Dublin Metropolitan Region?

We're not convinced. Administrative or bureaucratically defined boundaries are just that – administrative and bureaucratic. Historic county boundaries, being historic, are anachronistic and all too simplistic. In search of an alternative metropolitan region or new ways of looking at greater Dublin, we have created METROBUSLAND, METROPOLIA and CONTIGUOUS METROPOLITAN.

Route 66

go WEST young Dubliners

Western Frontier or Edge City ?

From Dublin city centre to exurb Co Kildare is a 1 hour, 35 minute bus ride westwards into the suburban, 'exurban' and edge city of the capital on route 66, courtesy of Dublin Bus. Route 66 leaves the city daily, approximately every 34 minutes, from 6.50am till 11.40pm. Overnight stays optional.

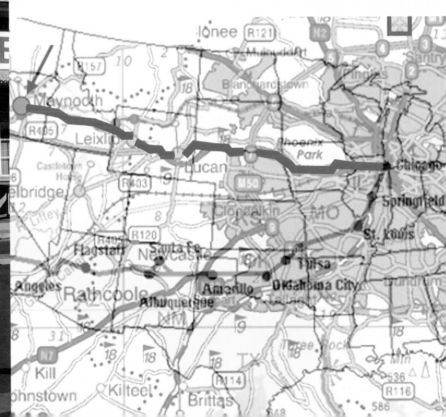

METROPOLIA

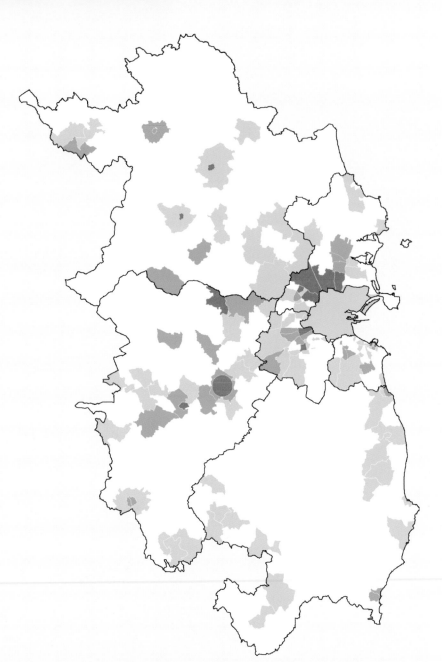

Population densities, commuting patterns, housing typologies tell an important metropolitan story; they give us clues as what type of 'city' we live in. They do, of course, paint a particular picture. How we live, shop and socialise, who our friends are, where they are from, what we do at weekends, where we go – if anywhere at all – on Sunday afternoons probably reveal much more about what type of city we really live in.

The presence and acceptance of new communities of foreign nationals, immigrants – the so-called 'new Irish' – has transformed the Dublin metropolitan region over the past decade. It informs and colours our lives and our city. Whether at work, at the supermarket, the petrol station, a café or post office, we encounter daily the smiles or the conversation of a foreign-born national. They are part of what we do, who we are. They are our neighbours, our friends, acquaintances and much more. In METROPOLIA we endeavour to capture a flavour of this multi-cultural landscape by mapping the density of the largest immigrant community – Polish nationals – across the entire eastern region.

So where have they chosen to live? The availability of affordable homes and decent well-paid jobs are presumably important determining factors in where Polish immigrants have chosen to live. The spatial patterns of METROPOLIA are remarkably similar to that of CELTIC TIGER METROPOLITAN which maps out the geography and density of new homes built during the Celtic Tiger boom between 1991 and 2006.

In 2006 it was estimated that one in 65 people living in Ireland was born in Poland. That rose to one in 45 in Dublin city. In the town of Naas, one in 14 of the residents was Polish. In parts of Dublin's North Inner City that figure rose to one in eight.[1] With the onset of acute economic contraction in late 2007, these numbers have substantially fallen. The census of 2006 perhaps represents the high-tide watermark for 'Celtic Tiger' immigration.

Poles per sq km

- ≥ 8%
- ≥ 4%   < 8%
- ≥ 2%   < 4%
- < 2%

source: Census of Ireland 2006

METROPOLITAN DENSITY

people per sq km

≥ 10,000

≥ 7,500 < 10,000

≥ 5,000 < 7,500

≥ 2,500 < 5,000

≥ 1,500 < 2,500

≥ 200 < 1,500

< 200

source: Census of Ireland 2006

CONTIGUOUS METROPOLITAN

people per sq km

≥ 10,000

≥ 7,500   < 10,000

≥ 5,000   < 7,500

≥ 2,500   < 5,000

≥ 1,500   < 2,500

≥ 200   < 1,500

< 200

source: Census of Ireland 2006

Contiguous Metropolitan

In CONTIGUOUS METROPOLITAN we have mapped out those areas in the greater Dublin region that have a minimum population density of 200 people per square kilometre, and also form a contiguous belt of density radiating out from the heart of the capital city.[1] Might this be metropolitan Dublin? Contiguous Metropolitan includes the northern suburban fringes of Co Kildare. This includes an unbroken finger of 'exurban' communities of towns and housing estates stretching from Leixlip to Celbridge and Maynooth, but excludes the 'island' towns of Naas or Newbridge, the latter better described as Dublin orbital suburban commuter satellites. Similarly, the towns of Arklow to the south, in Co Wicklow, and Skerries to the north, in Fingal, reside outside our metropolitan region. These dormitory towns, home to thousands of 'Dublin' commuters, are reasonably densely populated but are disconnected from the city proper either by green fields or low-density industrial estates.[2] In our Contiguous Metropolitan region they exist psychologically independent, just beyond its grip, definition or interest.

Contiguous Metropolitan captures the extent to which 'Dublin' expanded into neighbouring Meath, Wicklow and Kildare during the Celtic Tiger building boom period. It now extends as far south as Kilcoole in Co Wicklow, some 35km from the centre of the city. Those parts of the 'exurb' counties of Kildare, Wicklow, Meath and Fingal that form part of our new Contiguous Metropolitan area make up 59.7% of its land area and 25.8% of its population.[3] The geographical area of Dublin City Council, on the other hand, accommodates over 40% of the population of Contiguous Metropolitan, and occupies just 14% of its total land area.[4] Our Contiguous Metropolitan Dublin has a population of just over 1.25 million people. Its land area is marginally smaller and its population is marginally greater than Co Dublin itself (797km² and 1.25 million people, versus 921km² and 1.19 million). Our metropolitan region thus has a population density of 1,563 people per km² compared to 1,292 per km² for Dublin county.

So, having defined a version of our extended city, its boundary and its population, how does it compare to other great metropolitan cities globally? Interestingly, Contiguous Metropolitan Dublin has a similar area to New York City. The five New York boroughs (790km²) are, however, home to 8.3 million people, thus generating a population density of 10,630 people per km².[5] Greater Los Angeles, with a geographic area some 5.4 times greater than Contiguous Metropolitan (4,300km²), manages to accommodate a population 9.4 times greater (11.7 million), generating a population or urban density twice that of our metropolitan Dublin (2,750 per km²).[6] It's difficult not to conclude that the Irish east coast Celtic Tiger building boom has generated or outdone an American-style west coast 'CO2' settlement bust – a low-density, car-dependent metropolitan regional sprawl.

Might it have been done any differently? What went wrong? Are there any lessons to be learned? Was it the result of over-zealous land rezonings, weak regional planning structures, inept local planning, or does it reflect something much deeper – an Irish love of the front and back garden, a distaste or disinterest for apartment dwellings, and a subconscious distrust of city living?

CELTIC TIGER METROPOLITAN

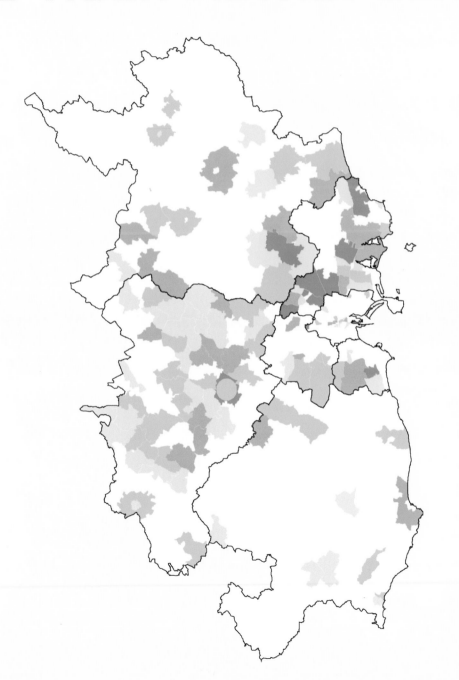

Celtic Tiger homes as a
percentage of all homes
(Celtic Tiger homes
= homes built 1991–2006)

≥ 70	
≥ 60 < 70	
≥ 50 < 60	
≥ 40 <50	
<40	

source: Census of Ireland 2006

METROVILLAGE

... close to or in existing towns and major villages?

Would life in these towns have been more vibrant?

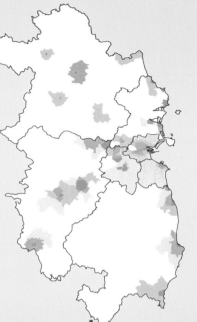

RAILWAYMETRO

... close to existing railway stations?

Would the environmental benefits have been significant?

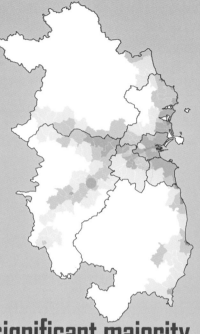

What would the metropolitan region have looked like if a significant majority of the new Celtic Tiger homes had been built ...

... in the heart of Dublin?

Would the city have been more dynamic?

METROURBAN

... along the eastern coastline?

Would people's quality of life have been better?

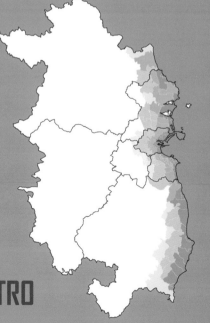

EASTCOASTALMETRO

27

How the East was Done?

The Celtic Tiger boom period (1991-2006) unlocked or unleashed (depending on one's perspective) an unprecedented transformation of the urban and suburban landscape of the greater metropolitan Dublin region. Some 185,000 new homes were built in the Eastern Region (the four local authorities of Dublin, and the counties of Wicklow, Meath and Kildare) during this fifteen-year period.[1] That constituted a staggering 47% increase in the number of homes built since 1990. Put another way, by 2006 one in three (32%) of all existing homes to be found in the counties of Dublin, Wicklow, Kildare and Meath had been constructed during this relatively short boom period.

The 'exurb' local authority areas all experienced more than a 90% increase in new homes built.[2] By 2006 almost half of all homes across these counties was a 'Celtic Tiger home'. Few of these 'exurb' homes were built in high-density consolidated village or town centre developments. By 2006, some 40% of all homes in Kildare and 55% of all homes in Meath were detached. Less than 5% of Dublin city homes are detached.[3] By 2006, in part because of the consolidation of high-density apartment building in Dublin city centre, almost one in four homes in the Dublin City Council area were purpose-built apartments or flats. This figure falls to 12.5% in Dun Laoghaire-Rathdown and 11.7% in Fingal.[4] Just 5.7% and 4.3% of all households in Kildare and Meath reside in purpose-built apartments.[5]

The counties of Kildare, Meath and Wicklow have firmly established themselves as the lands of detached houses, with almost half (47.5%) of all homes standing proudly alone. A further third (32%) of all homes are semi-detached. Just one in nine homes (11%) are terraced. Dun Laoghaire-Rathdown, Fingal and South Dublin, on the other hand, are the lands of the semi-detached house (47.7%); 17.7% of homes are detached, and a fifth of homes (20.8%) form part of a terrace. Dublin City Council is the only metropolitan authority area where a plurality of all homes are terraced (37%). In fact, less than 30% of all homes in the Dublin City Council area are detached or semi-detached, compared to more than 80% in Meath and Kildare.[7]

The environmental sustainability of these new low-density and largely detached 'exurb' homes is partially dependent upon the extent to which their residents are reliant on the private car (low-density public transport is, however, also environmentally unsustainable, and costly). The willingness to fairly 'economically price' and thus pay for this lifestyle through appropriate carbon-tax measures is also an important factor in determining their overall sustainability. 'exurban' Kildare, Meath, Wicklow and Fingal are all likely to fare poorly relative to city-centre Dublin on all these sustainable criteria. It is undeniable that the extent both geographically and quantitatively of the spread of 'exurban suburban' metropolitan Dublin represents significant environmental challenges for 'Dublin's' future.

City Expansion or City Eclipse?

The rise and sprawl of the population of the 'exurb' counties

In 1991, on the cusp of the Celtic Tiger boom, the city of Dublin, as defined by the functional boundary of Dublin City Council (then Dublin Corporation), had a population almost exactly equal to that of the combined surrounding 'exurban' counties of Wicklow, Meath, Kildare and Fingal County Council (then part of Dublin City Council), some 478,000 people each.[1] By 1996 that balance had begun to shift, with Dublin city registering a negligible rise of just 7,000, or a 1.5% increase. The 'exurb counties' on the other hand absorbed a 7% increase in their population.[2] By 2002 the divergence in population increase had begun to accelerate. Dublin once again witnessed a marginal increase (2.1%), with the city's population hitting 495,000. The 'exurb' counties over the same period saw their populations soar by 18.5%. Co Meath 'experienced' the largest increase at 23%.[3]

By 2006 the population of the 'exurb' counties had reached 715,000, a

17% increase on 2002. The population of the city of Dublin rose by a modest 11,000 to reach 506,000.[4] Between 1991 and 2006 – in effect, the Celtic Tiger boom years – the combined population of the 'exurban' counties had increased by 49%, with Fingal alone adding an additional 87,000 people (57% increase). Over the same period, the population of Dublin city increased by just 5%. This small increase masked considerable local variations, with the inner city witnessing a significant gain in population and older established suburbs a continuing loss.[5]

Has the star pulling power of Dublin city now being eclipsed by an 'exurban' rewriting of the urban and suburban geography of the metropolitan region? In just fifteen years, 'Dublin city' has shrunk from a level of parity to just 71% the size of its orbital exurban satellite counties. Was the City Eclipse inevitable? We believe not.

Dublin city, despite considerable popular perceptions to the contrary, is capable of accommodating a far greater increase in its population. Dublin City Council estimates that there is approximately 480 hectares of zoned land in the city that could be developed for residential use.[6] This calculation excludes vast industrial lands at Dublin port, and extensive areas of underperforming or derelict sites in its 'Arc of Disadvantage' in Dublin 1, 7 and 8. Even this conservative estimate, with densities of 100 residential units to the hectare and occupancy rates comparable to the rest of Dublin (currently 2.65 persons per dwelling), would potentially add a further 127,000 people to the city.[7] A more ambitious sustainable urban settlement policy might see three times that area (1,200 hectares) come into play.[8] Higher densities (140 homes per hectare) would potentially generate space for an additional 445,000 people.[9]

Despite a net outflow in population since late 2007, and substantial net emigration accelerating in 2008 and 2009, the ESRI predicted as recently as late 2009 that the overall population of Ireland would increase by 860,000 over the next decade.[10] Might doubling Dublin over the next twenty years prove to be a sustainable, ecologically friendly urban alternative solution to continued exurban sprawl? Can we reverse the City Eclipse now that the Celtic Tiger construction boom has elapsed?

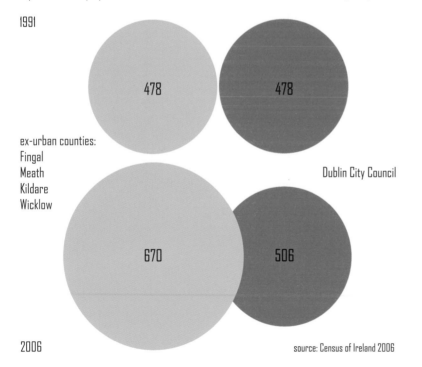

1991

ex-urban counties:
Fingal
Meath
Kildare
Wicklow

Dublin City Council

478   478

670   506

2006

source: Census of Ireland 2006

METROGRAPHIC 2006

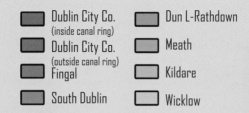
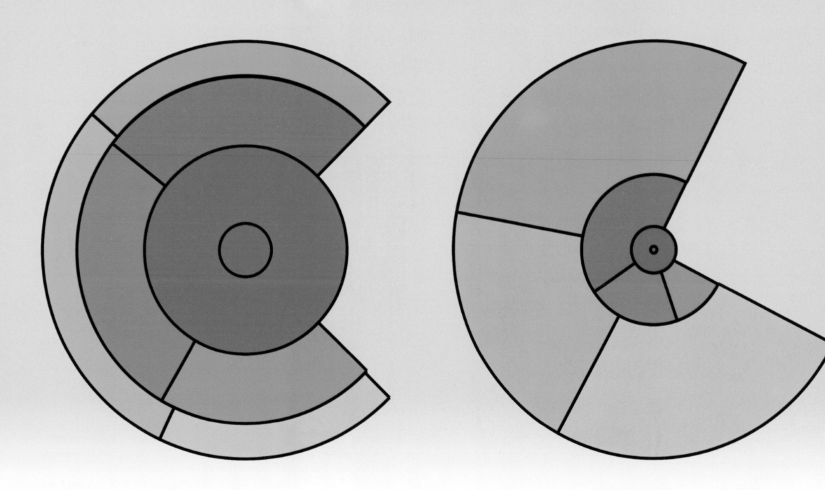

POPULATION

LAND AREA

Mapping Difference

Invisible Walls

fusing the past and the present

In INVISIBLE WALLS we playfully recreate the invisible walls from Dublin's past. Reconstructing an imaginary and magical historic city wall allows us to share with the citizen of today a now almost invisible urban history. This imaginary living history has recently come to life in Dublin's city's Wood Quay Venue exhibition space, where an unearthed and exposed part of the old medieval city wall is now visible. If invisible walls of history are hard to imagine, today's real social barriers are often harder to see.

Our urban ARC OF DISADVANTAGE is delineated by an imaginary wall or border representing real social divisions and psychological barriers. We have borrowed and temporarily reconstructed, somewhat provocatively, the Israeli separation barrier as our imaginary wall of social division. These imaginary walls, we believe, do not just simply reflect social or economic barriers of disadvantage, but a wider prejudice of the value or ambition of urban living in Dublin itself. Such walls may be higher and thicker than most people dare imagine or wish to believe.

The Arc of Disadvantage or Arc of Opportunity?

Dublin's 'Arc of Disadvantage' is a real place with flexible and moveable boundaries. It is currently home to 43,000 people, but could, if boldly re-imagined, be home to 40,000 more.[1]

The Arc of Disadvantage is also an imaginary space or a state of mind. While its geography is fixed, its boundaries and character are fluid, expanding and contracting to the alternatively pulsating beat of struggling ambition and jaded underperforming prejudice. The Arc of Disadvantage is located at the heart of Dublin's inner city, but occupies only a small proportion of Dublin city centre.[2] The Arc of Disadvantage is, if nothing else, entirely urban. It accommodates some of the poorest social housing flat complexes in the State, and is dotted with some of the worst-designed new apartment blocks in the city.

The Arc of Disadvantage is essentially an underperforming land bank. It is pocked with dozens of derelict sites. Despite its centrality, it remains somewhat disconnected, generally served by poor public domain, and criss-crossed by busy roads. It is fractured and edgy, home to too many broken streets and marred by common acts of anti-social behaviour. You are less likely to own your own home in the Arc of Disadvantage than in the rest of the city, and if you do, your home is likely to be smaller.[3] Small and ill-configured one-bedroom apartments dominate the housing profile of the area.[4]

The Arc of Disadvantage has less publicly accessible open green space and fewer tree-lined streets than either the rest of the city centre or the majority of the city's suburbs,[5] and, despite an unprecedented fifteen-year building boom, remains a challenging urban place to live.

Much has been written about the level of social deprivation in the Arc of Disadvantage or Dublin's inner city, the percentage of residents who are long-term unemployed, the proportion of lone teenage parents and early school-leavers. All are generally accepted as critical indices of social disadvantage. Few studies, however, of social disadvantage in Dublin's inner city discuss, let alone attempt to measure, indices of environmental deprivation or disadvantage. Issues as diverse and important as the size, design or the quality of homes, the cleanliness of streets, the density of trees and clean local parks are, for the most part, noticeably absent from an analysis of social disadvantage.

There are, perhaps, many possible reasons for this. Firstly, what gets measured gets valued, and vice versa. One reason why environmental measures of disadvantage are underplayed is that it is hard to measure or benchmark the visual performance of a neighbourhood. It is not easy to objectively evaluate the quality of neighbourhood architecture, to quantify whether public spaces are safe or well designed, or to measure the extent and impact of anti-social behaviour in public spaces.

True, these indices are harder to quantify than a desktop analysis of local unemployment rates, harder but not particularly hard. The lack of environmental data may also reflect a prejudice that these issues don't really matter to the lives of poorer people, or that somehow they are seen as a luxury or peripheral to more pressing and immediate concerns. It is, however, a prejudice that we imagine is not shared by poorer citizens in more disadvantaged parts of the city. Few of these residents are unlikely to be of the opinion that clean or safe streets, tree-lined pavements, well-designed public spaces, playgrounds and safe parks are somehow 'middle class' preoccupations. Perhaps the lack of academic or political interest in quantifying data in this field reflects another kind of prejudice, a kind of bigotry of low expectation for the areas themselves – in effect, a bigotry of place. Despite the often fawning flattery of local character, these areas were always poor and unattractive places to live and thus will remain so.

That lack of interest in quality of life or city-living environmental issues may also reveal an underlying anti-urban bias, a bias that fails to comprehend the challenge and importance of these issues in the making of successful high-density residential neighbourhoods. This is all the more peculiar in that urban 'benchmarking' is currently in vogue across a wide variety of social, economic and spatial-design professions. The Arc of Disadvantage is, after all, fundamentally urban. As an extensive residential urban area it is also diverse. It is not surprising that if indices of urban environmental disadvantage are underplayed, other measures of urban complexity are often misunderstood.

The Arc of Disadvantage is, after all, not a self-contained homogeneous community. Its challenges and opportunities are urban not suburban. It has a social structure and tenure typology that conventional suburbia struggles to understand. The high percentage of residents who rent as opposed to own their homes presents its own challenges, perhaps not the ones often imagined. Many of these people are foreign-born, many others are Irish who, for whatever reason, have decided to live in the city centre and choose to rent, not to buy. A significant proportion of both tend to have short-term leases. This is an unremarkable characteristic of residential living in urban areas.

In Dublin, however, renting is viewed through the prism of the Irish fixation with home-ownership. Those who rent are frequently and somewhat disparagingly called 'transient'. They are commonly faulted for having very weak connections to either the long-term existing residents and or the history of the local area. What is often misunderstood is that these so-called 'transients' often have a complex and engaging relationship with the city. They choose to be urban. They are also the first to choose to leave if local urban life and opportunity disappoints.

If these heterogeneous urban dwellers don't complain as loudly as their suburban cousins about dereliction, street cleaning or the lack of tree-lined streets, it is not because they are not interested, it is because they just don't see their relationship to City Hall and the city in quite the same way. They simply expect problems to be addressed, services to be delivered. As residents of a dense inner-urban neighbourhood, they don't view it as their role as individuals to remind the city of its job.

Environmental indices may also be underplayed for a variety of other reasons. There may be a fear, on behalf of the social researcher, that a deprivation index acknowledging and quantifying anti-social behaviour, such as public drunkenness or drug-induced harassment, is getting it back-to-front so to speak, a case of 'blaming the victim'. This is one of the strongest prejudices against disadvantaged areas. The biggest victims of anti-social behaviour are often the law-abiding poor and very often the most vulnerable in that community – the very young and the very old. There may also be a tendency amongst some on the academic 'left' that undue concern or interest in clean and safe streets, the delivery of quality homes and affordable local shopping doesn't quite fit well with ny grand 'structural model' or academic theory. To put it more bluntly, an alysis of disadvantage that focuses on such issues might be ceptible to criticism of being politically naïve.

The elite of the 'academic left' in Dublin invariably live somewhere else. It is usually a suburban somewhere else, and usually one with clean, green and safe streets. Mainstream economists in Ireland, until very recently, have also tended not to interest themselves in urban place-making. They don't see themselves as having any particular or meaningful role in city-planning. Instead, they tend to see its delivery as the natural, if not messy, outcome of the planning system and constrained local government bureaucracy.

For all the intense popular media and economic discussion on the role of the National Asset Management Agency (NAMA), there is remarkably little discourse or analysis on the impact NAMA may have on urban, specifically inner-urban, Dublin spatial planning.[6] Perhaps the economic opportunities of transforming the physical character of regeneration areas are not fully appreciated. Neither the local urban professional nor the national economist is really genuinely comfortable with the relatively 'new' (some might argue, fashionable) idea that the making of great urban spaces, spacious apartments, world-class city parks, tolerant clean and safe streets, efficient offices and great architecture actually generate real economic growth.

Despite a new-found interest in the rhetoric about competing global cities, urban regeneration, the knowledge economy and mobile creative workforces, most mainstream economists probably continue to believe that it is actually the other way round, that it is successful economies that deliver the real resources to make truly great cities. It is that opportunity to make a truly great city that is the most puzzling aspect of the Arc of Disadvantage. The Arc of Disadvantage is, after all, also an 'Arc of Regeneration' or 'Arc of Opportunity'. It has enormous economic and urban potential, possessing, almost uniquely in a greater Dublin context, historic inbuilt advantages and largely untapped resources. It boasts great geography, located immediately adjacent to, and in many places forming part of the core of the city. It is possible to walk to College Green in fifteen minutes from almost everywhere in the Arc of Opportunity. It has the city's greatest public space, the River Liffey, running through it, the country's greatest and largest walled urban park on its doorstep, and the two largest train stations in the State at its boundaries, with a recently extended light-rail system connecting the area to the Docklands and western edges of the city.

The Arc of Opportunity is home to a rich architectural heritage and some of the city's greatest historic set pieces, including the Four Courts, Henrietta Street, the GPO, Parnell Square and the Liffey quays and bridges. It houses some of the State's biggest tourist attractions and the city's most important cultural institutions – Collins Barracks, Guinness Brewery, the Abbey and Gate theatres, the Hugh Lane Gallery, and some of the city's more alternative or cutting-edge galleries. It is also home to the most diverse and cosmopolitan population in the entire State. Almost 40% of its residents, two in five people, are foreign-born. This compares to just over than one in seven for the city as a whole.[7]

The Arc of Opportunity is also fortunate in many ways to continue to have so many derelict sites, thus escaping the worst of the poor-quality construction of the early Celtic Tiger boom period. These derelict or underperforming sites are probably the biggest opportunity for the city moving forward over the next five or ten years.

The Arc of Opportunity land bank has the potential to transform Dublin into a truly great urban city. It can provide a model for high-density, quality urban living, a laboratory for 21st-century Dublin urbanism, a sustainable and dynamic urban alternative to both disenfranchised, sterile suburban sprawl and privileged, low-density, pseudo-urban two-storey redbrick Dublin. We say potential. It is not inevitable. It requires bold imagination and public commitment, an honest appraisal of its problems and an astute understanding of its needs as a heterogeneous urban area. It requires an acute understanding of high-density housing design, the need to deliver great public schools and the attentive management of public space. It also requires tackling out-of-date and sometimes paralysing community participation structures.

Most of all, it requires both public and private investment and ambition, an ambition that inner-city areas accustomed to generational poverty and disadvantage can attract and retain a whole new generation of mixed-income families, and that these areas will become genuinely desirable places to live. It requires nothing short of an ambition to eradicate a suffocating prejudice, so that some day it may be possible to use the term 'Dublin's inner city' without provoking or invoking either an implied pejorative or a jaded badge of romanticised underperformance.

Embryonic City

The Embryonic City is an unborn city. It is in gestation, evolving and growing inside the space of the Canal Ring City. The Embryonic City has been growing slowly for fifteen years, fed and sustained by hope and the lifeline of economic growth.

The Embryonic City is now at risk of a still birth or regressive mutation. The greatest threat to the Embryonic City is an economically depressed Dublin, choking the possibility of a successful birth.

WRITING SPACE DNA

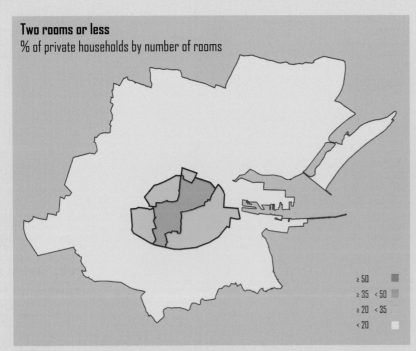

Two rooms or less
% of private households by number of rooms

≥ 50
≥ 35 < 50
≥ 20 < 35
< 20

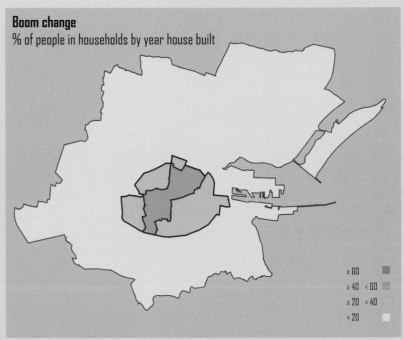

Boom change
% of people in households by year house built

≥ 60
≥ 40 < 60
≥ 20 < 40
< 20

THE EMBRYONIC CITY AND THE ARC OF DISADVANTAGE

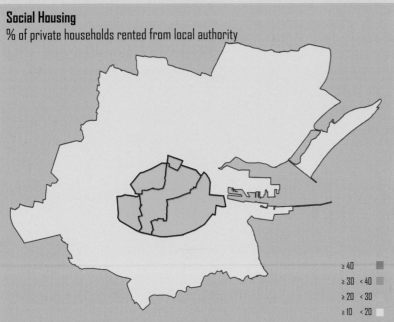

Social Housing
% of private households rented from local authority

≥ 40
≥ 30 < 40
≥ 20 < 30
≥ 10 < 20

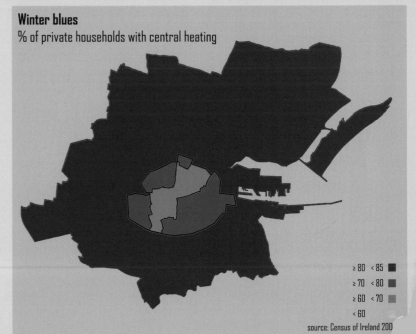

Winter blues
% of private households with central heating

≥ 80 < 85
≥ 70 < 80
≥ 60 < 70
< 60

source: Census of Ireland 200

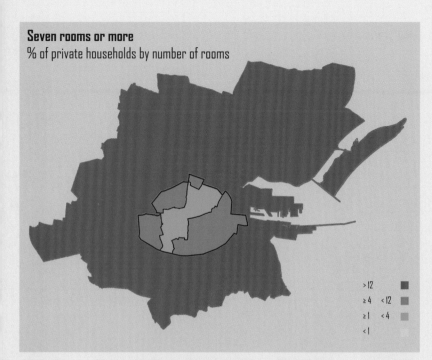

Seven rooms or more
% of private households by number of rooms

> 12
≥ 4   < 12
≥ 1   < 4
< 1

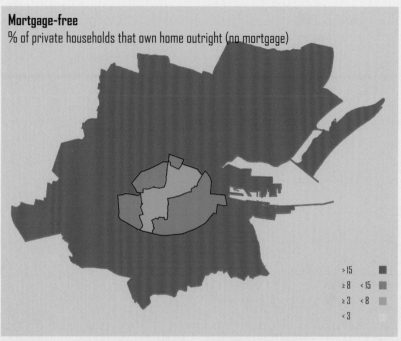

Mortgage-free
% of private households that own home outright (no mortgage)

> 15
≥ 8   < 15
≥ 3   < 8
< 3

THE EMBRYONIC CITY AND THE ARC OF OPPORTUNITY

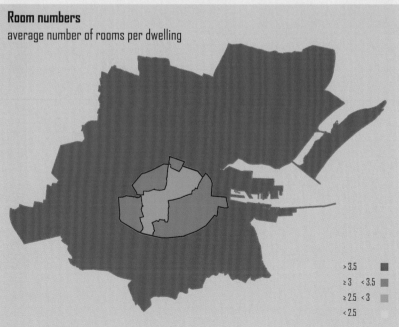

Room numbers
average number of rooms per dwelling

> 3.5
≥ 3   < 3.5
≥ 2.5   < 3
< 2.5

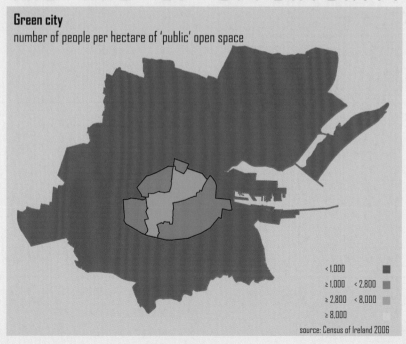

Green city
number of people per hectare of 'public' open space

< 1,000
≥ 1,000   < 2,800
≥ 2,800   < 8,000
≥ 8,000

source: Census of Ireland 2006

41

Two rooms or less
% of private households by number of rooms

≥ 50
≥ 35 < 50
≥ 20 < 35
< 20

Boom change
% of people in households by year house built

≥ 60
≥ 40 < 60
≥ 20 < 40
< 20

Social housing
% of private households rented from local authority

≥ 40
≥ 30 < 40
≥ 20 < 30
≥ 10 < 20

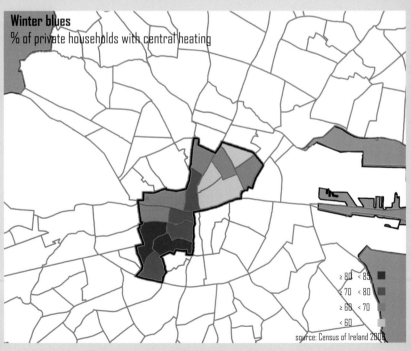

Winter blues
% of private households with central heating

≥ 80 < 85
≥ 70 < 80
≥ 60 < 70
< 60

source: Census of Ireland 2006

Seven rooms or more
% of private households by number of rooms

> 12
≥ 4   < 12
≥ 1   < 4
< 1

Mortgage-free
% of private households that own home outright (no mortgage)

> 15
≥ 8   < 15
≥ 3   < 8
< 3

Room numbers
average number of rooms per dwelling

> 3.5
≥ 3   < 3.5
≥ 2.5 < 3
< 2.5

Green city
number of people per hectare of 'public' open space

< 1,000
≥ 1,000   < 2,800
≥ 2,800   < 8,000
≥ 8,000

source: Census of Ireland 2006

43

Dublin's North **West**
Urban Land **Bank**

The Arc of Disadvantage

The Old City

The Promised Land

UNBORN STATES OF MIND AND PLACE

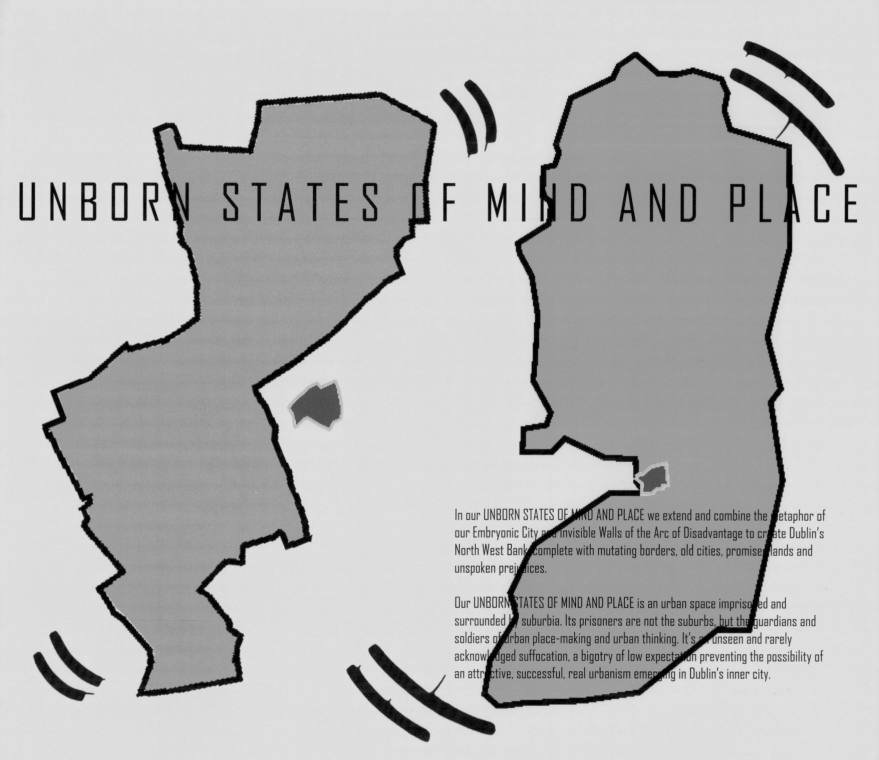

In our UNBORN STATES OF MIND AND PLACE we extend and combine the metaphor of our Embryonic City and Invisible Walls of the Arc of Disadvantage to create Dublin's North West Bank complete with mutating borders, old cities, promised lands and unspoken prejudices.

Our UNBORN STATES OF MIND AND PLACE is an urban space imprisoned and surrounded by suburbia. Its prisoners are not the suburbs, but the guardians and soldiers of urban place-making and urban thinking. It's an unseen and rarely acknowledged suffocation, a bigotry of low expectation preventing the possibility of an attractive, successful, real urbanism emerging in Dublin's inner city.

In Dublin's North West Bank ...

37.5% of all homes have two rooms or less – this compares to 15% for the city as a whole.

The average number of rooms per home is **2.8** – this rises to 4.3 in Dublin city.

Just **1 in 100 homes** have 7 rooms or more – almost 1 in 8 homes in Dublin city have 7 rooms or more.

North West Bank homes are colder – 69% of homes have central heating, compared to 85% in Dublin city

... put another way, **1 in 4 homes have no central heating** as opposed to 1 in 9 for the entire city.

North West Bankers are renters – one quarter of homes are rented from the local authority – this compares to 1 in 8 homes for all of Dublin city. A further 1 in 3 homes are rented this figure falls to less than 1 in 4 in the city.

Just **1 in 14 householders own their homes outright** – that is, they have no outstanding mortgage. This compares to 1 in 4 across the city.

Almost **1 in 2 live in Celtic Tiger homes**.

– over 45% of all people living in private households live in homes built during the Celtic Tiger boom (1991-2006) – for the city as a whole this figure is less than 20%.

More than 2 in 5 homes in the North West Bank are Celtic Tiger homes. Almost all of these homes are apartment-style housing.

source: Census of Ireland 2006

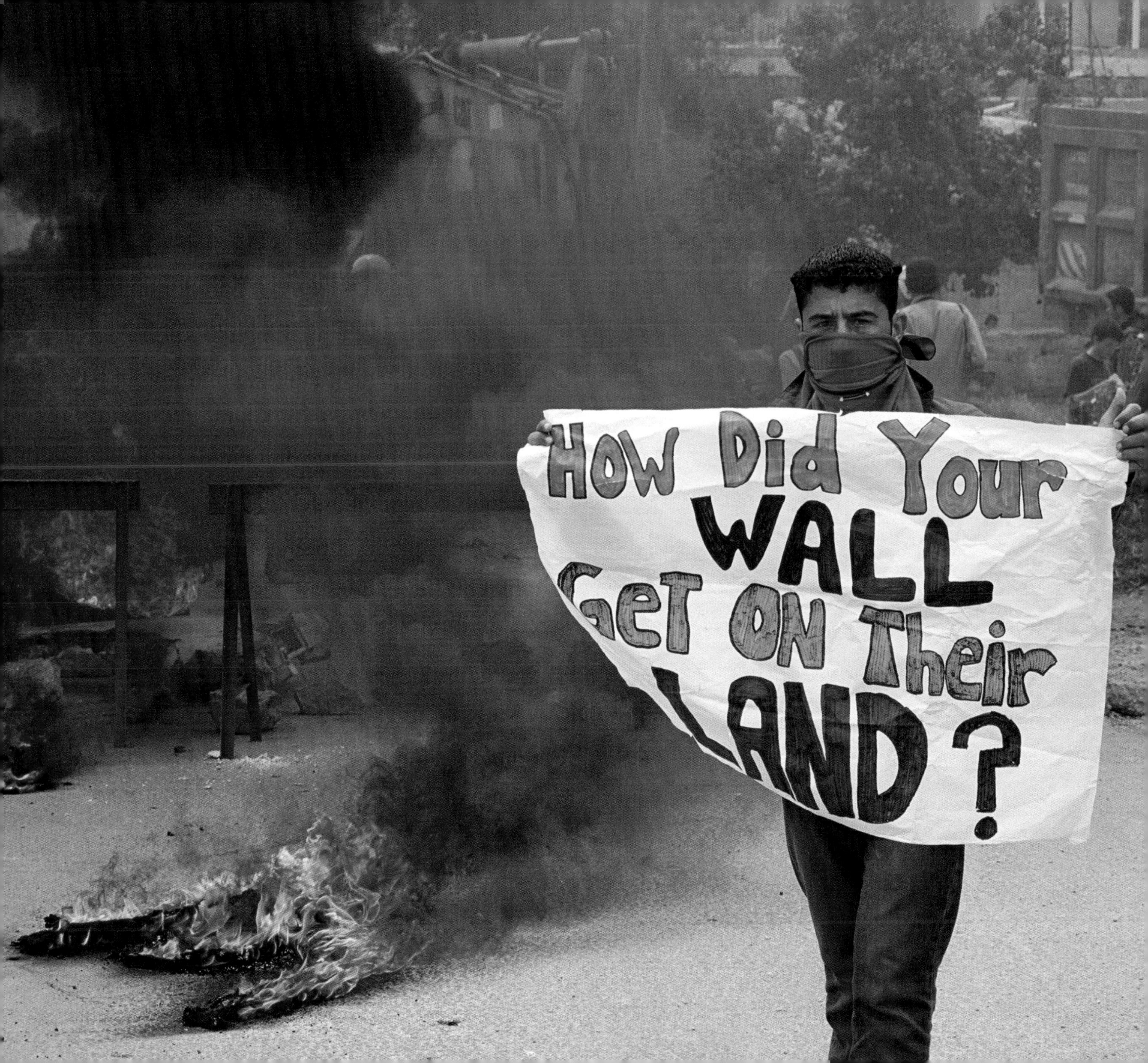
How Did Your
WALL
Get ON Their
LAND ?

Homeless

If Dublin's inner-urban Arc of Disadvantage is home to 43,000 people (8.5% of the population of the Dublin City Council area), it is also home to 32.7% of all people residing in state or city homeless and emergency hostel accommodation in Dublin city.¹ If one includes emergency hostel accommodation just one street, or less than 200m away, from the 'border' of our imaginary but very real Arc of Disadvantage, that figure rises to 58.2% of all Dublin city homeless provision.

Just 8.7% of all homeless and emergency hostel accommodation in Dublin city is located outside Dublin's Canal Ring. Some 80.2% of Dublin city's population resides outside the Canal Ring.

Is city or state emergency hostel accommodation service deliberately concentrated in less affluent parts of the city because of perceived potential local need or low local property prices?

Does the density of concentration of the homeless service provision in poorer parts of the city communicate civic generosity to and public investment in disadvantaged local populations or communicate public disinterest in and abandonment of struggling disadvantaged communities?

The Regeneration Paradox

Following the property bubble burst and onset of severe economic contraction in late 2007, it became somewhat *de rigueur* in populist economic and social discourse to dismiss the phenomena of the entire Celtic Tiger boom period. A smug, almost self-satisfied glee could be detected in those who felt a lot more comfortable in a Dublin where the possibility of rapid social change didn't challenge either the status quo or personal choices. There was, and continues to be, an almost ghoulish delight in the flagellation of developers, and a hollow celebration at the empty or half-completed housing estates. A peculiar post-Celtic Tiger mob analysis has emerged in certain circles that fifteen years of unparalleled growth was all a mirage, a comical joke, an exercise in 'binge economics', a kind of economics of bloated housing overindulgence.
We didn't and don't deserve wealth and full employment.

This collective giddy, but ultimately debilitating mood has given the broad church of the anti-development lobby enormous sustenance and thin ideological cover for wholesale attack on development of almost any kind. This is damaging for any city, but in Dublin it is potentially devastating for inner-city areas still in need of regeneration. Instead of less development and fewer developers, Dublin's inner city actually requires much more – more discerning perhaps, but a lot more.

It is worth remembering that during the unprecedented period of wealth creation, Ireland experienced national growth rates in GDP averaging 6.8% for a full fifteen years (1993-2007). In the years 1995 to 2000, widely accepted as predating wreckless bank-lending and the property bubble, growth averaged 9.3%.[1] Some 497,000 new homes were built in the Irish state during the Celtic Tiger period (1991-2006). This remarkable figure means that a third of existing Irish dwellings were built during the Celtic Tiger boom.[2] Dublin city experienced a more modest increase in its housing stock, but nevertheless added an additional 35,000 new homes during this period. Celtic Tiger homes thus account for a fifth of all Dublin city homes.[3]

Extensive areas of Dublin's inner city, ravished by decades of poverty, neglect and decline, witnessed considerable transformation. The city centre has experienced a physical and cultural renaissance. Recent years has seen the construction of the O2 arena, the Samuel Beckett Bridge,

the Grand Canal Theatre, the Convention Centre Dublin, two world-class sports stadia – the Aviva and Croke Park – a new city courts complex, and significantly improved commuter and mainline rail and Luas transportation infrastructure.

There is, however, a lingering sense of being somewhat underwhelmed by the extent of the new development, visually at least, in the historically disadvantaged parts of the city. Many parts of Dublin 1, 7 and 8, outside the city centre core but often very close to it, remain derelict, vacant or untouched by the biggest building boom in the State's history. Much of what was actually built during this boom period is, by common consensus, rather mediocre. More importantly, many of the tax-driven new apartment schemes dating from the late 1980s and 1990s are small in size, have awkward layouts and poor-quality finishes, and have arguably contributed to a further sense of social marginalisation of gritty and deprived inner-urban areas.

It's not that change didn't happen. A lot did, and it would be churlish not to recognise the level of change. The population of the inner city has significantly increased in the past fifteen to twenty years. But one is forced to ask, with national growth levels averaging 6.8% for fifteen years, why more development did not take place in Dublin's disadvantaged inner city. Had national growth rates been a healthy and internationally respectable 2.8% instead of a heady 6.8%, would these areas have changed at all? Where exactly did all the growth go?

Our CELTIC TIGER METROPOLITAN maps (Chapter 1) demonstrate that a lot of development was diverted to the 'exurb' counties of Kildare, Fingal and Wicklow. During this period, entire towns and townlands outside, but within commuting distance of Dublin have being totally transformed. From Swords to Leixlip, from Naas to Greystones, the story is the same. The suburban, indeed rural, landscape has been radically changed by new motorways, flyovers, spanking new industrial estates and shopping centres, marinas, multiplex cinemas, and more and more new tree-lined, manicured-lawn Celtic Tiger suburban town house-style housing estates.

Walking along the Luas line in the heart of Dublin's North Inner City, driving through Summerhill or Seán McDermott Street, or meandering through the back streets of The Liberties in the South Inner City around Marrowbone Lane, one could be forgiven for thinking that the city and the State's economy had actually contracted in the last fifteen years, let alone grown at unparalleled international or historic growth rates.

The fact that these inner-city areas may have looked a lot worse in 1988 both misses the point and betrays a somewhat unconvincing defensiveness in the context of a national economy that almost doubled in size between 1990 and 2007. Yes, the inner city population doubled, and, yes, extensive areas of dereliction were developed, but after fifteen years of a property boom, one cannot help concluding this was an opportunity lost, a failure to deliver quality urbanism. A simple question, perhaps tellingly, reveals a lot: has the perception of Dublin's inner city meaningfully changed after these fifteen years of record economic growth? Outside the Docklands area, do Dubliners perceive their inner city as a desirable place to live? One could also be forgiven for asking a very simple but more troubling and potentially provocative question: did the State require annual growth rates of 7.8%, possibly 8.8%, or perhaps 10.8% for fifteen years to transform these underperforming areas? Rephrasing that slightly: had 'the City', or its citizens, for that matter, been told in 1992 that they faced a decade-and-a-half of national growth rates averaging 6.8%, culminating in almost full employment in 2007, might they have expected a better, greener, more beautiful inner city?

There are, of course, a number of urban assumptions here. The first is that the citizens of the city, the vast majority of whom live and continue to live in a house with a front and back garden, are actually interested in the quality of life of those who live or might choose to live in the inner city. Perhaps more worryingly is the possibility that the underperformance of the inner city somehow doesn't reflect on them as citizens of Dublin; the inner city simply doesn't matter to suburban Dubliners. This indifference to the inner city is not to be confused with a desire to visit or shop in the city centre. Dublin's inner city and Dublin's city centre are of course fundamentally different worlds. To the unfamiliar visitor, the city centre and the inner city may seem, superficially at least, linguistically close cousins; they are, however, for Dubliners, immediately understood as very distant, albeit neighbourly relatives.

The second assumption is that city policy-makers have a genuine

ambition or vision that high-density, mixed-income quality urban living – with the possible exception of the Docklands area – is either really possible or even desirable in Dublin's inner city. Everybody believes in regeneration. The ambition, however, to actually transform places into genuinely thriving mixed-income communities that would attract middle- or high-income families somehow continues to elicit lukewarm enthusiasm.

Regeneration has itself become a jaded term, and has increasingly lost its edge, its hopeful or radical intent. Today, regeneration for many means nothing more than 'stitching' in a few missing blocks, refurbishment of social flat complexes, providing yet another community centre, and perhaps hoping for the best. This is ultimately nothing short of a kind of bigotry of low urban expectations, a failure in imagination of the possible. This unspoken bias is rarely openly acknowledged or discussed, and, of course, harder to prove. It can, however, reveal itself by asking a simple and singular question to key decision-makers: what would it take for you to live in the inner city? The reaction to this question tends to range from the startled to the perplexed and the defensive. The question strangely intimidates. The questioner and question become oddly accusatory. In how many other European cities would such a simple question about city-centre living provoke such verbal gymnastics and emotional hand-wringing from the very people empowered to deliver quality urbanism?

This bigotry of place is driven not by some sort of defeatist social pragmatism – a recognition that we will always have the poor, they will always be with us – but rather by a much more reactionary belief that we will always have poorer disadvantaged areas, and that those poor areas are destined, no matter how much they are marginally improved, to remain that way. The fact that these inner-urban socially deprived areas enjoy enormous advantages of geography, are close to the city centre, within walking distance to major city or state transport hubs, are close to some of city's best urban parks and are peppered with national city tourist attractions and great museums makes the bigotry against these areas all the more perplexing and acute. These prejudices, nevertheless, exert a powerful force, one that betrays not just an acquiescence of challenging generational poverty, but rather an unconscious mistrust or suspicion of the value or possibilities of quality urban living – well, at least of quality urban living in Dublin's inner city.

Regeneration: Seven Deadly Risks

There are many varied and complex challenges to the further regeneration of the Arc of Disadvantage, not least stubborn pockets of acute social disadvantage, continued negative perceptions of the area, and a national economy in temporary retreat. We believe there are, however, more deep-seated, less tangible, and perhaps unspoken challenges that pose an equal, maybe even greater risk to the successful regeneration of disadvantaged inner-city neighbourhoods. These challenges may be harder to identify, more difficult to measure, and, for some people, easier to dismiss. This does not, however, make them any less real or diminish their threat or risk.

We have endeavoured to describe a few. There are, perhaps, many more lurking out there in the media, academia, professional institutes, voluntary organisations, in local government, or indeed in the local community itself.

1 – Gentrivilification

'Gentrivilication' is, for some people, an irrational fear or dislike of urban change; for others, however, it is a very real rational fear of loosing political power or influence over the citizens (voters) of a disadvantaged area. 'Gentrivilification', as the name suggests, is derived from the term gentrification. Gentrification can be defined as the process of urban-renewal and rebuilding which accompanies the influx of middle class or affluent people into hitherto deteriorating areas that may displace earlier, usually poorer residents.

The term gentrification, when employed by academics, planners or community activists is widely understood as a pejorative, a not-so-thinly disguised term of abuse. It is a term, we argue, that is widely used and abused in Dublin. There is actually little or no evidence of housing 'displacement' in Dublin's inner city. Young couples and families who 'choose' to move to far-flung suburbs were more likely to do so because of a lack of local housing choice. This lack of housing choice is primarily the result of a failure to meaningfully increase the supply of newly built, spacious, quality, high-density homes in the heart of the city.

'Gentrivilification', as the term implies, is very different and runs much

deeper. It is a vilification of social change masquerading as a critique of gentrification.

The potential displacement of economically disadvantaged communities as a result of local rising property markets is, of course, a genuine and legitimate concern when areas undergo a period of rapid regeneration. The fear, however, of those who adhere to 'gentrivilification' is not one of social displacement, but rather one of social dilution. 'Gentrivilification' usually stems from a fear of the other, of newcomers, of change. It fears the dilution of the values of some pre-existing or endangered, perhaps romanticised, indigenous community. Some adherents of 'gentrivilification' also fear losing political control over the local 'indigenous' community, and thus a monopoly on the authenticity of the voice of that community. 'Gentrivilification' is, in many ways, another variant form of NIMBYism (Not In My Back Yard).

The provision of a better food choice in new supermarkets, employment opportunities, new office blocks, or additional local services arising from a growing population are often dismissed or belittled by the adherents of 'gentrivilification' as being of little or no benefit to 'their' disadvantaged community. This is one of the most destructive characteristics of 'gentrivilification', a deliberate failure or, perhaps, myopic inability to acknowledge the many genuine benefits urban regeneration can bring or may have brought to a disadvantaged community.

There is a second type of gentrilvilifier, who unashamedly publicly bemoans, perhaps disingenuously, gentrification (confusing it with social change) of other areas whilst simultaneously privately and desperately pining for a similar kind gentrification of their own neighbourhood. They are surprisingly common.

Gentrivilification

"slanderous defamation of dilapidated areas becoming attractive to middle classes through improved services, access or a perception of trendiness"

Abandonment of hope is the belief on the part of the residents or businesses of a regeneration area that their previous 'urban hope value' – as reflected in their decision to choose to live or open a business there – has proven to be disappointedly misplaced. It is important to distinguish between abandonment of hope and the natural fear a resident in a regeneration area may have of an economic slowdown. Abandonment of hope is altogether different. It is the strong belief or conviction, rightly or wrongly, that the local authority lacks commitment to, or has simply given up on the regeneration of their local area. When abandonment of hope takes hold and becomes widespread amongst new homeowners or businesses in a regeneration area, it can become a self-fulfilling prophecy, potentially devastating possibilities of any further positive change. Abandonment of hope can quickly, almost suddenly, send a

regeneration area into reverse. All previous successes can rapidly begin to unravel or unwind. Vacancies, dereliction and accelerated declines in property values can assert themselves with a vengeance.

Abandonment of hope is fed by many things. This includes streets that are not kept clean, the perceived sense that the city is concentrating unwanted problematic land uses, a municipal indifference to anti-social behaviour – in effect, a general unease that the city has lost interest in the challenging problems of managing emerging urbanism in the area. All are devastating to continued private commitment and investment to a regeneration area. If hope is lost, money and people quickly flee. It is extraordinarily difficult to rebuild that hope after expectations have been dashed. Confidence in urban regeneration when lost is hard to rebuild.

Abandonment of Hope

"the act of giving up the general feeling that some desire will be fulfilled"

3 – Bigotry of Low Expectation

Bigotry of low expectation is the belief by policy-makers that socially disadvantaged areas of the inner city – areas that middle income families have historically abandoned and have no desire to return to – will always remain just that, socially disadvantaged and undesirable places to live. The regeneration ambitions of the practitioners of bigotry of low expectation do not look beyond an almost patrician attitude to rehousing the poor. Transforming the perception of these areas for the better is neither possible, nor, perhaps, desirable.

Adherents of bigotry of low expectation are usually held hostage by a constrained imagination. They tend to lack the vision that an area, usually one with enormous inbuilt urban advantages, can actually become a different sort of place, a place where successful new urban possibilities can be imagined, where new parks, great public spaces, better homes, excellent schools are made, built supported and managed. They do not see regeneration areas as potential drivers and innovators in the urban economy, but rather as areas deserving perhaps of charitable 'trickle-down' benefits of a 'real' economy made elsewhere. Ultimately, it's a belief that inner-urban areas can never become genuinely desirable or attractive places to live, at least attractive enough for the adherents of bigotry of low expectation to choose to live there.

Bigotry of Low Expectation
"obtuse or narrow-minded intolerance of little prospects, especially of success or gain"

Nostalgia

"a bittersweet longing for things, persons, or situations of the past"

4 – Nostalgia

Nostalgia can be defined as a longing for the past, often in an idealised form. Disadvantaged areas in need of urban regeneration are very often seen through the prism of a form of 'urban nostalgia'. This is perhaps natural, but nevertheless quite unhealthy. The past is somehow imagined as a better place when confronted with what seems like the overwhelming challenges of the area today. Nostalgia, however, is a potentially destructive recipe for urban paralysis.

The 'nostalgic city' is one where past poverty is romanticised. It is a city where overcrowded tenements are sanitised and recreated as potential interesting sources or typologies for 21st-century high-density communal living. The historic social urban realities of deprivation, inequality, disease, overcrowding and stifling social suffocation are ignored, glossed over, re-imagined or dusted down as the virtues and stories of a bygone era. Urban nostalgia is blind to the past, indifferent to the present, and hopelessly pessimistic and hostile about the possibilities of our urban future.

Of the many great risks to successful regeneration, nostalgia is probably one of the least understood and yet most openly tolerated. It very often provides a thinly veiled disguise for more malign political forces that are intimidated by cultural diversity, immigration and progressive social change.

5 – Phoney Urbanism

Phoney urbanism is perhaps the most perplexing and dangerous of all the risks to urban regeneration. The advocates of phoney urbanism are very often found in positions of real power, or at least in positions of potential influence to advance the acceptability of their theories of urbanism.

The phoney urbanist can be found anywhere. They tend to prioritise or advance theories in architecture, urban design and city living – most of which are impenetrable and many of which are unworkable – as to how others should live their urban lives, whilst they shamelessly and simultaneously live out a closeted suburban lifestyle. The phoney urbanist endlessly explores and deconstructs miniaturised cardboard models of urban architecture at a scale of 1:250. Living in the city, Dublin's inner city, at a scale of 1:1 somehow either terrifies or bores them.

The phoney urbanist is endlessly fascinated by the sustainability of a single building but is usually indifferent to the environmental costs of suburban settlement. They are usually indifferent to or suspiciously suspicious of large inner-city apartments. An exploration or elaboration of quality spacious domestic design is somehow too easy. The phoney urbanist is instead bafflingly intrigued by the design challenges of miniaturised apartment-living. We term this movement 'bespoke nano-apartment architecture'. The advocates of bespoke nano-apartment architecture market their theories as a sustainable 21st-century response to the challenges of eco-friendly, high-density living. We suspect, however, it betrays a deeper and far more personal affliction – a form of spacious begrudgery infused with a heavy dose of bigotry of low expectation.

Phoney Urbanism

"insincere, pretentious or bogus specialists in the study of planning and cities"

Sub-urbanism, unlike most of the other SEVEN DEADLY RISKS to regeneration, is neither ideological nor irrational, hypocritical nor devoid of vision. It is, however, uninformed. The sub-urbanist comes to the subject of city-making with the analytical tools or rational experience of suburbia. It is important to understand that the sub-urbanist is well intentioned, their motivations well meaning. They bring with them a language of hope and inclusivity, of utopian integration and social neighbourliness. It is also important to state that not all suburbanites are sub-urbanists.

The sub-urbanist risk to regeneration lies in their efforts to impose inappropriate models of behaviour, to transpose or 'suburban graft', a suburban value system of how urban people should live their lives. The sub-urbanist stresses integration and assimilation; the true urbanist values choice and tolerant co-existence. The sub-urbanist wants us all to know each other and to share similar values. Neighbourly disinterest or warm indifference is disturbing for the sub-urbanist.

Urban areas are, for good or ill, more complex than suburbs. Their social structure is not simply a denser version of the suburb nor a concentrated magnified village. Urban areas behave differently. It's perfectly fine for some people to choose not to know the name of their immediate neighbour in the city; furthermore, it's okay not to want to know. To the sub-urbanist, such mutterings is a form of residential or communal dysfunctional heresy. It is the very social complexity of successful cities, the proximity of strangers that necessitates neighbourly tolerance, yet doesn't require friendly intimacy, that the sub-urbanist fails to understand.

Sub-Urbanist

"just below, or somewhat imperfect specialists in the study and planning of cities"

7 – Denial

Denial can be defined as an unconscious willingness to recognise painful realities. In the context of urban regeneration, denial manifests itself in primarily two ways, both equally damaging for the capacity of an area to embrace positive change. The first form of denial is the inability or refusal to see what is actually there. We call this 'urban denial of existence'. The second form of denial is almost a perverse flip of the first, a closely related cognitive dissonance. This is the ability to see things that are no longer there and have long since gone. We call this 'urban denial of disappearance'.

In Dublin, the regeneration risk of the urban denial of existence is the refusal of decision-makers to acknowledge, prioritise or adequately engage with various forms of anti-social behaviour. It is that anti-social behaviour or edginess in the city, particularly in areas most in need of regeneration, that are enormously challenging for the quality of life of those who live there. It may be street drunkenness, drug dealing, vomiting and urinating in doorways or laneways. They all pose real risks to successful further regeneration.

The failure to see empty sites or dereliction anymore is another classic form of urban denial of existence. We've termed these urban BLIND spots (Big Land Islands of Non-Development). We walk by them everyday. They are a seemingly permanent fixture in parts of our urban landscape.

The urban denial of disappearance is altogether more intriguing. It's a particular affliction of many archaeologists, architectural historians and conservationists. Architects and planners are equally prone to occasional bouts of denial of disappearance. Those who suffer from urban denial of disappearance primarily see place and space through the prism of a distant, imaginary, but nevertheless non-existent past, what was or might have been there, not what is actually there. Derelict sites, vacant plots and rundown spaces are discussed in effusive historic architectural language as if the buildings continued to exist and their occupants glide by in ghosted carriages and suitable historic evening attire. Those afflicted with urban denial of disappearance do not prevent the destruction of our heritage in these places (it has already happened); they can, however, and very often do prevent the reimagination of the possibilities of our urban future.

Denial

"an unconscious defence mechanism characterised by a refusal to acknowledge painful realities, thoughts or feelings"

Urban Burden-Carrying Capacity

The 'urban burden-carrying capacity' of an area is its capacity to absorb a given amount of negative externalities before a critical urban stress or tipping point is arrived at, whereupon serious and very often irreversible damage occurs to city living. The urban burden-carrying capacity of an area is dependent upon the simple relationship between its stresses and the attractiveness of its liveability. What might irrevocably damage or destroy one urban area may be of no consequence to an urban area of equal size, but one of a very different character.

In 'proto-urban spaces' – places with a weak or slowly emerging quality urban way of life – an urban vulnerability exists. These areas cannot absorb additional stresses or strains. It is more distressing for disadvantaged areas with existing vacant or derelict sites to absorb acts of anti-social behaviour. Busy, successful, attractive streets can absorb such temporary, albeit unwelcome, blips or shocks because of their otherwise energetic and attractive city street life. Poor-quality pavements or broken kerbs that seem not to matter in downtown New York, central Paris or Dublin's bustling Exchequer Street are more visible in distressed areas. In distressed areas they communicate neglect and civic disinterest. Ironically, they are simply not that important in safe, visually exciting and interesting places.

Emerging urban spaces cannot afford pedestrian lights at traffic signals that never seem to go green (or more annoyingly stay red when the light remains red for vehicles). These urban areas cannot afford the stress of uncollected rubbish on public streets, broken trees or the visual pollution of sawn-off galvanized steel poles masquerading as street furniture. What matters little in vibrant, successful urban places can often prove fatal in embryonic urban areas with a very weak urban immune system or low urban burden-carrying capacity.

Such stresses tend to be magnified in distressed urban areas, and yet it is one of those urban paradoxes that those areas with the smallest urban burden-carrying capacity – areas that are often already blighted with dereliction and poor-quality housing, limited shopping or poorly maintained public spaces – are very often the very same areas that are stressed to their 'tipping point' by the sometimes deliberate, more likely, indifferent decision-making of city or state policy-makers.

Desert Island Risks or Baby Urbanism

Why is it that some of Dublin city's greatest tourist attractions are accessed on foot along some of its poorest-quality and edgiest streets? Is it simply an accident of urban typography or an act of municipal indifference to social geography? Most Dubliners would probably see it as neither, but rather view it as, well, just the way it is... and probably the way it always has been.

In DESERT ISLAND RISKS we highlight the peculiar and perhaps little acknowledged urban taboo that Dublin, a city that prides itself as an important international city of tourism, appears to be oblivious to the damaging branding image it communicates annually to hundreds of thousands of overseas visitors.

Six of the top ten fee-charging and free tourist attractions in Dublin city (as measured by attendance),[1] including Dublin Zoo, IMMA, Guinness Storehouse and the National Museum at Collins Barracks, are either located inside the Arc of Disadvantage or located immediately to the west of the city, thus necessitating a walk through the Arc of Disadvantage if arriving by foot from the city centre. All are accessed along Thomas Street, Benburb Street or the city quays. These pedestrian routes are deeply distressed, sometimes edgy, rarely as clean as the rest of the city and, for the most part, pretty joyless, lacking any resemblance to the bustling energy of the city centre.

Why does the city risk its image and perhaps the safety of its tourists? Why is it that the city's premier tourist attractions appear ambivalent to the challenges of their immediate surroundings? And why do Dubliners not believe it reflects badly on them as citizens of their city? Are Dublin's premier tourist attractions destined to be underperforming drivers of urban regeneration or can they, alongside the city, become engaged by the citizen to energise and engage with the challenges and opportunities of its urban streets. Can the Arc of Disadvantage become the Arc of Opportunity? Has Dublin the urban ambition to make the connection between the city's tourist economy and the city's walkable streets?

"What would it take you to *live* in the inner city?"

E R U V

In modern Jewish practise, eruv refers to a symbolic fence which creates and denotes the boundaries of an emblematic walled courtyard within which certain religious activities are permitted or can take place. The 'planning eruv' is a similarly symbolic fenced-off area. It is delineated by connected wires linking poles that designate a defined zone where quantitative planning rules such as plot ratio (area of site divided by total gross floor area of development) are relaxed in favour of excellence in architectural or urban practise. The planning eruv is a state of mind that is almost invisible. Entry is subtle, conceptually flexible, but legally defined. The planning eruv can be expanded and contracted depending on its success.

Over time, one senses where the eruv begins and ends as a distinct eruv urban landscape is built. Within the planning eruv, an urban architectural laboratory evolves and mutates, germinates and flowers repeatedly. A hybrid urban and architectural condition emerges: a kind of experimental architecture and elastic urbanism governed by the singular rule of the eruv. This singular rule is the dispensation sought and granted from the limitations of mathematical planning abstractions on condition of delivery of excellence in urban living. Diversity, originality, quality and beauty are favoured and prized over the restrictive shoulder heights, bed spaces per square metre of open space, plot ratio and the maximum governors of the mediocre and the formulaic.

In the planning eruv, a parallel design universe expands and contracts. The laws of this universe stretch inhabitable space to infinite possibilities, its material qualities emerge unknown and unplanned. It's a place where glass and metal collide, where brick solidifies shape, and light liquefies space. The planning eruv is governed by a council of guardians practised in the virtues of architectural and urban innovation. These are not the arbiters of taste or the enforcers of universal parapet heights, but the wizards and magicians of design, capable of liberating a fantastical three-dimensional wonderment of space and spaciousness.

The planning eruv is necessarily a planning heresy. It is not imprisoned by doctrines or vacuous rules, but instead aspires to the ambitious heights of volumetric and light-filled voids. The practitioners in the planning eruv are innovators and experimenters. Most of all they are urbanites. They delight in the excesses of consumption of the imagination. They are neither spatially puritan nor physically constrained, but instead have cultivated a taste for heights and views, a passion for light and roominess. Decisions are immediate and final in the planning eruv. Excellence and creativity are rewarded not postponed. Urban gratification is celebrated and embraced, not shunned or censored.

Eruvurb

"an erotic love or desire of excellence in experimental urbanism"

ARCHITECTURAL EXCELLENCE

Y = 3 Houses

Architecture Republic

Architecture Republic's infill housing project for a site on North Circular Road – commended in the AAI Awards 2010 – was refused

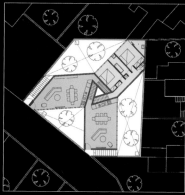

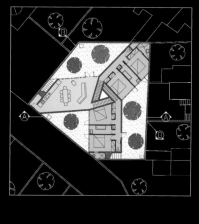

RE USED

permission by An Bord Pleanála because of 'Mathematical Planning Bedspace Theory'.

"The other relevant standard is that private open space should normally be 12-15m² per bedspace (section 15.9.6). Each of the proposed three units has four bed spaces, resulting in a private open space requirement of at least 48m². While two of the units have open space of 45m², the third unit has only 30m². I conclude, therefore, that private open space provision, notwithstanding the innovative design, falls short of development plan requirements for mews dwellings." [1]

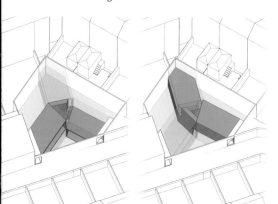

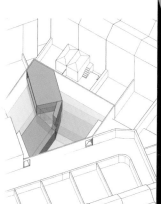

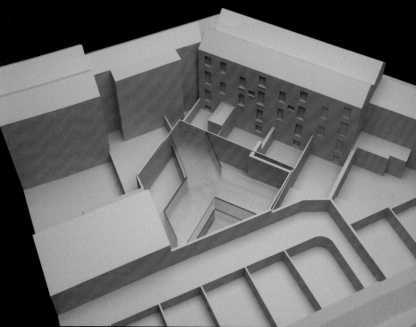

Carbon Footprint

Ratio of those who walk or cycle to school, college or work and between those who drive or are passengers in a car:
>6
>4 <6
>1 <4
>0.5 <1
<0.5

Class in No Time

This is Class

% of working population employed at higher and professional

% of households manual skilled, semi skilled and unskilled.

The Graduates

Cosmopolitans

Apartment Dwellers

% of usually resident population that are non-Irish national:
>50
>40 <50
>30 <40
>20 <30
<20

% of all private households residing in apartments and flats:
>80
>60 <80
>40 <60
<40

70

Postcards from Dublin

MAPPING DIFFERENCES tells a story of the spatial diversity, disparities and inequalities that makes up life in Dublin city. MAPPING DIFFERENCES is a simple snapshot or photograph of a city at any one point in time. It does, however, paint colourful geographies, some perhaps fleeting, others longer lasting. These colourful geographies reveal many unexpected patterns of lifestyle choices, imposed hardships, personal beliefs and built realities. It teases us with potentially weird but wonderful casual and causal spatial connections.

There is a striking relationship between the maps POST-GOD AND TRUE BELIEVERS and WINTER BLUES, evidence of a strong spatial correlation between those who state a belief in a Catholic God and those who are most likely to have central heating in the their homes. The relationship however is unlikely to be causal. Young working-class couples with young children (likely to profess attachment to Catholicism) are also more likely to disproportionately live in new outer suburban homes (almost all of which have central heating). They are to be found in great numbers in the North Fringe.

In addition, many third level students or young adults who might be less likely to state an attachment to a religion, also find themselves living in older converted flats with no central heating. Perhaps it is not surprising that those who find themselves in colder homes are less likely to profess a belief in the generosity or benevolence of an all-seeing God.

In MORTGAGE FREE, MAPPING DIFFERENCES also reveals surprisingly that fewer people own their own homes outright in Dublin 4 and 6, the wealthiest areas of the city, than in the predominantly working-class suburbs of the city's northside. The colourful geographies of MAPPING DIFFERENCES and the social and economic realities informing them may be of interest to some. They may amuse, fascinate or perplex others. An understanding of these diversities and inequalities is critical to effective urban policy.

Creative visualisations or visual storytelling can also play an important role in stimulating the citizen's interest in city-making. A city is never static. While some geographies tend to freeze or solidify, others are altogether more fluid. It is opportune that POSTCARDS FROM DUBLIN should find a voice in 2010. It is a year that conveniently straddles, on the one hand, the story of the recent past as encapsulated in the census of population of 2006, and the vision of the immediate future as outlined in the new Dublin City Development Plan, which will shape the city from 2011 to 2017.

1 in 12 people living in the Walkinstown area are widows.

This figure compares to only 1 in 25 widows citywide.

1 in 45 Walkinstown residents are widowers.

For every **1 widower** in Dublin there are **4 widows.**

In only 1 of 162 wards do widowers outnumber widows: Rotunda, North Inner City.

Widows Speak

% of entire population
who are widows

≥ 8

≥ 6   < 8

< 6

source: Census of Ireland 2006

1 in 5 people live in a Celtic Tiger home.

This rises to 2 in 5 inside the Canal Ring. In the South Docks it is 1 in 2.

In 10 north inner-city wards, housing over 29,000 people, 53% live in a Celtic Tiger home.

Fewer that 1 in 20 homes in Terenure are Celtic Tiger homes.

On Arran Quay and Usher's Quay, 3 out 4 people live in a Celtic Tiger home.

1 in 7 Dubliners live in an Edwardian, Victorian or Georgian home, including 1 in 750 Ballyfermot residents.

Celtic Tiger Homes

% of all persons
residing in homes built
during the Celtic Tiger
boom (1991-2006)

≥60%

≥50% <60%

≥30% <50%

<30%

source: Census of Ireland 2006

1 in 40 homes in Dublin

are classified by their occupants as **bed-sits**; that's a total of **4,829 homes** citywide. This rises to almost 1 in 13 in Rathmines.

25% of all bed-sits in the city can be found in Rathmines.

13 of the city's 162 wards don't have any at all; a further 18 wards have just one bedsit each.

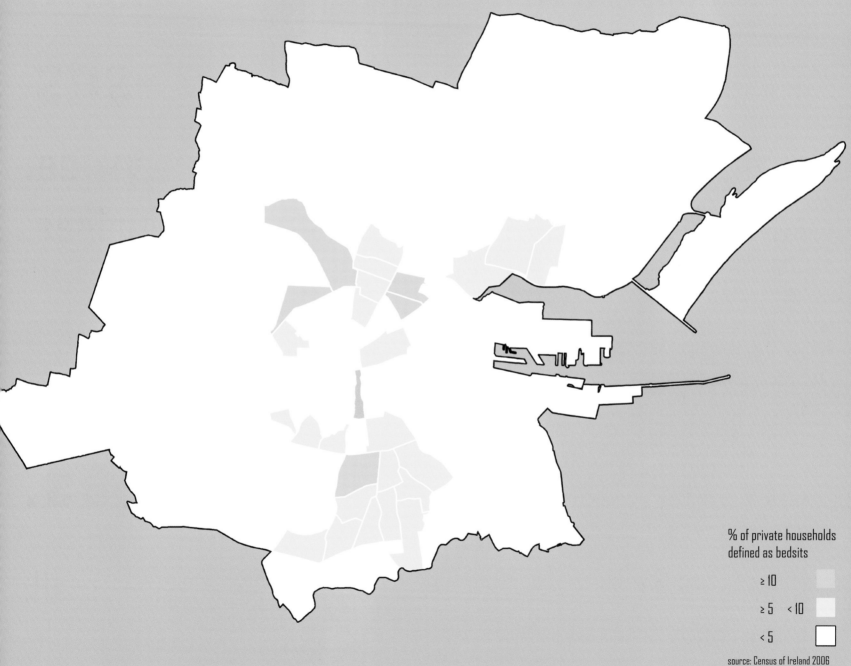

Bedsit Land

% of private households
defined as bedsits

≥ 10

≥ 5   < 10

< 5

source: Census of Ireland 2006

1 in 9 Dubliners live alone

1 in 10 live in homes with 6 or more people;
1 in 7 southsiders live alone, versus 1 in 10 northsiders.

You are two-and-a-half times more likely to live alone in the city centre than live with a family of 6 or more. For the rest of the city it's a 50:50 chance of either.

1 in 5 residents of Cherry Orchard live in households with 6 or more people.

1 in 4 people live in 2-person households. That rises to 40% in South Docklands.

Home Alone

Full house

% of people living in households with 6 or more people

≥ 20

≥ 15

% living in households with 6 or more people, or 1 person only, is less than 15%

Home alone

% living in households with 1 person only

≥ 15

≥ 20

source: Census of Ireland 2006

1 in 6 homes in Dublin city have 2 rooms or less.

Over a third of all homes in the North Inner City have 2 rooms or less.
Only 1 in 8 homes have 7 rooms or more.

Almost 40% of homes in the North Inner City have 2 rooms or less. 1 in 50 homes have 7 rooms or more.

Almost 1 in 10 homes have just 1 single habitable room.

In Terenure South, 66% of homes have 7 rooms or more.

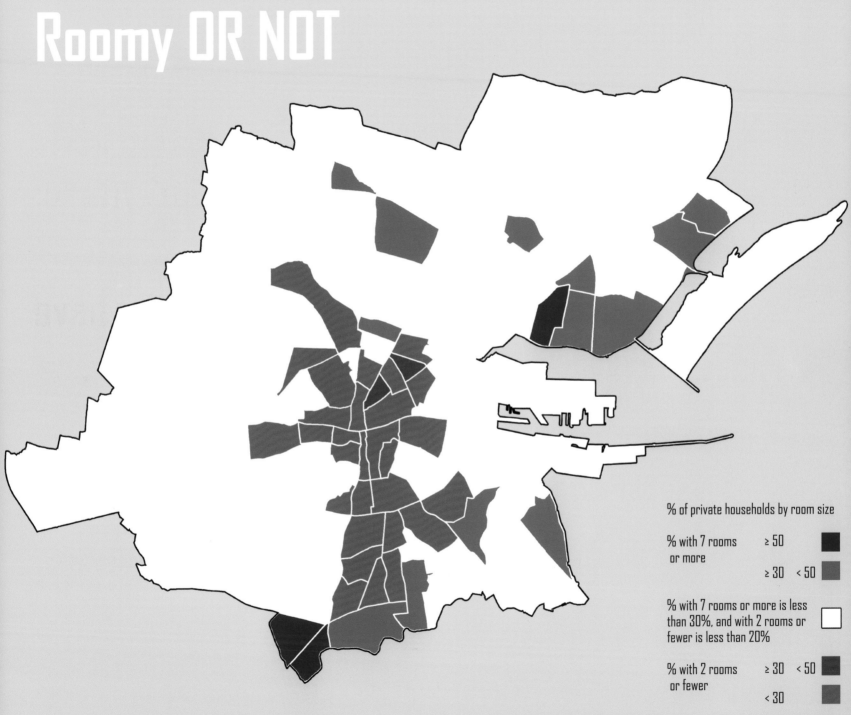

Roomy OR NOT

% of private households by room size

% with 7 rooms
 or more
≥ 50

≥ 30   < 50

% with 7 rooms or more is less
than 30%, and with 2 rooms or
fewer is less than 20%

% with 2 rooms
 or fewer
≥ 30   < 50

< 30

source: Census of Ireland 2006

1 in 4 households have no mortgage to repay, **owning their homes outright.**

This rises to 1 in 2 in Walkinstown. This is the highest pocket of 'real' homeowners in the city.

Contrary to popular perception, **more northsiders own their own home outright** than southsiders, and the south city centre has more local authority renters than the North Inner City. **1 in 9** of all households are **local authority renters.**

These are concentrated in the South Inner City and in the north and west suburban fringes of the city.

Mortgage Free

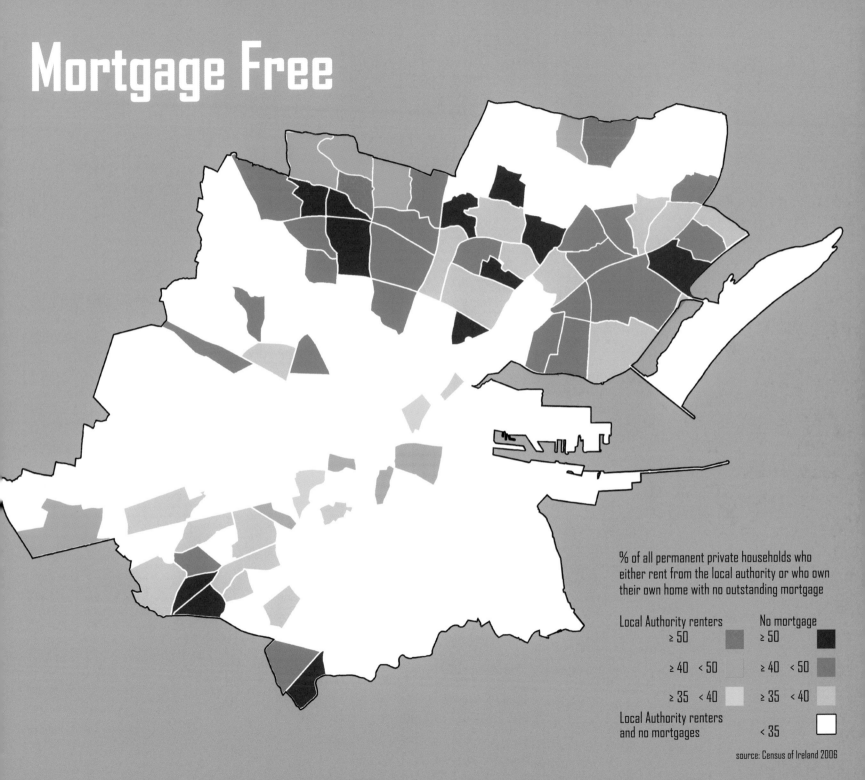

% of all permanent private households who
either rent from the local authority or who own
their own home with no outstanding mortgage

Local Authority renters | No mortgage
≥ 50 | ≥ 50
≥ 40 < 50 | ≥ 40 < 50
≥ 35 < 40 | ≥ 35 < 40

Local Authority renters
and no mortgages | < 35

source: Census of Ireland 2006

1 in 30 Dubliners define them-selves as 'Asian' or 'Asian-Irish'.

Asians are urban

In the 11 wards that make up the entire North Inner City (population 33,000), 1 in 8 are Asian. **This rises to 1 in 5 in the ward of North City.**

Asians are thin on the ground in Dublin's working-class suburbs; just 1 in 283 Finglas residents and 1 in 258 Ballyfermot residents are Asian.

Eastern Promises

% of private households
defined as bedsits

≥ 15

≥ 10   < 15

≥ 5   < 10

< 5

source: Census of Ireland 2006

1 in 9 homes in Dublin city have **no central heating.**

Northsiders are warmer than southsiders. Almost 1 in 7 southside homes do not have central heating, compared to 1 in 11 northside homes.

Rathmines and the North Inner City have the **coldest** homes in winter, with almost 1 in 5 homes having no central heating.

That rises to 1 in 3 in the ward of North City. The 'cosiest' place is the North Fringe suburbs. The ward of Ballymun East is one of the toastiest of them all; 99 out of every 100 homes there have central heating.

Winter Blues

% of permanent private households that have central heating

≥ 94	■
≥ 75 < 94	□
≥ 60 < 75	■
≥ 50 < 60	■

source: Census of Ireland 2006

Are 1 in 12 Dubliners post-God?

Almost 1 in 12 Dubliners deliberately chose the category of 'No Religion' in the census of 2006. This rises to almost 1 in 8 in the Rathmines area.

In the 11 wards that make up the **North Inner City** (a population of 33,000) **1 in 6 are post-God.**

Working-class suburbs, however, are remarkably at one with God – a Catholic one. 92% of Ballyfermot residents identify as Catholic; fewer than 1 in 40 are post-God.

79.9% of Dubliners identify themselves as **Catholic**.

In only 4 of Dublin's 162 wards, all located in the inner city, are Catholics a minority. In the ward of North City, for every 3 Catholics there are 2 with 'No Religion'.

Post-God + True Believers

% of people who don't
adhere to a religion

≥ 20

≥ 15 < 20

≥ 3 < 15

< 3

source: Census of Ireland 2006

Women and girls outnumber men and boys in Dublin by a ratio of 51:49.

MEN ARE ON TOP

in the city centre area with a ratio of 52 to 48 in favour of males.

In one area of the city – Cherry Orchard – **males outnumber females by 20%, or a ratio of 3:2.** It is also the location of Wheatfield Male Prison.

Sex and the City

% of population that is male

≥ 52

≥ 51 < 52

≥ 50 < 51

< 50

source: Census of Ireland 2006

What is STREET DNA ?

"Street DNA is the building blocks of, or genetic blueprint for the physical characteristics of all living streets."
In other words, it's what makes our streets tick.

Street DNA

Metro Walk

In METRO WALK we map out an imaginary Dublin pedestrian Metro, an interconnected network of people's pathways, urban junctions and destination stops, all colour-coded to allow you to navigate the good and the great, or assist in avoiding the bad and the dreary streets of the capital city.

METRO WALK is necessarily subjective, and no doubt many will passionately disagree or summarily dismiss our ranking of Dublin's inner-urban streets. METRO WALK is nevertheless a useful guide, a simple tool or framework of thinking for the citizen, the tourist, or the city policy-maker. If it does nothing other than provoke a civic discussion about streets in general, and Dublin's streets in particular – what makes some of them work and others fail – then we have succeeded.

So what makes an urban street great? It is many things. Most are obvious, some less so. One doesn't need an architect, a planner or an urban designer to tell you how an urban street feels, whether you should like it or not. It's instinctive. It either feels good or it doesn't. It's the look of a particular building or group of buildings, the trees lined along the pavement, the glimpses of other streets, your favourite restaurant, shop or pub, the people walking on the street. Recognising great streets, enjoying them, requires little effort; making them, on the other hand, paying for them, keeping them working, keeping them safe, vibrant, clean, interesting and beautiful, is altogether more civically demanding.

There are, we believe, a few common traits to all great streets. Great streets are safe. Great streets are usually clean (busy market streets perhaps are the exception). Great streets, even some of the most disarmingly simple or the very short, are visually interesting. Great streets usually go places. They are not physical or social cul-de-sacs. Great streets are generally shared with other people.

Great urban streets can be busy or they can be quiet. Not all great urban streets need to be bustling with shops and restaurants, be peppered with or possess multiple public entrance points or doorways. It is perfectly acceptable, even desirable, to have calm, predominantly residential streets in the heart of a city with a singular entrance and little or no active commercial ground-floor uses. Such successful, calm, high-density residential urban streets understand the importance of extended lobby entrances, elevated ground-floor living rooms, and protective semi-private green space at street level.

Striking the appropriate balance between the business and the quietness of inner-urban streets is a challenge for any city, and a particular challenge for inner-city Dublin. Many Dublin urban streets often tend to fail, underperform or generate stress for two deceptively simple reasons: they are either busier or noisier than they should be, or the very opposite – they are not as busy as they could or should be.

Both residential and commercial streets can be too busy or noisy. Dublin streets are no exception. Urban commercial streets that are too busy or noisy are not to be confused with streets that are vibrant, thriving and successful. 'Too busy' and 'too noisy' doesn't imply fewer people or less commerce, less density or less intimacy. It does very often require more pedestrian space, wider public pavements, traffic-calming, pedestrian-friendly crossings and greater respect from people for people. That respect includes reduced tolerance for noisy anti-social behaviour, be it screeching bellowing or boorish drunken abuse of others. Many of Dublin's inner urban streets at 1am on a Saturday or Sunday morning are anything but great.

Commercial streets that are too quiet, on the other hand, are easy to recognise. They are usually devoid of people. They are either home to too many vacant premises and derelict sites or have extensive dead street frontage with minimal doorways from the street. Either way, they are usually eerie and very often visually uninteresting. The visual interest of a street is critical. It attracts, it can excite, it can stimulate; it can also calm and welcomingly sedate and comfort. It rarely bores. Short-term visual interest is not to be confused with long-term affection or attachment. Broken streets, abandoned spaces and dilapidated historic buildings may momentarily excite the visiting photographer or the curious art student, but they tend to tire and depress the long-term resident.

It is much more difficult to identify urban residential streets that are too

picture this

DUBLIN

OFF SIDE

STREET WALKING

quiet. They do exist. They also have their own unique particular problems. These quiet streets are not the sleepy cul-de-sacs of suburbia, but rather the streets of partly abandoned or half-empty homes in the city. They are also incomplete or broken residential streets. These are streets pock-marked by dereliction with isolated islands of residential blocks or houses.

It's a peculiar irony of 'empty' or quietly abandoned urban residential streets that they often attract occasional but acute forms of invasive noise pollution and aggression. An 'underperforming' quiet inner-city residential street is much more likely to attract or 'permit' the audible raucous passer-by, the drunken or howling out-of-towner who, because of the real or perceived lack of local passive residential surveillance, have little respect for those who live there.

Inner Dublin has many quiet quality residential streets, but it has very few quiet quality high-density apartment residential streets. Quality high-density apartment residential streets are usually calm for its residents. Many are 'leafy' and green. They may or may not have many people walking along them. They may or may not have other ground-floor uses. They are likely to have spacious apartment entrance foyers in the form of great communal entrance halls or doorways. These streets are not to be confused with residential streets housing ill-configured ground-floor apartments where bedrooms directly front onto the pavement, with habitable room windows centimetres from the street at ground level, invariably protected by guardrails. This is a failed street, and they are surprisingly common in Dublin's inner city.

Successful streets have many more varied and diverse origins or reasons for their success. In METRO WALK we have chosen a few of our favourite Dublin streets. We have photographed some of the things that we think makes these streets great. Choice, diversity, interest and comfort are common to all.

STREETWATCHING

metro war

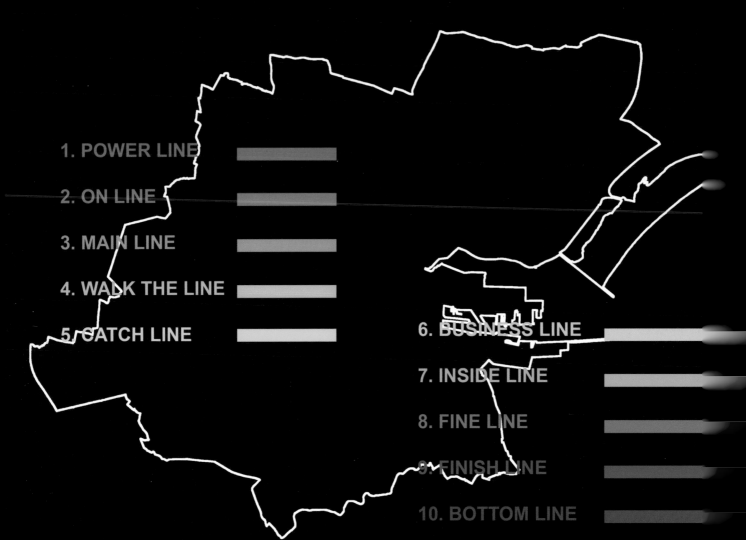

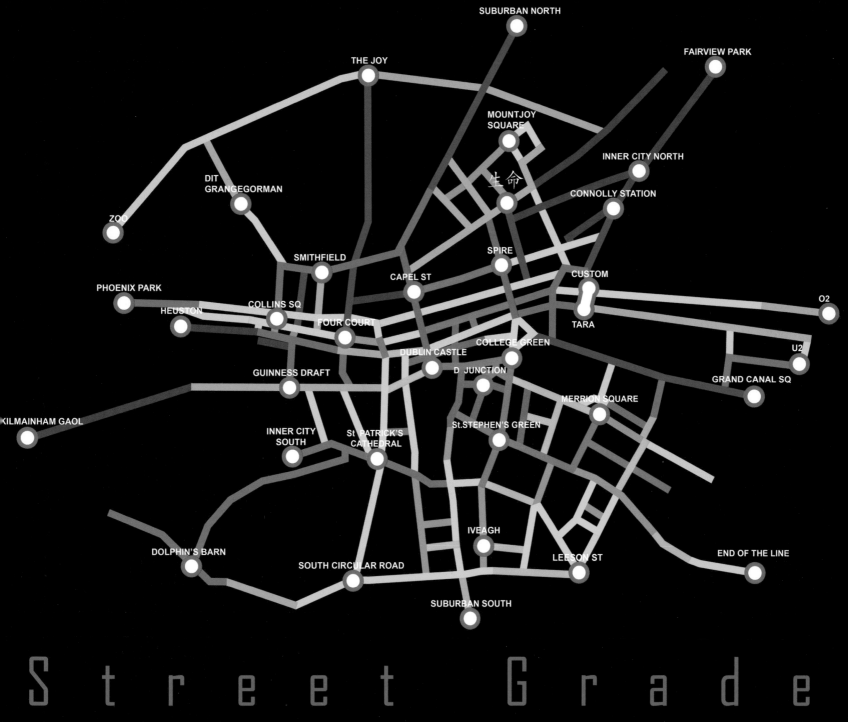

Thomas Street / James's Street

Parliament Street

Nassau Street

Usher's Street

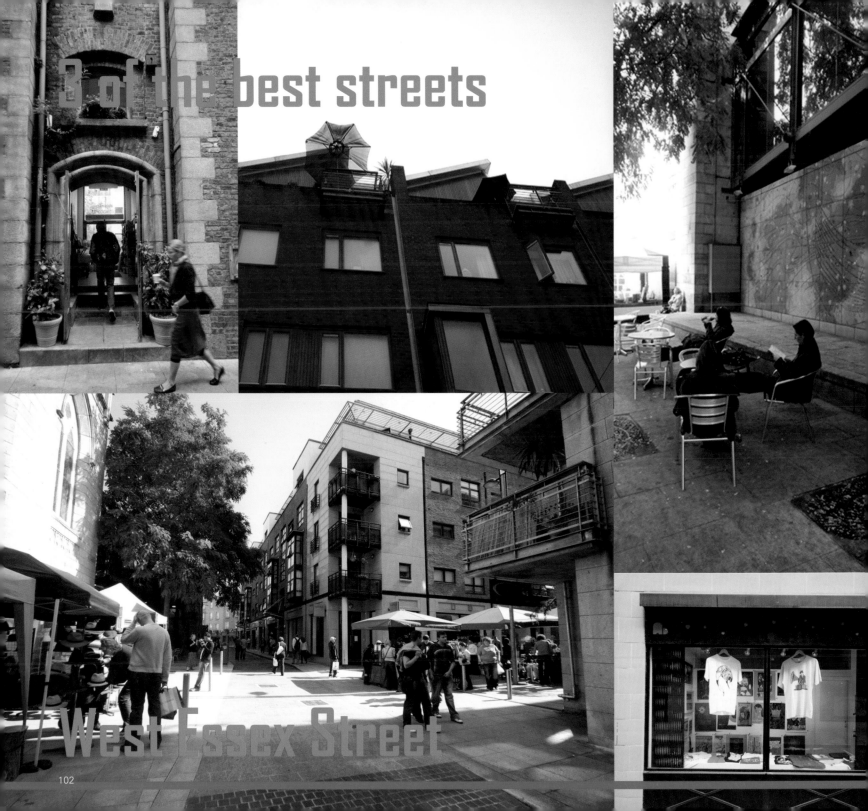

3 of the best streets

West Essex Street

Capel Street

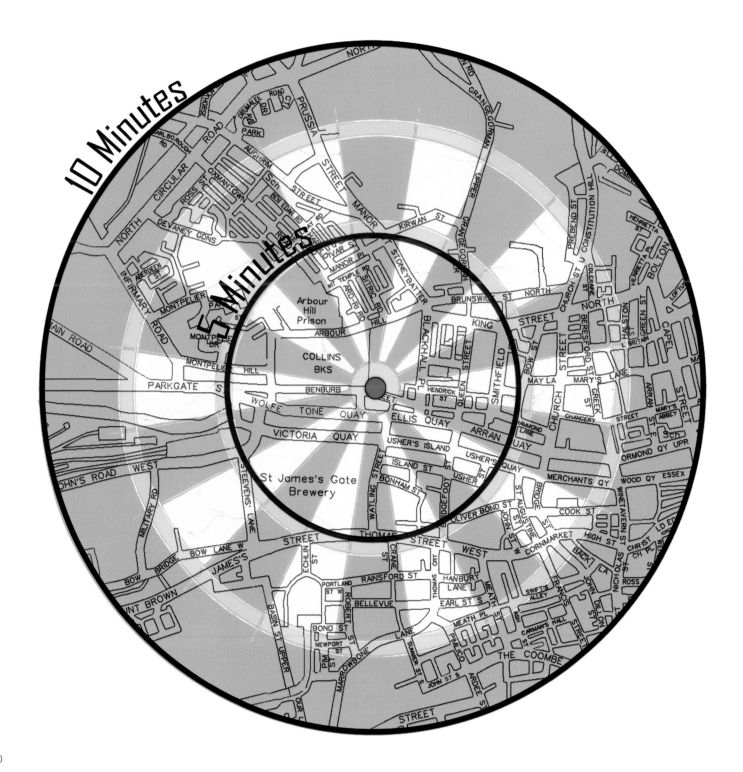

Reality Urbanism

So what makes a great neighbourhood?

There are many things that make a great neighbourhood. Some are easier to define than others. Community spirit, a sense of place, respect for newcomers, and civic participation are all hugely important, but somewhat difficult to quantify. The presence of a great park, tree-lined streets, a quality and affordable supermarket, a good school or a local children's playground are altogether easier things to identify and measure. Most people also understand them as both practical and desirable.

The things that detract from or diminish an area are, of course, equally important in any evaluation of the quality of life in a neighbourhood. Few people want to walk past derelict buildings, boarded-up shops or vacant premises. Even fewer would prefer not to have to walk over uncollected rubbish or avoid dog waste on the streets they walk every day.

The list of what contributes to or detracts from a neighbourhood is as infinite as it is subjective. We have, however, endeavoured to narrow it down to 50 reasonably tangible items – 25 of the best and 25 of the worse things that you would want or definitely not want to find in your neighbourhood. They are pretty timeless, as valid today as they would have been twenty or forty years ago or likely to be in decades to come.

10 minutes away

50 of the Best and the Worst

things you want and don't want to find in a 10 minute walk from your home

50 of the Best and the Worst things you want and don't want to find in a 10-minute walk away from your home

Take the Quiz

Grab a map of your local area and start mapping and plotting the best and the worst of what is close to your home. Local circumstances can differ, but as a rule of thumb a ten-minute walk is approximately 800m. You know your local area and your own speed of walking, so you are the best judge of a ten-minute walking range.

25 of the Best in your area

Give yourself one point if you can find any of the following within a ten-minute walk from your home. Triple the points if any are just a five-minute walk away from your front door.

1   A local public park
2   A great job you can walk to
3   A cinema
4   A friendly local bar (that you visit)
5   Good friends
    (that doesn't include acquaintances or polite neighbours)
6   A great city park
7   At least one building you truly like
8   A delightful garden (shared or otherwise)
9   An urban tram or metro stop
10 A least one tree-lined street
11 A truly beautiful view
    (must be less than five minutes walk away)
12 Café dinning al fresco
13 A museum to wander around
14 A post office, an ATM or a pharmacy
15 A place to swim
16 Your dream home
17 A great view from at least one window of your home
18 A good school
19 A quality supermarket
20 At least one local greengrocer, fishmonger or butcher
21 Children's playgrounds
22 Good restaurant(s)
23 A new building you truly like
24 A cosmopolitan buzz (you can easily tell when and where it exists)
25 A taxi that can take you to an airport (international) for under €25

25 of the Worst in your area

Deduct yourself 1 point if you can find any of the following within a ten-minute walk from your home. Triple the deduction if any are either a five-minute walk away or if any are visible on your daily or preferred walk home from work, college, the local shops, etc

1   Derelict sites that seem to be there forever
2   Places you avoid after dark
3   A locked local park
4   Too many or too few police
5   Boarded-up buildings
6   Rubbish dumped or uncollected
7   Too many dreary and ugly buildings
8   Drunken people and drug-dealing
9   Black gunge on the pavement (that's never hosed)
10   Parks with nowhere to sit
11   Obstacles to walking
12   Pedestrian traffic lights that seem to stay red
13   Drivers that see you as a target
14   Blocked-up doors or windows
15   Closing-down signs or abandoned factories
16   Polluted river
17   Poor street-lighting
18   Cycle lanes inside bus lanes
19   Suffocating car fumes
20   Ugly street furniture (including poles with nothing on them)
21   Offensive graffiti
22   Narrow pedestrian pavements
     (road space is plentiful or underused)
23   Streets peppered with dereliction.
24   Badly designed and substandard housing
25   Human or animal waste that's never cleaned

Bonus Green Points – Give yourself bonus green points for the following:
– A job that you enjoy within ten-minutes walking distance of your home
  (10 points)
– A quality school that children can safely walk to (5 points)
– A tram, light rail or metro stop within a five-minute walk from your front
  door (5 points)
– A local park within a five-minute walk (2 points)
– A 'city'-scale park within a ten-minute walk (2 points)
– A recycling facility such as a bottle bank within a ten-minute walk
  (1 point) (if however the noise is unbearable from your home, deduct 5
  points for noise pollution)

Your Score

50 to 100 points

The chances are that you are living in a truly great part of a great city. Our advice (you obviously don't need much guidance in this field) is to stay put. Your neighbourhood is both a desirable and interesting place to live. Extend the lease, or remortgage and invest in your home in this dream urban area.

0 to 50 points

Your neighbourhood score here sends out mixed messages. There is a possibility that you are living in one of the following: a settled affluent suburb, an area close to the heart of a middle-sized town, or an inner-urban area with true potential. If you are living in a settled affluent suburb you are obviously missing some of the attractions that make the city so satisfying – the vitality, energy and accessibility of urban living. You are, of course, avoiding some of the grit and grime or edginess that comes with most cities. If you are living in an inner-urban area with true potential, hang in there. There would appear to be many strong local positives. The chances are the area has considerable regeneration potential and – notwithstanding any temporary national economic down turn – is likely to change for the better.

0 to -50 points

You are either living in a distant and/or badly planned suburb or an edgy and gritty urban area. Either way, city or suburb, you are likely to be living in a kind of residential twilight zone, with below-average local services. Look out for the municipal commitment to your area, and its commitment or understanding of urban living in general. Dumping 'unattractive' municipal uses or services in your locality, indifference to street cleaning or failure to improve the local park or plant a tree are clear warning signals of municipal indifference to your neighbourhood.

-50 to -100 points

Where exactly are you living? We reckon it's time to get out, and get out fast. If, for whatever reason, you insist on staying or can't afford to move, try to get involved in local community politics to change things for the the better. You are either living in a very tough or peripheral suburb or a historically depressed and socially disadvantaged part of a city, and its time to either get organised to fight back or start packing and move on. An alliance of like-minded community locals armed with an ambitious civic determination and a reasonable understanding of municipal or local city politics has the power to literally transform any area for the better.

Our advice? If you do insist on staying and want to improve your area, steer clear of the following:
– Ideologically driven solutions or ideologically driven people, particularly if they don't live in your neighbourhood.
– Municipal plans or plan-makers that have neither a clear commitment to nor an understanding of how to deliver real resources to realise their plans.
– Meddling, well-intentioned outsiders who don't live in your neighbourhood and patronise or flatter you and don't tell it as it is. You are more likely to know your own area's strengths and weaknesses.
– 'Nostalgia' of any political persuasion. Nostalgia is a barrier to logic and effective change.
– The cynic doubter or naysayer. Avoid the peddlers of 'bigotry of low expectation'; they surprisingly and deceptively come in all sorts of political stripes and guises. They can lurk within your own community; more often they communicate their prejudice or lack of ambition through a prism of well-meaning or well-intentioned 'it will do-ism'.
– Technocrats and bureaucrats who talk impenetrable gobbledygook non-speak. Clean city streets are clean city streets, even if some prefer to call them quality landscapes of valued animated urban public domain.

Instead embrace the following: Trust your instincts. Focus on small, short-term, high-profile actions. Seek and welcome change. Demand to know how city monies are spent on everything from tree-planting to street cleansing. Cultivate relationships with developers to invest in your area. Make the most of local expertise, but stay sceptical of those who talk about 'the community' at the expense of real issues. Be ambitious. And finally, most of all, fight for resources both public and private for your neighbourhood as opposed to fighting against developments in your neighbourhood.

10 minutes away

DUB-*URBS*
Finding 'Urban' Dublin

If Dublin is a predominantly suburban city, with a vibrant albeit small downtown or city centre, where exactly is 'urban Dublin'? Where does it begin and end?

Dublin's city centre may be small, stretching probably no more than a couple of kilometres north to south, and even less as one moves east-west, but what it lacks in size it certainly compensates for in energy and vibrancy. The city centre has an undoubtable buzz, with the density and intensity of ground-floor pubs, cafés, restaurants and shopping comparing favourably to most European cities of a comparable size. Probably the best time to experience this city buzz is either early Thursday evening or Saturday afternoon, preferably in late spring or early summer, when gallery openings can be crashed, urban markets explored, early drinks enjoyed and a general air of urban expectation and pedestrian vitality fills the city. This street life is arguably one of the city's, and, by implication, the State's, biggest economic assets. It helps attract people to the city, be they local suburbanites, short-stay tourists, or foreign citizens who may, for a variety of economic reasons, choose to stay.

If, however, one wanders (inadvertently or otherwise) a block or two beyond this bustling downtown, one enters a peculiar, confusing and somewhat unique Dublin urban transitional zone. We call these streets the 'Dub-urbs'. The first thing you notice about the Dub-urbs is that footfall (planner-speak for the number of people walking along the street) dramatically drops, shops and restaurants curiously begin to disappear. The transition is usually abrupt and unexpected. On the north side of the city it's west of Capel Street, north of Parnell Street, and one block, or two at most, east of O'Connell Street. On the south of the city, the George's Street to Camden Street axis provides the western boundary of the downtown.

The Dub-urbs aren't simply about reduced pedestrian footfall. The Dublin urban 'transitional zone' ('Dub-urbs'), are usually characterised by an increasing proliferation of poor architecture, reoccurring pockets of dereliction, significantly reduced visual interest, inconvenient road traffic junctions and, occasionally, a general sense of unease. There are few quality incidental spaces. Walking through much of the Dub-urbs can be a somewhat harried pedestrian experience, the objective primarily to negotiate getting from A to B. The exception to this fractured transitional geography is the Georgian south-east quadrant of the city. But even the southeast Georgian core – a phenomenal architectural and cultural asset – is generally forlorn and usually drained of any interesting street life by early weekday evening and most weekends. This potentially dynamic district, fortunate to 'inherit' a rich and largely intact architectural heritage, is, for that very reason, a peculiarly underperforming area. What could be a thriving, bustling mixed-use residential quarter with a much sought-after Dublin 'village Redbrick' (an equivalent of the much sought-after New York 'village Brownstone'), is, for the most part, instead a dreary mono-use office belt.

It's perfectly common and understandable, of course, that a city centre has an intermediary area, an edge, a beginning and an end. What makes the Dub-urbs transitional zone particularly unique is the near total absence of either a significant intact or newly created urban quality residential district. Isolated pockets of apartment blocks and individual islands of social housing complexes, disconnected by pedestrian-unfriendly traffic junctions and generally poor quality streets, do not constitute a coherent urban residential district. A high-density residential belt, an ordinary livable urban district, usually rings most European city 'downtowns'. This residential belt is characterised by building heights comparable to the commercial or recreational downtown with residential densities that far exceed suburban locations. They are usually well connected by a legible network of streets with reasonable quality public spaces and served by local shops, cafés and services. Safe cycle paths are not uncommon.

Yet despite a fifteen-year property boom and tens of thousands of new homes having being built, Dublin's inner city continues to lack an extensive, coherent legible inner-urban residential neighbourhood with a plentiful supply of quality, spacious, high-density homes. Much of the revamped and radically transformed Docklands area of the city unfortunately still exudes a somewhat sterile high-end office/retail park atmosphere. The DDDA (Dublin Docklands Development Authority) attempt to capture or replicate the busy vitality of city living or the charm of a green and child-friendly local neighbourhood remains, for now at least, elusive. There are some exciting new public spaces, yet few are green or particularly child-friendly. New homes are relatively small.

Reasonable sized supermarkets are oddly absent. Despite its close proximity to the city centre, the area remains disconnected from the business of city life. Its greatest charm – extensive water frontage – existed long before the DDDA was handed authority and significant public subsidy to redevelop the area.

Isn't the downtown or city centre itself residential? In places yes, but partly because of its limited size and the nature of existing commercial land-use, remarkably few people actually live there. We have estimated that it is no more than one in seventy or 1.6% of the city's entire population resides in its centre.[1] This figure falls to approximately one in every 150 for those who live in the Greater Dublin region.[2] Dublin's downtown or city centre is a great place to shop, work, socialise and to generally walk about, but given its relatively small size, it is disingenuous to characterise it as anything other than a lively downtown dotted with isolated micro-pockets of residential urban living.

Why is this analysis of Dublin's urban character so important? There are many reasons. Providing attractive, high-density urban residential alternatives to predominantly car-dependent suburban living is the best way to combat environmental and financially unsustainable sprawl. High-density urban living allows for the efficient provision of local shops, services, schools and public transport. An attractive, dense and liveable urbanism is widely accepted as being a critical factor in the creativity, innovation and dynamism of cities. High-density quality urban space is also critical in attracting and retaining creative workers, both Irish and foreign born. Getting the capital city right is a direct investment in Ireland's economy.

Providing the choice of attractive, high-density urban residential living also utilises a significant national underperforming asset – namely, inner-urban land. Quality liveable urbanism also gives meaning and coherence to the city's character and legibility. It sustains economic vitality, including tourism. Many of the city's top tourist attractions – Guinness, the National Museum at Collins Barracks, IMMA, Dublin Zoo and the Phoenix Park – continue to be somewhat disconnected urban 'islands' separated from the city centre by dereliction and poor-quality streets. Improving the attractiveness and urban livability of these areas would, simultaneously, sustain the city's tourist economy.

When we talk about high-density residential urban, we mean, of course, city living, that part of the city where building heights are predominantly four storeys or higher, where the local residents can walk or cycle to work or school, walk to a local park, playground, shop, restaurant, bar or café. It is not uncommon to have city-wide services and amenities: hospitals, museums and colleges all sit comfortably within these communities. This is not just an attractive place to live, but also an interesting place to visit. This is a reasonably safe place, relatively clean, a place where the streets are hosed down regularly, and it feels comfortable to walk in late at night. There is a plentiful supply of affordable and family-sized homes. This is a place locals don't walk more than five or six minutes to buy fresh bread, fruit or vegetables, visit a doctor or a pharmacy. This is a place where children walk to school, where elderly neighbours sit and chat on a local park bench or where newly arrived immigrants feel comfortable. The neighbourhood doesn't have to have any particular historical set pieces or award-winning architectural interventions. It is not a stage set for iconic architecture. It is a real place for living.

This is an urban landscape that needs no interpretation. It doesn't require an artificial 'district' or 'character label' or any other planning euphemisms to function effectively. It just is. It's ordinary. It's comfortable. It's a desirable place to live. Whilst history or a sense of place is understood and respected, the past or the lives of those who lived there are not romanticised; instead the present quality of life is strongly valued. This is a place where the local people are both welcoming and yet warmly indifferent to newcomers who choose to live amongst them. It's a place where the community doesn't have to have a shared identity, a common history, a collective personality other than they get on with their lives and each other, and there's the necessary minimum social level of respect and tolerance.

Assimilation and integration are imposed abstractions; friendships and choice, on the other hand, are real, are valued and are understood. Community participation is not sitting in a draughty local municipal hall listening to community 'activists' berating local officials. Rather, it's partaking in the life of the local neighbourhood, it's a casual friendly hello, a cup of coffee, an invitation or a conversation. It's an ordinary place but also a place capable of extraordinary possibilities. Now that's urban.

Planet Dublin

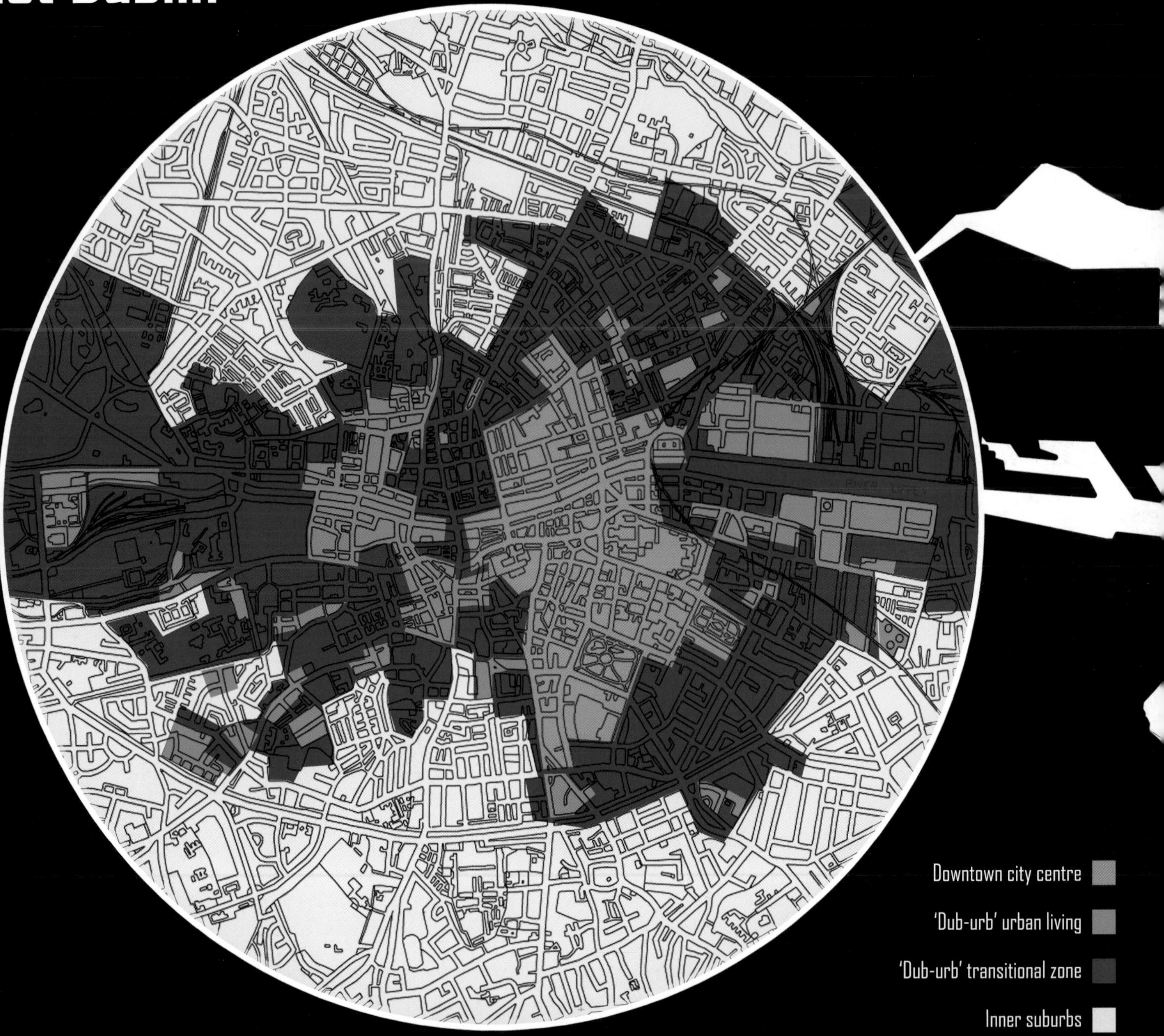

Downtown city centre
'Dub-urb' urban living
'Dub-urb' transitional zone
Inner suburbs

Ledge City

In PLANET DUBLIN we map out Dublin's city centre (orange). This is the commercial downtown core of Dublin. High-density private inner-city apartment and social flat complexes are shown in green. These blocks are predominantly four-to-five storey in height, with densities averaging 150 to 200 residential units per hectare. Encircling the city core, a residential ring, mostly two-storey, makes up the inner suburbs (pale blue).

Our 'Dub-urbs' (dark blue) is less a transitional urban/suburban zone than a fragmented built-up area. These Dub-urbs have no predominant use, no principal unifying built form. There are individual, special, sometimes exceptional attractions, but little legible overall spatial coherence. The Dub-urbs are, in effect, partially built-up spaces waiting to become connected, pedestrian-friendly places. Our inner-urban residential flat complexes and apartment blocks (green) appear to float somewhat disconnected inside the Dub-urbs in LEDGE CITY.

In LEDGE CITY we protrude our city centre or downtown. Ledge City captures the sometimes dramatically changed, often fractured urban landscape experienced a block outside Dublin's city centre. Leaving the urban core north or west is like falling off a ledge of coherent or quality urbanism. The transition is usually abrupt and unexpected. On the northside of the city it is immediately west of Capel Street and north of Parnell Street, and one or two blocks east of O'Connell Street. On the southside of the city, the George's Street / Camden Street axis is effectively the western boundary of the downtown area.

Inner City Outer Space

Why the FUSS? And what it tells us about urban Dublin

Why is it that an urban (predominantly low-quality) residential Dublin dominates the inner city, and an urban (predominantly high-quality) non-residential, recreational Dublin dominates the city centre? Why the functional urban spatial segregation (FUSS)? What does it tell us about the desirability of an urban life in Dublin? Evidently, an urbanism to be temporarily consumed, but not permanently lived.

"*Suburbia* is the place where major life decisions have already been made or futures foretold. The *City* is a space for stories of dreams and desires yet to unfold."

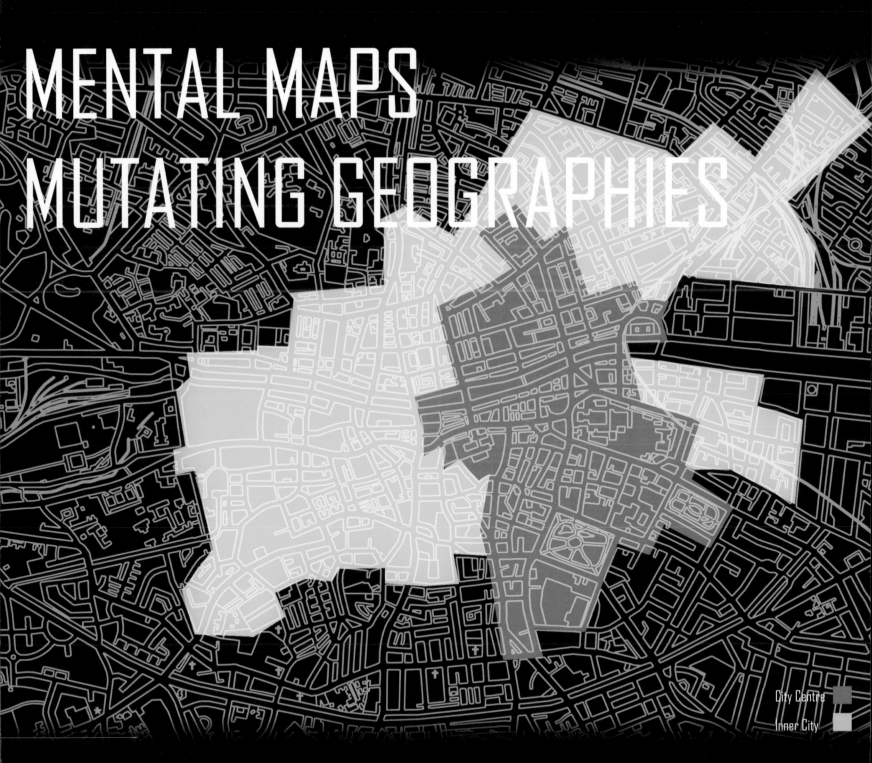

MENTAL MAPS
MUTATING GEOGRAPHIES

City Centre
Inner City

Central Area

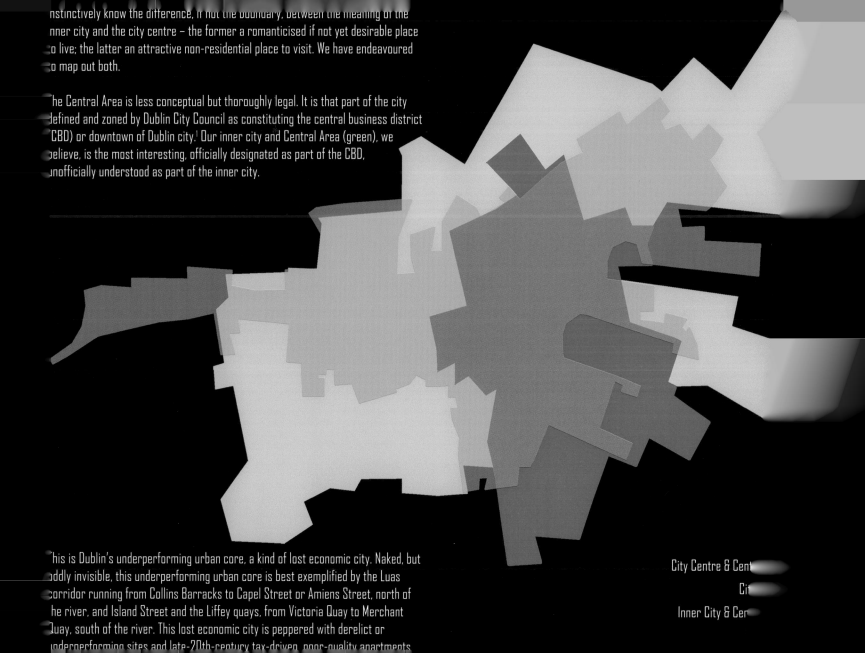

nstinctively know the difference, if not the boundary, between the meaning of the inner city and the city centre – the former a romanticised if not yet desirable place to live; the latter an attractive non-residential place to visit. We have endeavoured to map out both.

The Central Area is less conceptual but thoroughly legal. It is that part of the city defined and zoned by Dublin City Council as constituting the central business district (CBD) or downtown of Dublin city.[1] Our inner city and Central Area (green), we believe, is the most interesting, officially designated as part of the CBD, unofficially understood as part of the inner city.

This is Dublin's underperforming urban core, a kind of lost economic city. Naked, but oddly invisible, this underperforming urban core is best exemplified by the Luas corridor running from Collins Barracks to Capel Street or Amiens Street, north of the river, and Island Street and the Liffey quays, from Victoria Quay to Merchant Quay, south of the river. This lost economic city is peppered with derelict or underperforming sites and late-20th-century tax-driven, poor-quality apartments

City Centre & Cent

Cit

Inner City & Cer

131

Is Ranelagh Urban? And does it matter?

The neighbourhood of Ranelagh in Dublin is increasingly being trumpeted as a model of successful high-density, walkable urbanism. In 2010 the incoming president of the Royal Institute of the Architects of Ireland (RIAI) suggested that in order to ensure 'compact and sustainable communities', we should aspire to 'the quality of life you might find in Ranelagh, Dalkey, Kinsale or Westport'. So is the 'compact and sustainable' quality of life in Ranelagh urban, and if it isn't, does it matter?

Ranelagh is just one kilometre south of Dublin city centre and, by common consensus, is a very desirable place to live. Boasting leafy avenues and streets, Ranelagh is home to a dense concentration of fine two-storey 19th and early 20th-century Victorian and Edwardian redbrick homes. More than 10,000 people live in Ranelagh,[1] that's just over 7,200 people per km^2 – a reasonably high density of population relative to the rest of Dublin city.[2] The residents of Ranelagh are relatively wealthy.[3] Two in five of them walk to school or work compared to just one in four citywide.[4] Ranelagh has good local parks, and a light-rail line runs through its centre, connecting it to the city centre in minutes. The centre of Ranelagh provides an attractive choice of local shops, restaurants and bars, all within 5-10 minutes walk of its 10,000 residents. This neighbourhood is surely a model of successful Dublin urbanism? Or is it?

Ranelagh is often invoked as the quintessential Dublin equivalent of the many inner 'city villages' of London that are undeniably urban. Ranelagh, however, isn't just any 'city village'; it is frequently held up as the exemplar of high-density, attractive, connected and walkable Dublin urbanism. It occupies a pre-eminence in the consciousness of a particular strand of the Dublin city middle class that is consciously aware of its status and eager to differentiate both their own local neighbourhood and themselves from more distant outlying wealthy suburbs and suburban residents.

A fairer London comparison to Ranelagh is, perhaps, the neighbourhood of Kensington and Chelsea, one of the wealthiest and more fashionable 'urban' villages in London. Ranelagh, however, is no Chelsea. Chelsea is home to a diversity of London attractions – museums, shopping, galleries, Chelsea FC, Saatchi & Saatchi, etc This isn't simply a matter of

scale, London versus Dublin, its a matter of choice, a choice that an 'urban' village like Chelsea can and does offer (thus attracting others to visit) and one that an inner suburban village like Ranelagh doesn't and rarely can. Perhaps quality urbanism is, if nothing else, about choice and diversity. (Failed urbanism rarely offers either.) How attractive urbanism distinguishes itself from attractive suburbanism is that the former offers sustainable, often extraordinary levels of real choice – choice of housing type, choice of shopping, choice of work, and choice of recreation. It also potentially excites. Attractive suburbanism rarely excites anymore than it provides real choice. Unless one is visiting friends or family, there is actually no particular reason for the non-Ranelagh resident to visit Ranelagh. This is, not surprisingly, a common characteristic of most suburbs. Suburbs invite visitors. If permission is not sought and given by local residents, one can often feel like a trespasser. Non-locals are viewed somewhat suspiciously. Urban areas are open to all; anonymity is a virtue not a vice.

The Ranelagh/London 'urban village' comparison also misses a critical difference between the urban geography of London and Dublin. In part because of differences of scale, Dublin has an altogether different typology. Unlike London, Dublin is not made up of a series of neighbouring polycentric urban villages; it has a strong identifiable urban core, and unlike London possesses a vast underperforming urban residential ring (the inner city). Ranelagh is self-evidently not of this core. It happily exists outside this ring of underperforming urbanism. Its street pattern is not hardwired or connected to the network of Dublin's urban streets in the way Chelsea is in London. The fact that Ranelagh exists outside this ring of underperforming urbanism is an undeniable factor in its attractiveness to Dubliner's. It is a successful and performing neighbourhood that charms with attractive redbricks, quaint coffee shops and restaurants and boutique wine stores.

But what makes it so special or different from other (superficially, at least), comparable inner-Dublin-suburban neighbourhoods? What is the difference between Ranelagh and Stoneybatter? They are both approximately one kilometre from the city centre. They are both historic Dublin city villages peppered with attractive Victorian and Edwardian terraces, and have similar densities. Stoneybatter is reasonably close to a light-rail line, and has quality local parks on its doorstep. Ranelagh is, however, a far wealthier place than Stoneybatter. It is that wealth that sustains those quaint eateries and specialist retail stores. It might appear obvious, but it is nevertheless worth stating: Ranelagh's wealth does not convey an automatic badge of urbanism.

If Ranelagh evokes any Irish comparison, it's not the diversity, dynamism, opportunity or, indeed, challenges of inner-city or city-centre Dublin, but rather interestingly the humdrum hub of the quaintest towns and villages on Ireland's west and south coasts. Ranelagh, as the president of the

RIAI acutely observed, looks and feels remarkably like the fashionable villages and towns of Kenmare, Westport or Kinsale. Outwardly, at least, they are visibly and functionally apparently very similar. They all offer the same range of 'small town', quality local services. They all celebrate the best that a small, dense, wealthy Irish town has to offer.

Ranelagh is, of course, in Dublin city. Its close proximity to, but safe distance from the city centre is a critically important factor in accounting for its wealthy status, a reality that many of its suburban residents possibly do not consciously care to acknowledge. It is its 'urban distance' just as much as its 'city-centre proximity' that explains Ranelagh's unique Dublin attraction. There is an inescapable feeling, for good or ill, that the life of a city, a sense of real urbanism is somewhere else, over there, over the canal, to be visited but safely contained, not threatening, and consumed at a safe distance. This perhaps says less about Ranelagh or its residents than it does about Dubliners' views on the attraction and quality of Dublin urbanism itself.

So if Ranelagh isn't urban, but instead a relatively wealthy inner suburb, does it really matter? It probably matters very little to most of the residents who live there. What does matter is that urban professionals and citizens are honest about our city, that we understand the challenges and opportunities of real urban living. It is also important to try to understand why, as citizens, we eagerly embrace and promote Ranelagh as a model for future urban Dublin development. Is it simply because Dublin doesn't have an existing successful extensive real urban residential district and that this relatively exclusive, self-contained inner suburb is superficially viewed as the next best thing? Is it because we collectively believe that Dublin can't actually have a real attractive urbanism (a bigotry of low expectation – we just can't do it here), or is it because we don't really believe in real urban living and are perhaps unable or unwilling to admit it? After all, if the best 'urban' place in our city to live is neither really 'in the city' nor 'urban', what does it say about the urban liveability of this city?

The relatively high density of over 7,000 people per square kilometre also masks an interesting story. Ranelagh, despite its obvious wealth, has a remarkably high proportion of very small homes. The number of homes with two rooms or less is greater than one in three.[5] One in 13 homes are classified by their residents as bedsits.[6] Most of these are not visibly purpose-built flats or apartments, but 'unseen' sub-divisions of period houses. Most are student flats. It is reasonable to presume we are not aspiring to build a new high-density urbanism where a third of all new homes have just one-bedroom.

A final thought, if Ranelagh really is urban, and Ranelagh is one of the wealthiest and most 'fashionable' neighbourhoods in Dublin, can Dubliners imagine a better urbanism? And if so, what might it look like?

True Dubs and Adopted Dubliners

I'm a Developer Liam Carroll

Name three things you like about Dublin?
Its energy, scale and setting – the bay, Liffey, Wicklow mountains.
And three things you don't like about the city?
The sprawl, traffic congestion, and the bureaucratic obstacles.
Apart from the immediate economic difficulties, what do you think is the biggest challenge facing Dublin over the next 10 years?
Avoiding the temptation of crawling into our shells as a result of damaged confidence and to enable committed people to jump-start recovery as soon as possible.
What is the greatest opportunity facing the city over the next ten years?
To build on the progress already made.
What was the biggest 'mistake' the city made during the boom?
The slowing of development in or near the city centre.
What would you like Dublin to be known for?
As a sophisticated, modern and energetic city.
What do you think Dublin is actually known for?
A weekend destination of historic and cultural importance which has suffered from the credit crisis and a compromised image.
If you could change one thing about the city, what would it be and why?
To resurrect the development of near-city-centre lands in the short term, and to reinforce the consolidation of a living compact city.
What city, outside Ireland, has most impressed you and why?
Bordeaux. The old and the modern are reconciled, people seem to enjoy living there.
Where do you live and why?
Mount Merrion, because its calm quietness suits my family while nevertheless being relatively close to the city centre.
Did you ever live in the inner city?
Yes, as a student.
What cities do you think are Dublin's competitors?
Similar-sized cities that manage and support a real and meaningful quality of urban life – Bordeaux, Copenhagen, Vienna.
Do you think a directly elected mayor with political powers is a good idea?
Not necessarily. It would depend on the vision and capacity for real and positive change.

Word Association Test

The River Liffey:	What the city is all about
Guinness Brewery:	Waste of space
Croke Park:	Very brave of the GAA. Bertie talked about the 'Bertie Bowl'; they [GAA] went ahead and did it.
St Stephen's Green:	Fantastic place
Inner city:	Lots of tourists and foreigners make it almost a cosmopolitan city
Dublin Bay:	Doesn't have a lot of water; think it needs the eastern bypass
The Liberties:	Great area, lovely people up there
O'Connell Street:	Good attempt at regeneration
Dublin 4:	Should it be part of the city or not? I'm not sure.
Dublin City Council:	I would be for enterprise.
James Joyce:	Great man. I don't know very much about him.
An Taisce:	A very good body. We have them in one of our buildings. We have to say that.
Temple Bar:	One of the areas that does draw people.
Dublin Castle:	A beautiful place, but I don't think it affects the daily life of the city.
Planners:	There are some good planners, but a lot of planners are afraid to make decisions.
Moore Street:	Maybe past its sell-by date
The Irish Times:	Best paper, the only paper
Georgian Dublin:	Not what it's all cracked up to be. The Wide Streets Commissioners had huge imagination and vision; the buildings, however, are bland.
Liberty Hall:	Should be knocked down.
Northside:	A lot of positives about the north inner city.
Southside:	There's been huge change.
Trinity College:	Great institution
Dublin Bus:	Needs competition
Smithfield:	Didn't work out
Apartment-living:	Will become more accepted over a generation; the Irish man wants his front and back garden
Liffey Boardwalk:	An excellent idea; policing it is a major problem
RTÉ:	Privatisation should be brought into these areas
Docklands:	The future, the city moving east

I'm an ex-Taoiseach
Bertie Ahern

Name three things you like about Dublin?
> Its people, clearly. In my view, it's still a very safe city. And we have a huge amount of open spaces, all close to the city.

And three things you don't like about the city?
> It can be an untidy city. We are far too tolerant of derelict houses, of allowing the state of buildings decline ... and of litter on streets. In development terms, things are just too slow: from the time we start a project, the lead time, to the time we actually do it is just ridiculous, it just kills us. There shouldn't be such bureaucratic ways, with the Bord Pleanálas and all the rest of it...

Apart from the immediate economic difficulties, what do you think is the biggest challenge facing Dublin over the next ten years?
> Trying to get more people, especially families, living in the city ... and dealing with the traffic issues. We are going to have to deal with quality-of-life issues. The reality is that there are not that many families living in the places that have been built up over the last few years. We really need to make it attractive for families.

What is the greatest opportunity facing the city over the next ten years?
> Dublin is a fantastic city, its one of the most popular cities in Europe. It has tourist and business potential, and it will continue to attract people...

What do you think was the biggest 'mistake' the city made in the last fifteen to twenty years, during the boom?
> Allowing far too many small apartments to be built. It excluded the families.

What would you like Dublin to be known for?
> It's a fantastic city ... but it could be a cleaner and more attractive city.

What do you think Dublin is actually known for?
> It is known as a safe and friendly and fun city.

If you could change one thing about the city, what would it be and why?
> It would be the traffic management. We are losing very good businesses and families.

What city, outside Ireland, has most impressed you and why?
> My favourite city in the world is Sydney. We are no Sydney! We should be using all our waterways better. I like Paris also. I love the concept of people living in the city. A living city has to mean living in the city.

Where do you live and why?

Drumcondra. It's so close to so many good facilities – the 'Bots' [Botanic Gardens] – it's relatively safe, there is little crime; it has old houses, well-built houses...

Did you ever live in the inner city?

All my mother's people are from it... I spent my life here... I don't have a problem with it – I regularly walk from here to Marlboro Street. I've no hangups about it, no problems toddling through it. Except for the shitty buildings...

What cities do you think are Dublin's competitors?

I suppose we're just about keeping our nose ahead of Rome and Vienna...

Do you think a directly elected Dublin mayor with real political powers is a good idea?

My fear is someone who'd talk total bullshit and deliver nothing. It would tempt me, if it was to be a mayor of Dublin with real powers and the ability to raise revenue.

Word Association Test

The River Liffey:	Excellent
Guinness Brewery:	Historic
Croke Park:	Home of dreams
St Stephen's Green:	Top class, family
Inner city:	Massively improved, but...
Dublin Bay:	Now a fantastic asset
The Liberties:	In decline
O'Connell Street:	Nearly a capital street
Dublin 4:	Needs more high-rise buildings
Dublin City Council:	Excellent
James Joyce:	Character
An Taisce:	Abolish
Temple Bar:	Better than a bus station
Dublin Castle:	Top class
Planners:	Should be listened to
Moore Street:	Time to move on
The Irish Times:	Could do without it
Georgian Dublin:	History
Liberty Hall:	Should be gone
Northside:	Better than the south
Southside:	In decline
Trinity College:	World class
Dublin Bus:	Improving
Smithfield:	More life needed, more nightlife
Apartment-living:	Nothing wrong with it, more families needed
Liffey Boardwalk:	Good effort; more Gardaí required
RTÉ:	Sell them
Docklands:	A work in progress

I'm an Architect
Yvonne Farrell

Name three things you like about Dublin?
People, the scale and cultural choice. Scale is quite a low city, a lot of sky, walkable city, sense of connection, the cultural vibrancy of a capital city, and a sense of diversity.

And three things you don't like about the city?
Cyclist are treated very badly, infrastructure, decentralisation. The idea of decentralising from a capital is an oxymoron.

Apart from the immediate economic difficulties, what do you think is the biggest challenge facing Dublin over the next ten years?
The contemporary meaning of citizenship; how policies affect our daily lives; what it means to be a contemporary citizen; what projects of modest scale it is possible to build.

What is the greatest opportunity facing the city over the next ten years?
More architects blurring the line with planning, and planning blurring with architecture.

What do you think was the biggest 'mistake' the city made in the last fifteen to twenty years, during the boom?
Believing that it wouldn't end. Speculation, by virtue of its nature, things become separated as products rather than places. We weren't prudent, the value of money went up and the value of the common good got lost.

What would you like Dublin to be known for?
For what it *is* known for – where people still value time and work and cultural opportunity.

What do you think Dublin is actually known for?
Guinness, Joyce, U2, Trinity, music and literature ... a product of media, voice, sound, language and literature. We do like to chat, to talk.

If you could change one thing about the city, what would it be and why?
That it values cyclists.

What city, outside Ireland, has most impressed you and why?
Stockholm. Its engages with the sea, it has very distinctive parts, its sense of scale... Also New York City. It's a liveable city, with diversity, ordered chaos, and a wonderful sense of city.

Where do you live and why?
In a 19th-century square in the Ringsend/Sandymount area, within walking distance of the city. I have good neighbours, it forms a human landscape, this little square – a collection of houses that defines something else, large trees that show the changing

seasons, a 24-hour shop close by, a walk to the theatre on a balmy summer's night.

Did you ever live in the inner city?

I did live off Camden Row in the 1970s. While the Grafton Street space didn't become our flat because it wasn't zoned residential, it has become our office. It's a real privilege.

What cities do you think are Dublin's competitors?

Amsterdam and Berlin for fun and culture.

Do you think a directly elected Dublin mayor with real political powers is a good idea?

Yes. It's necessary for civic engagement and citizenship awareness. They should have a vision, manage budgets and work to a deadline. Good architects juggle to do this all the time.

Word Association Test

The River Liffey:	Dublin
Guinness Brewery:	Tradition
Croke Park:	Wonderful athletes
St Stephen's Green:	Flowers and pleasure
Inner city:	Intensity, choice, accent
Dublin Bay:	Sunrises, Howth to Bray
The Liberties:	Real citizens of Dublin, retained its character
O'Connell Street:	History, GPO
Dublin 4:	A slandered intelligentsia
Dublin City Council:	On whose shoulders rests huge responsibility
James Joyce:	Had to leave Dublin
An Taisce:	Minders
Temple Bar:	Grain, complexity, fun life
Dublin Castle:	A building island in the city
Planners:	People with more impact than I realised
Moore Street:	Characters who sell bad tomatoes
The Irish Times:	Part of Dublin life
Georgian Dublin:	Beautiful legacy
Liberty Hall:	Part of Dublin skyline
Northside:	Nearer than I thought
Southside:	Home
Trinity College:	Rooms in the city
Dublin Bus:	Stillorgan route is brilliant
Smithfield:	Wish it was more simple
Apartment-living:	High ceilings are wonderful
Liffey Boardwalk:	Extremely successful
RTÉ:	Radio I love
Docklands:	Public space is good

I'm a Planner
Dick Gleeson

Name three things you like about Dublin?
Georgian houses, the IFI, Dublin Bay.
And three things you don't like about the city?
The complaint culture, the inscrutability of Dublin Bus, the lack of typologies in architecture.
Apart from the immediate economic difficulties, what do you think is the biggest challenge facing Dublin over the next ten years?
I see the economic downturn as a huge opportunity to realign the city in fundamental ways, the sustainability challenge being the most important; also the liveability, making culture more accessible, energising the citizen to take responsibility for the city.
What is the greatest opportunity facing the city over the next ten years?
Making connections in the inner city – for example, making a great cycle network connecting disconnected people, and really getting to grips with what we mean by the knowledge economy.
What do you think was the biggest 'mistake' the city made in the last fifteen to twenty years, during the boom?
Fragmented and weak institutional set-up of regional planning, three separate local authorities for too long doing their own thing to the detriment of the core, not managing to find a more effective voice in bringing government onside for Dublin.
What would like Dublin to be known for?
Delivering a quality of life for everyone ... to be able to say it's great to live in the city, that citizens have an appreciation of what they have.
What do you think Dublin is actually known for?
An energy and liveliness. It has an attraction and unique character for people who live here. We don't always know what it is.
If you could change one thing about the city, what would it be and why?
We should be at one with our councillors. I'd like a constructive and enduring partnership where we could share their endorsement for the local, and they take real responsibility for the strategic.
What city, outside Ireland, has most impressed you and why?
Copenhagen. There's a long-established appreciation of what good planning and good design means. It's a process as well as a product, a shared belief in the process and value of plan-making.
Where do you live and why?
I live in Naas, mainly because my kids go to school there, and I love the Kildare hinterland for its cycling and walking.

Did you ever live in the inner city?

As a student. I moved away for job reasons.

What cities do you think are Dublin's competitors?

There is a sense of generous co-operation in the cities we compete with, an open source of collaboration, those scale of cities – Stockholm, Copenhagen, Amsterdam, Lyon, Barcelona. A lot of those cities have strong tradition of civic infrastructure.

Do you think a directly elected Dublin mayor with real political powers is a good idea?

I think so. I do admire a lot of cities that have good lord mayors. It would engage the citizen with a sense of civic engagement. It would allow for a strong political voice for Dublin.

Word Association Test

The River Liffey:	Identity of the city
Guinness Brewery:	Smells wonderful, almost emotional
Croke Park:	Amazing achievement for an amateur body
St Stephen's Green:	Peaceful reflection, beautiful environment
Inner city:	Unbounded potential
Dublin Bay:	Magical, interface between bay and the city
The Liberties:	Organic, argumentative, inspirational name
O'Connell Street:	Ceremonial, symmetrical
Dublin 4:	Annoyance
Dublin City Council:	Pride
James Joyce:	Complexity
Phoenix Park:	Gift from Heaven
An Taisce:	Be a member if I wasn't doing what I was doing
Temple Bar:	Resourceful, evolving, always surprising
Dublin Castle:	Just love being there
Planners:	A mixed church
Moore Street:	Colourful, ethnic, badly in need of new role
The Irish Times:	A curates egg, but I have to see it everyday
Georgian Dublin:	Sustainable, adaptable, beautiful
Liberty Hall:	Elegant, of its time
Northside:	South-facing
Southside:	Could do with more of northside edginess
Trinity College:	Magical, terrific example of urban design
Dublin Bus:	Always operating from the back foot
Smithfield:	Needs further decisive moves
Apartment-living:	We are beginning to understand the culture of living in apartments. Tenure is still an issue.
Liffey Boardwalk:	Slightly awkward in design terms, but works enormously well
RTÉ:	Shallow discourse
Docklands:	High quality, yet an opportunity to review where we go from here

I'm a Builder
Mick Wallace

Name three things you like about Dublin.

The Guinness. If I left the city it's the thing I'd miss the most. The further you go way from the quays the worst it gets. I love the river – it's the heart of the city for me. And the wit of its people.

And three things you don't like about the city?

Firstly, the way the place is run, I find abysmal – not so much at city council level, but at top government level... Secondly, the huge level of poverty is disturbing. It impacts on everybody. 20% of the city living in social deprivation translates as drug-abuse and alcohol-abuse, with a direct impact on the city; we haven't addressed these problems... Thirdly, the litter. I see people just throwing stuff out of their cars.

Apart from immediate economic difficulties, what do you think is the biggest challenge facing Dublin over the next ten years?

Addressing the major fact that 20% of the city has been left behind, because it affects everybody, especially them.

What is the greatest opportunity facing the city over the next ten years?

Maybe now we could take a fresh look at how we do things. There a window of opportunity to do things differently. Maybe we can inject a little bit of honesty.

What do you think was the biggest 'mistake' the city made in the last fifteen to twenty years, during the boom?

We allowed development for development sake. We really didn't curtail it, and there wasn't a big input into the quality of it. We built an awful lot of stuff poorly.

What would like Dublin to be known for?

Honesty.

What do you think Dublin is actually known for?

Its fame is very close to its drinking culture. People see it as a town to have good craic in.

If you could change one thing about the city, what would it be and why?

There's too much social division, that's the most unhealthy thing in the city.

What city, outside Ireland, has most impressed you and why?

I'd be very fond of Turin. It's an unsung city, a wonderful place to eat. They are an unusual Italian, a mixture of the north and the south. You can walk around at 3am on a Saturday morning, you don't have to be afraid in Turin.

Where do you live and why?

I live in Fairview. I do like it. I love the sea.

Did you ever live in the inner city?

I stay here [on the quays] sometimes. I love living here. I've two bedrooms here. If I was drinking I'd stay here!

What cities do you think are Dublin's competitors?

Belfast. It's all about supply and demand. People stay when jobs and money are good.

Do you think a directly elected Dublin mayor with real political powers is a good idea?

I do. My one fear is they won't give him enough power, but I would like to think a mayor with powers should only be allowed to stand once. Between you and me, I'm going to stand for it!

Word Association Test

The River Liffey:	Wonderful
Guinness Brewery:	Lovely
Croke Park:	Monstrosity, ugly to look at
St Stephen's Green:	Lovely
Inner city:	Alive
Dublin Bay:	Dirty
The Liberties:	Hidden
O'Connell Street:	Chippers
Dublin 4:	Private schools
Dublin City Council:	Fettered
James Joyce:	Fantastic
An Taisce:	Irrational
Temple Bar:	Cesspit
Dublin Castle:	Locked away
Planners:	I find most of them bright. Believe it or not, I do.
Moore Street:	Finished
The Irish Times:	Right of centre
Georgian Dublin:	A Myth
Liberty Hall:	Green, it's painted green
Northside:	Soul
Southside:	Money
Trinity College:	Exclusive
Dublin Bus:	Late
Smithfield:	Disappointing
Apartment-living:	Depends on the size of it
Liffey Boardwalk:	Good
RTÉ:	Sad
Docklands:	Overrated

DUBLINERS

DUBLINERS maps the population of the top twenty foreign-born nationalities living in Dublin city. The relative size of their country reflects the relative size of their population living in Dublin city. The figures date from 2006, prior to the onset of a sharp downturn in the fortunes of the Irish economy, and therefore possibly represent a recent peak immigration or 'peak globalisation' point in the city's emerging diversity.[1]

144

1 in 1820 LATVIANS
1240
0.2% DUBLINERS

1 in 1270 LITHUANIANS
2637
0.5% DUBLINERS

1 in 236506 CHINESE
5632
1.1% DUBLINERS

1 in 7424 UK
8302
1.6% DUBLINERS

1 in 3539 POLES
10736
2.1% DUBLINERS

1 in 145852 PAKISTANIS
1145
0.2% DUBLINERS

1 in 46172 GERMANS
1776
0.4% DUBLINERS

1 in 10026 CZECHS
1044
0.2% DUBLINERS

1 in 22468 FRENCH
2893
0.6% DUBLINERS

1 in 30498 FILIPINOS
3024
0.6% DUBLINERS

1 in 158247 US
1940
0.4% DUBLINERS

1 in 3207 SLOVAKIANS
1684
0.3% DUBLINERS

1 in 405556 INDIANS
2880
0.6% DUBLINERS

1 in 23274 ITALIANS
2578
0.5% DUBLINERS

1 in 11139 HUNGARIANS
898
0.2% DUBLINERS

1 in 27883 MALAYSIANS
285
0.2% DUBLINERS

1 in 17729 SPANIARDS
2589
0.5% DUBLINERS

1 in 3333 ROMANIANS
8,000
1.6% DUBLINERS

1 in 106354 NIGERIANS
1448
0.3% DUBLINERS

1 in 17572 AUSTRALIANS
1252
0.2% DUBLINERS

"We wanted to live abroad for a while, for the experience. We got an offer in Dublin."
"A few more years."

"We had a large project being built here, and part of our family is living here also."
"Could be for good."

"Accidental. I was offered a job in Dublin."
"It depends on work situation. I don't think I like to rear my children here. You never know."

"To travel Europe, and basically I don't like London."
"A minimum of two years, a maximum of whatever."

"Followed my partner; he dragged me here."
"Indefinitely. Until they kick me out."

"Another year, let's say."
"Four months. We'll see. As soon as I find a job in Italy."
"I heard it was a young, vibrant city."

"My parents emigrated. I was seven, I had no choice."
"Another year, I think."

"To work."
"Maybe two more years, but not more then that. I miss home."
"As long as I have a job."

"To study English. I came for a holiday for six months."
"I don't know. The plan is for five years."

"Initially just a working holiday for six months."
"I don't know. The plan was for five years."

"To study English."
"Probably a few more years, and then we move back to China"

"Job."
"Forever. I have a wife and kids here."

4 years in Dublin
Meital Bendayan, 33
Alon Bendayan, 33
ISRAEL + ISRAEL

3 years in Dublin
Robin Lee, 43
Donagh Collins Lee, 36
UK + returning IRISH

3 years in Dublin
Magdalena Ladka, 30
POLAND

8 months in Dublin
Megan Willows-Munro, 27
SOUTH AFRICA

3 years in Dublin
Juan Carlos Cordovez, 38
EQUADOR

8 years in Dublin
Ivana Pitten, 35
Alesandro Tavernaro, 35
CROATIA + ITALY

10 years in Dublin
Marianna Coccuza, 38
29 years in Ireland
Martijn Vermolen, 37
ITALY + HOLLAND

2 years in Dublin
Pinar Ekerbicer, 32
Harun Ekerbicer, 32
TURKEY + TURKEY

2 years in Dublin
Fabio Lopas, 31
BRAZIL

10 years in Dublin
Jo Anthoni, 42
NEW ZEALAND

10 years in Dublin
Lida Hughes, 36
CHINA

12 years in Dublin
Alfred Sankoh, 40
SIERRA LEONE

mietalrobinoonaghmagdameganjuancarlosivana
alemartjinmariannapinarharunfabiojolidaalfred

LIKE

"the energy" "cosmopolitan" "good walking city" "lively, good vibe, young people" "easy to make friends, people talk" "walkability of it" "good salary, a quality of life better than in italy" "the liveliness, the vibe" "multicultural" "multicultural" "i really like the joy of dubliners" "it's safe, we know where not to walk" "irish people are fun" "the people, it makes the place" "people are friendly" "close to local amenities" "amount of green space" "good to walk around" "scale of the city" "opportunities" "small enough to walk around" "literary history" "friendly people" "the people" "lots of gigs" "job opportunities" "the culture" "blackrock park" "old and new together" "compact, i can cycle everywhere" "full of green" "short distance to work" "its size, compact" "like that ireland sees itself as european" "wandering street pattern" "compact, cosy" "people, the irish and all the other people too" "phoenix park" "relaxing atmosphere at work" "easy to meet up, make friends" "lively" "irish people, irish attitude towards life" "its green parks, they're in your daily life" "dublin is green" "new experiences" "the clean air" "the freedom, people are not nosey" "easy to make friends in the city"

DISLIKE

"drug addicts and drunks on luas" "poorly lit at night" "river is ignored" "standard of apartments" "weather sucks" "drunks and junkies at jervis" "the horrible traffic" "the weather" "people drunk" "the weather" "the smell of pee" "in a spoilt way it's expensive" "first the weather" "traffic chaos, fighting to get from a to b" "some parts are very dodgy" "expensive" "difficult to walk with a buggy in the city centre" "too much traffic" "lack of city neighbourhoods" "dangerous in places" "difficult to get answers here" "bathroom plumbing" "the weather" "public transport" "scumbags" "lifestyle, pubs" "prices are too high" "no fish market in dublin" "it's so small, where do i go now? another seat?" "lack of integrated transport" "racism" "trouble in the city centre" "level of vandalism" "the northside southside thing" "drunken suburbanites" "dirty" "nothing huge i dislike so far" "drinking culture" "its expensive for me" "cost of living" "transportation is crap" "inner-city roughness" "not easy to find a handyman" "people passionate about their cars" "city is finished at 7 or 8pm" "it's on an island behind an island" "drugs, alcoholics, beggars" "too crowded"

NON-NATIONAL

"no problem" "strange" "official" "very bureaucratic" "i'm assuming it's a non-irish national" "what do you mean?" "i think it's strange" "i think it's strange" "it's ok, feels like third generation irish descent" "bland" "it's a fact, doesn't bother me" "what's non-national?" "odd concept" "no identity" "what comes after that matters"

FOREIGN WORKER

"feeling of alienated" "implies transient" "implies physical labour" "class-ist" "i'm working in a foreign country" "i don't find it very derogatory" "blasé about it" "it's a non-integrated word" "yeah, that's what i am" "working robot" "that makes sense" "it's ok" "descriptive" "don't feel nice" "not abusive, correct"

NEW IRISH

"no, wouldn't consider myself new-irish" "denying my identity" "hard to define" "welcoming, i like that" "i don't feel it, i feel a bit different" "if i was making long-term plans to make citizenship" "i'm not really irish, i'm not new fucking irish" "it's conceitful, no thank you" "it's funny" "welcoming, implies long term" "no" "oh my god, italian-spanish maybe but not new irish?" "kinda nice, technically I am, even if in denial" "could be alright if you want" "yes, of course i'm new"

FOREIGN NATIONAL

"suppose a reality" "implies not meant to be here" "sounds professional" "doesn't bother me" "yep" "i find it a bit bizarre, either you're a foreigner or a national" "i've no idea what that means, how can you be foreign and national at the same time?" "it's a contradiction" "it's strange" "not welcoming, indifferent" "i'm against that" "it's ok" "it's the tone for me, the voice that uses it" "alright, ok" "can be used as a negative"

IMMIGRANT

"not me" "historically loaded, as if you had to leave" "negative, old style" "perhaps wishful thinking" "i feel like an immigrant" "it's fine" "i have never been called that" "i feel very irritated by this, doesn't have a choice" "are they refugees or immigrant? i think it's used for non-eu" "makes me feel like a refugee" "i didn't come here because i had to, i chose to" "it's my life" "not sure about that" "quite formal, wouldn't be offended"

SKILLED MIGRANT

"fine with it, a big strange" "antiquated" "sounds very bad" "doesn't appeal" "don't like that" "technical" "neutral" "horrible, if you are not, do you have to leave?" "that's what we are for the moment" "best out of the list" "it's an intellectual way of saying it" "it's a little bit strange" "again very descriptive" "neutral" "might be seen as positive"

FOREIGNER

"a bit alienating" "colloquial, dismissive" "normal" "i guess i am" "yes, it's ok" "i suppose so" "sounds like you here on holiday" "it's fine, neutral" "ok" "insulting, hints at being a tourist" "correct, yeah" "yeah ok" "what other word could you use?" "ok for chinese, in china all foreigners are westerners" "ok for now"

NON-IRISH NATIONAL

"fine with it" "not offensive, simply descriptive" "neutral" "that would be correct" "it's ok" "complicated" "neutral no feeling about this" "too complicated" "i understand non-eu, but not non-irish national" "fair, i suppose" "i wouldn't be happy, means i want to be irish" "i don't know" "if i was granted irish citizenship am i a non-irish national?" "alright" "wont be offended"

Do foreigners love Dublin more than the Irish?

Some 11.8% of the Irish-born population of Ireland lives in Dublin city.[1] This compares with an average of 14% for those foreign-born and now living in Ireland.[2] If one excluded those who were born in the United Kingdom, the figure rises to 20%. In other words, one in five of all foreign-born residents of the Irish state (excluding those born in the UK) live in Dublin city compared to just one in eight Irish-born residents. Remarkably, of the top 24 foreign nationalities living in Ireland, only those born in Latvia, Lithuania, Nigeria and the UK are less likely to live in the capital city than the Irish; apparently all others are more attracted to cosmopolitan urban Dublin living.

So do foreigners love Dublin more than the Irish? Yes, is the simple answer. One might of course expect immigrants or citizens of other nations to gravitate to the State's busiest point of entry, the country's largest city, and the place of greatest economic opportunity, but the preference for city living, or Dublin city living to be more precise, varies enormously between these citizens of immigrant nations. The Chinese are apparently most attracted to life in the city. More than half of all those born in China (50.4%) and living in Ireland live in Dublin city.[3] The Italians and Spanish are also attracted to Dublin, with just over 41% of all Italian- and Spanish-born Irish residents living in Dublin city. Those who were born in Sweden, Finland and Denmark also prefer Dublin city life, with 30% of these Nordic-born residents living in Dublin. Other 'Dublinphiles' include Indians (31%), Filipinos (31%) and Malaysians (30%). Asians are obviously urban.

The British are least likely to favour living in Dublin city. Just 8.1% of all those born in the United Kingdom and residing in the Irish state live in Dublin city.[4] Apart from the British, the Dutch are least likely of all west Europeans to find Dublin favourable, with just 12.7% of those living in Ireland choosing to make a home in the capital city.

The Human Entrepot

Entrepot – "a seaport through which exports and imports pass without incurring duty"

The human entrepot is a city of coming and going, a city of journeys unfolding and stories yet untold. This is neither a city of static destination nor final immigration, nor is it a city of immigrant labels such as New Irish, Lost Irish or Non-Irish. The human entrepot doesn't speak pejoratively of city-living transients or classify immigrants and migrants by convenient but meaningless labels.

The human entrepot is a public arena for private individuals to act out their urban lives free of discrimination, categorisation and classification. In the human entrepot, identities overlap, fluid communities mutate and evolve, interact and co-exist, free of the prying magnifying glass of municipal tick-boxes or community-art-inspired outreach access programmes.

This is a city in a permanent state of flux, a never-ending party of conversation and chattering excitement, a city of musical chairs, a 'cityspace entrepot' with a constant revolving open door.

Can Dublin become the first 21st-century human entrepot?

"A city space through which people arrive and leave without incurring prejudice or barriers".

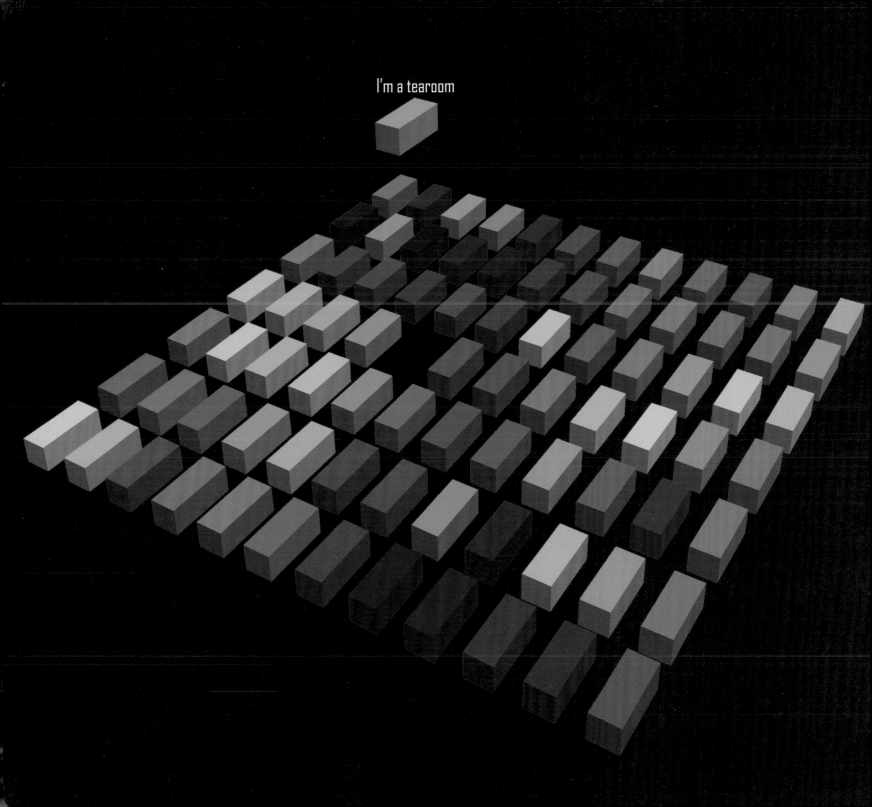

Zoned Out

Zoning Uncovered

Zoning can be defined as a designation given to a particular geographic area by local government to regulate the type of use and the density of development permitted for properties in an area. Probably every city has some form of urban land-use zonings. Zoning is the building block of the planner's universe. It's that dark mysterious planning matter that is hard to see, impossible to touch, and sometimes unfathomable to comprehend. It is, nevertheless, very real and a hugely powerful force in determining the shape, functioning and expansion or possible contraction of our cities.

Zoning is everywhere. Just as nature abhors a vacuum, city planning maps abhor non-zoned lands. They simply don't exist. With the singular exception of road and railways, zoning is ubiquitous. It is omnipresent. No urban land or urban plan escapes its clutches.

Zoning can determine where we live, what we can build, how and when we work or shop. It can dictate how big a city gets or how high it reaches. Dublin city zoning is no different. Currently Dublin has fifteen categories (with an additional sub-category) of land-use zonings.[1] They are each given a distinct colour code for ease of understanding and pictorial recognition. Do you know what zone you live in? How many have you visited in the last week or year? Can you tell one zone from another?

There are some obvious clues, but few or no signposts to tell you when you are entering or leaving a new zone. Does it matter? We believe it does. We believe it affects your daily city choices and the quality of your life, but perhaps, at times, not in the manner in which the planners intended or citizens understand.

ZONISM

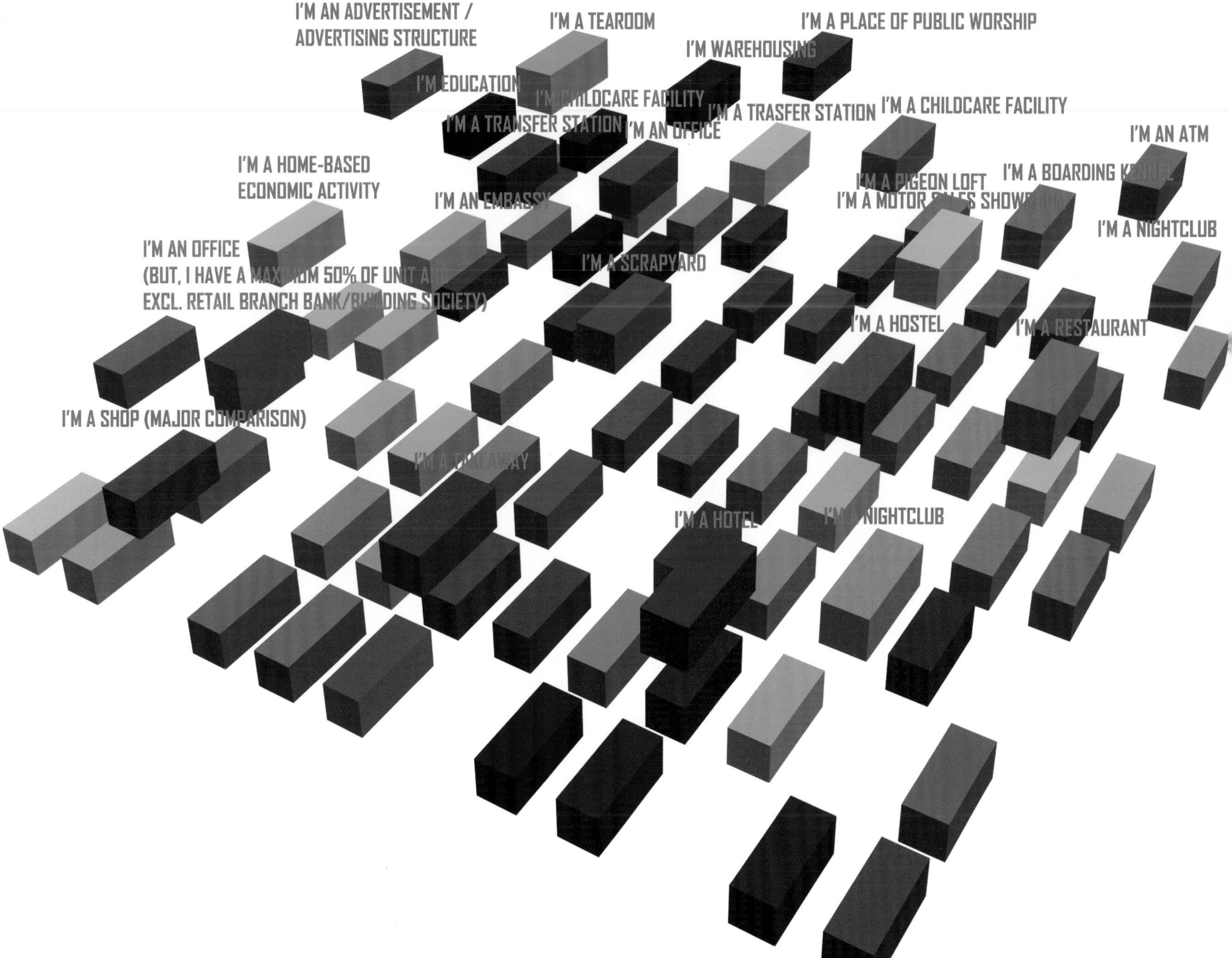

I'M AN ADVERTISEMENT /
ADVERTISING STRUCTURE

I'M A TEAROOM

I'M A PLACE OF PUBLIC WORSHIP

I'M WAREHOUSING

I'M EDUCATION

I'M CHILDCARE FACILITY

I'M A TRASFER STATION

I'M A CHILDCARE FACILITY

I'M A TRANSFER STATION

I'M AN OFFICE

I'M AN ATM

I'M A HOME-BASED
ECONOMIC ACTIVITY

I'M A PIGEON LOFT

I'M A BOARDING KENNEL

I'M AN EMBASSY

I'M A MOTOR SALES SHOWROOM

I'M AN OFFICE
(BUT, I HAVE A MAXIMUM 50% OF UNIT AND
EXCL. RETAIL BRANCH BANK/BUILDING SOCIETY)

I'M A SCRAPYARD

I'M A NIGHTCLUB

I'M A HOSTEL

I'M A RESTAURANT

I'M A SHOP (MAJOR COMPARISON)

I'M A TAKEAWAY

I'M A HOTEL

I'M A NIGHTCLUB

1	Advertisement and advertising structures	29	Garage (motor repair/service)	57	Petrol station
2	Amusement/leisure complex	30	Garden centre	58	Pigeon lofts
3	ATM	31	General industrial uses	59	Place of public worship
4	Bed and breakfast	32	Golf course and clubhouse	60	Port-related industries and facilities
5	Betting office	33	Guest house	61	Public house
6	Boarding kennel	34	Halting site	62	Public service installation
7	Buildings for health, safety and welfare of the public	35	Heavy vehicle park	63	Public service installation which would not be detrimental to the amenity of Z9 zoned lands
8	Car park	36	Home-based economic activity	64	Residential
9	Car park ancillary to and subject to the main use remaining as community or institutional	37	Hostel	65	Residential Institution
		38	Hotel	66	Restaurant
10	Car trading	39	Household fuel depot	67	Retail park
11	Caravan park/camp site (holiday)	40	Incinerator/waste to energy plant	68	Science and technology based industry
12	Chemical processing and storage	41	Industry (light)	69	Scrap yard
13	Childcare facility	42	Internet café	70	Shop (district)
14	Civic and amenity/recycling centre	43	Kiosk	71	Shop (major comparison)
15	Civic offices	44	Live/work units	72	Shop (neighbourhood)
16	Club house and associated facilities	45	Media recording and general media associated uses	73	Storage depot (open)
17	Community facility			74	Support office ancillary to primary use
18	Conference centre	46	Medical and related consultants	75	Takeaway
19	Craft centre/craft shop	47	Motor sales showroom	76	Tearoom
20	Creche	48	Municipal golf course	77	Training centre
21	Cultural/recreational buildings and uses	49	Nightclub	78	Transfer station
22	Education	50	Office	79	Transport depot
23	Education (excluding a night-time use)	51	Office (max 300m²)	80	Veterinary surgery
24	Embassy	52	Office (max 600m²)	81	Warehousing
25	Enterprise centre	53	Office (maximum 50% of unit and excluding retail branch bank/building society)	82	Warehousing (retail/non-food)
26	Factory shop			83	Warehousing (retail/non-food) / Retail park
27	Financial institution	54	Open space	84	Water-based recreational/cultural activities
28	Funeral home	55	Outdoor poster advertising		
		56	Park and ride facility		

Zoning and Uses

Zonings derive their power, sustain their logic, and give sustenance to their meaning neither from their classification colour or titles, nor from their scale or boundaries, but primarily from the variety of land 'uses' that may be allowed to reside within them. Dublin has conceived 84 different types of land-'uses' for the city.[1] That's one for every 6,000 citizens, less than six for every zoning classification, or 0.7 separate land-uses per square kilometre.

It doesn't, of course, work quite like that. These land-uses are diverse, many as obtuse as they are meaningful. They include 'Tearooms' and 'Transfer Stations', 'Pigeon Lofts' and 'Boarding Kennels'. If zoning areas, on the one hand, are fixed and demarcated with enforceable borders to control, uses, on the other hand, are more light-footed and transient. They can travel across the city, finding a home in more than one zoning place at any one time.

USES

USES MULTIPLEX

What if 'The City' could conceive of some 840 land-uses instead of a mere 84? Would we, as consumers and citizens, have more choice and planners less control, or would we have less choice and The City more control? Is it possible it could be neither, possibly even a little bit of both? Would it really matter? Who decides?

Why are additional schools or educational uses not permissible in predominantly 'redbrick' residential areas, or Internet coffee shops in Georgian squares? Why can't we study openly at night in inner-urban regeneration areas? What explains the mysteries of the zoning that permits us to stay in a 'Hotel' or a 'Bed and Breakfast' but not a 'Guesthouse' in the suburb, yet allows us to stay in a 'Hotel' and a 'Guesthouse' but not a 'Bed and Breakfast' in a city centre Georgian square?

And what exactly is a 'Transfer Station', and how many 'Tearooms' have recently been granted planning permission or have recently been built?"

Zs

In 'Zs' we have constructed a singular and colourful alphabetical zoning world. Each land-use zone is given its officially designated colour, and their size reflects the proportion of land each zone currently occupies in the city.[1]

Z1 (yellow) is the largest zone in Dublin city. It is the primary residential zoning objective area, and covers (alongside the smaller Z2 residential zone) just over 44% of all zoned land.
Z7A (deep purple) is the smallest, covering a mere 3.4 hectares or 0.4% of the city's area. Z7A 'provides for the protection and creation of industrial uses'.

Z5 (blue) or Central Area is the land-use zone that delineates the city centre. Z5 covers 231 hectares or just 2.3% of all zoned land in Dublin city. Z9 (green) seeks to preserve, provide and improve recreational amenity and open space. This includes Bull Island and the Phoenix Park among others. A quarter of all zoned land in the city is zoned Z9.

Zs = DENSI

site coverage: 100%
plot ratio: 3:1
building height: 3
GF open space: 0%

site coverage: 75%
plot ratio: 3:1
building height: 4
GF open space: 25%

site coverage: 50%
plot ratio: 3:1
building height: 6
GF open space: 50%

site coverage: 25%
plot ratio: 3:1
building height: 12
GF open space: 75%

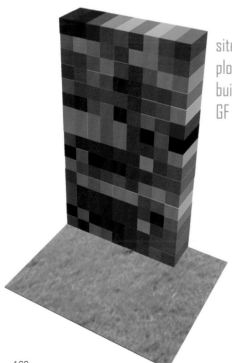

site coverage: 18.75%
plot ratio: 3:1
building height: 16
GF open space: 81.25%

site coverage: 8.3%
plot ratio: 3:1
building height: 36
GF open space: 91.7%

162

site coverage: 50%
plot ratio: 1.5:1
building height: 3
GF open space: 50%

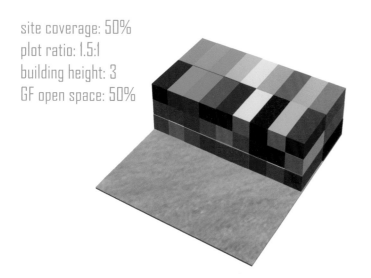

site coverage: 25%
plot ratio: 1.5:1
building height: 6
GF open space: 75%

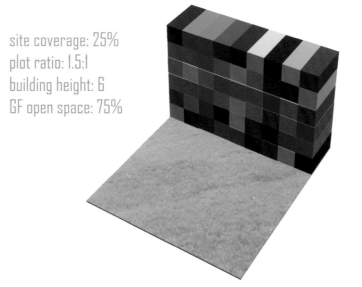

site coverage: 22.2%
plot ratio: 1.5:1
building height: 6-7
GF open space: 77.8%

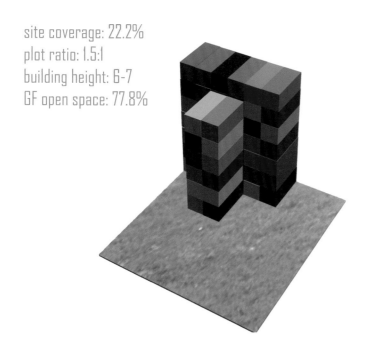

site coverage: 16.6%
plot ratio: 1.5:1
building height: 9
GF open space: 83.4%

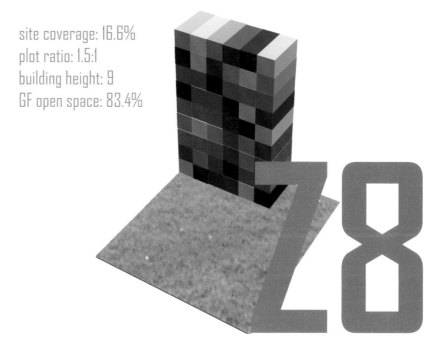

GEORGIAN AND RESTORATION PERIODS

Dublin City Map by Thomas Larcom (National Library of Ireland)

"Rapid growth produced a fragmented urban landscape" p.69 "brought new types of urban design" p.69 "much uncoordinated development" p.69 "property speculators" p.11 "appalling traffic congestion" p.69 "uncontrolled physical expansion" p.70 "congestion within the city" p.70 "lack of continuity between the centre and the various new suburban developments" p.70 "Vision of European urbanism" p.10 "the recovery of a city and its emergence as a monumental capital" p.67 "introduction of apartment-style buildings with residences over shops" p.117 "imminent danger of bankruptcy of the city as a result of the poor economic and political climate..." p.81

source: *Dublin Through Space and Time* by Joseph Brady and Anngret Simms (Dublin, 2002)

GEORGIAN DUBLIN?

Dublin is famed – not least, by Dubliners themselves – as a Georgian city. The city may not have the Georgian stature of Edinburg or Bath, and has shamefully 'lost' in relatively recent years perfectly intact Georgian buildings – in places, entire streets – but the city does continue to boast a significant number of grand Georgian squares, many great Georgian streets and terraces, and hundreds of 'isolated' Georgian buildings.[1] The actual area extent of these Georgian squares, terraces and buildings, whether acknowledged or not by the urban professional or the local city tourist guidebooks, is, however, remarkably small.

The built reality is that the 'Georgian city' of Dublin, a city of over 500,000 people,[2] is in fact predominantly made up of vast tracts of two-storey housing, a significant proportion of which were built by the city authorities between the 1940s and 1960s to house working-class families who had previously being living in crowded tenement buildings in the inner city, many ironically of Georgian origin, many subsequently demolished.[3] Today, fewer than one in seventy of the city's population lives in the city centre, let alone actually live in its remaining Georgian streets and squares.[4]

Where exactly is Georgian Dublin? Dublin City Council designates a mere 0.8% of its zoned land area as one of outstanding historic value.[5] The vast majority of these areas are made up of Georgian streets and squares. Invariably known by city planners as Z8-zoned land, these areas include all of the city's Georgian squares – Merrion, Fitzwilliam, Mountjoy and Parnell squares. Z8 also includes Dublin's most important historic set pieces The Customs House, Four Courts, Trinity College and all of the last remaining Georgian terraces of city significance, including North Great George's Street, Gardiner Place on the north side of the city and Baggott Street, Leeson Street and Fitzwilliam Street on the southside.

Dublin's City centre or Central Area, as defined by the City Council (lands zoned Z5), is also home to a considerable number of intact Georgian terraces and buildings. The entire Z5 Central Area makes up just 2.3% of the zoned land of the city.[6] A considerable amount of historic fabric built during the 'Georgian period' and subsequent Victorian and Edwardian periods are designated 'protected structures' or classified as special 'residential conservation areas' (zoned Z2) outside Z8 zoned lands. These lands make up just a further 6.6% of the zoned land, but are primarily

Victorian in character.[7] We estimate that Georgian Dublin probably constitutes no more than 3.8% of the total zoned fabric area of the city.[8]

So, if Dublin's primarily 20th-century two-storey suburban housing stock accounts for the vast proportion of its residential built-up area and accommodates approximately 75% of the city's population (most of the remainder living in 20th-century purpose-built apartment blocks), can Dublin legitimately define itself as a truly Georgian city? [9]

Interestingly, Dublin is currently seeking official UNESCO approval for the designation of Dublin as a Georgian city deserving of World Heritage status. The UNESCO approval of Dublin as a World Heritage Georgian city is not entirely academic. It is much more than a historic, geographic or qualitative headcount of buildings or recognition of the grand legacy of street layouts. Its importance is greater than simply the telling of a story of the evolution of the city, its buildings, its squares or street patterns. If such status is sought and approved, it is likely to have real influence on how the city is perceived, how it perceives itself and how it potentially evolves in the future.

An interesting comparison of a World Heritage City is that of Tel Aviv. In 1999 UNESCO designated part of the city a World Heritage City on account of its rich and unique Bauhaus and International Style architectural legacy. The critical difference, however, between 'Bauhaus Tel Aviv' and 'Georgian Dublin' is that Tel Aviv, a city of 300,000 people (metropolitan Tel Aviv has a population of three million), remains essentially a Bauhaus city, with the significant proportion of its built fabric continuing to date from that period or style. A significant proportion of the city's population also resides in purpose-built Bauhaus and International Style residential apartments. The latter fact, in particular, gives real meaning and credibility to the city's urban identity and designation as a World Heritage City, and was an important factor in both the application for and decision to grant the city its UNESCO status. Georgian Dublin, in this regard, compares unfavourably to Tel Aviv. Tel Aviv is a living, breathing Bauhaus or International Style city. Georgian Dublin is largely devoid of residential life. Just 869 persons reside in Dublin's South Georgian Core. Just 388, however, live in private households, with a mere 217 persons living in homes built prior to 1919. The Georgian homes of the South Georgian Core, therefore, including all

its grand squares, currently accommodate fewer people than three double-decker buses. It is a particularly peculiar irony that the most elegant and historically beautiful urban part of Dublin city is largely uninhabited. Why have the super Dublin affluent – apart from a few noticeably absent residents – forsaken a quality urban life? [10]

So, does the apparent disconnect between the perception and reality of Dublin as a Georgian city matter too much beyond a debate amongst academic historians or urban professionals? We believe it does. Misunderstanding the urban geography of the city, a city of suburban residents, ignoring the reality of this typology – effectively a city of two-storey housing which also includes extensive areas of underperforming 'non-Georgian' inner-urban land – has real implications. Protecting the remaining Georgian built fabric and character of Dublin city is critically important, and in the light of recent past destruction it is an obligation – indeed, a moral civic urban imperative.

Understanding the story of the legacy of that heritage, and, critically, the reality of its fragility and rarity will also help to secure its future. To designate an essentially suburban two-storey city with an extensive diverse and underdeveloped inner-urban core as a World Heritage Georgian city, however, is a muddled misunderstanding of Dublin's present built geography and a potentially destructive limitation on the possibilities of its urban future.

Dr Ronald Tallon
An ode to Georgian Dublin

"The scale, it's very human. The four squares. The simplicity of the architecture, it is unpretentious. Unique in its simplicity. Elegant and logical, it is beautifully done. If they extended the windows another six inches the whole place would collapse. The living areas of the higher scale overlooking the park. It is a beautiful concept – as you go up, the scale reduces. The discipline of the brick. There is a quietness."

167

Historical Archipelago *and the* Georgian Islands

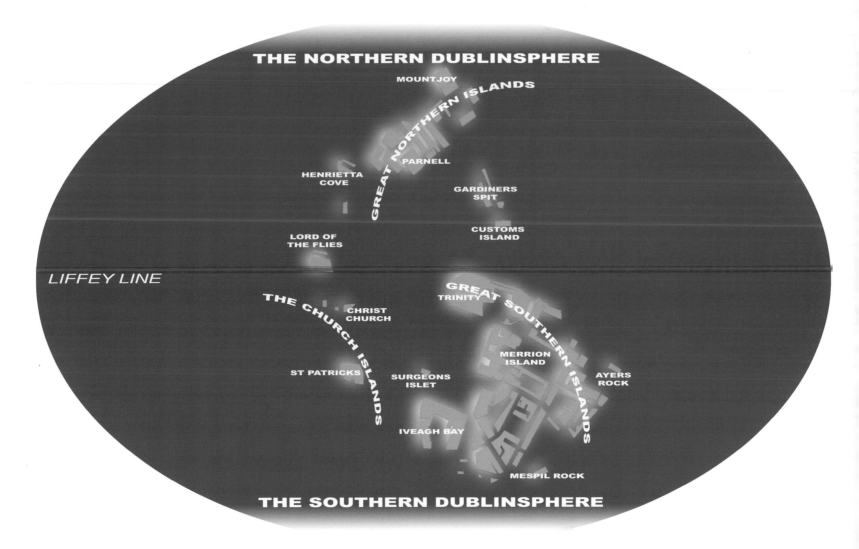

THE NORTHERN DUBLINSPHERE

MOUNTJOY

GREAT NORTHERN ISLANDS

PARNELL

HENRIETTA COVE

GARDINERS SPIT

LORD OF THE FLIES

CUSTOMS ISLAND

LIFFEY LINE

GREAT SOUTHERN ISLANDS

THE CHURCH ISLANDS

TRINITY

CHRIST CHURCH

MERRION ISLAND

ST PATRICKS

SURGEONS ISLET

AYERS ROCK

IVEAGH BAY

MESPIL ROCK

THE SOUTHERN DUBLINSPHERE

In HISTORICAL ARCHIPELAGO AND THE GEORGIAN ISLANDS we create a fantasy Dublin composed of the Northern Dublin-sphere and the Southern Dublin-sphere, separated by the equatorial Liffey Line. This Historical Archipelago is a world of epoch-making architectural islands and islets, design formations, constructions spits and rock compositions. The archipelago is made up of all those lands and buildings zoned Z8 in the zoned world of Dublin. These Z8 islands are those areas or land fragments designated Conservation Areas.[1] They include the great

Georgian squares and Trinity College. HISTORICAL ARCHIPELAGO AND THE GEORGIAN ISLANDS paints an oceanic or aquatic metaphor of the fragmented and fragile nature of our historic fabric, splendid and at sea in its vulnerability and isolation. Understanding the isolated realities of our precious architectural island heritage allows us to better equip ourselves to fight for its continued protection and use. Perhaps it may also liberate us as to what may emerge in the vastness and sometimes emptiness of the geographic oceans of land of the rest of the inner city that surrounds it.

GEORGIAN DUBLIN

Z1 Zoned lands (predominately sub-urban two-storey non 'red brick' residential built fabric) constitutes 38.8% of all zoned land in the city. This is ten times the quantum of our Georgian Dublin (3.8% of all built fabric)

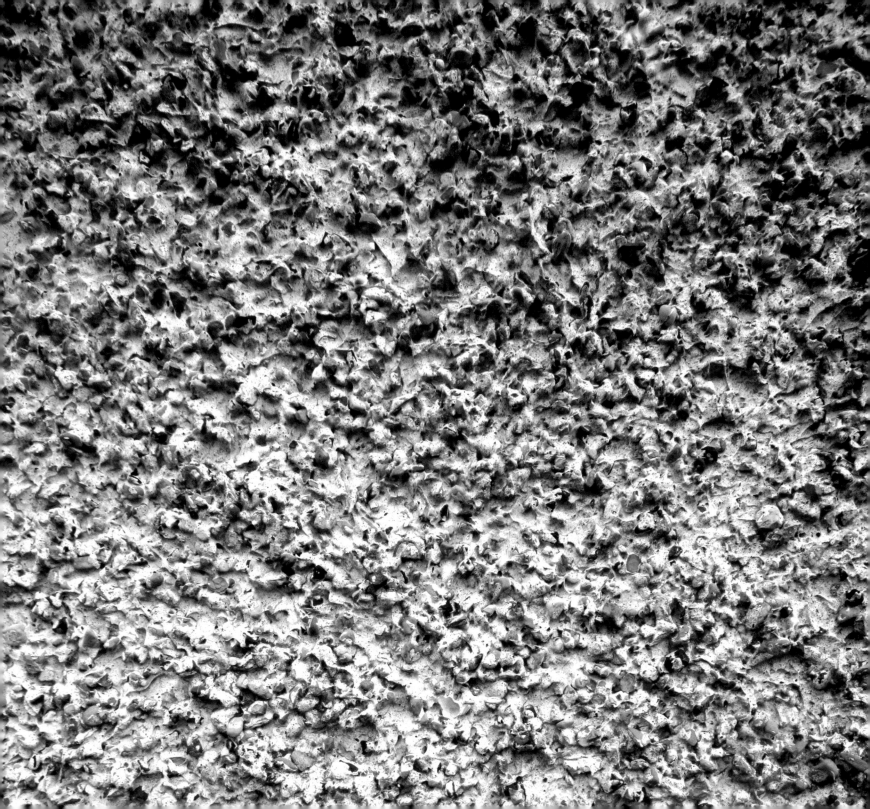

Republika Suburbia and Mixed-Use Enclaves

In our imaginary Republika Suburbia but very real monocultural zone of Z1 suburban lands, just 21% of all conceivable land-uses are automatically tolerated and accepted. In contrast, in the mixed-use enclaves of the Federation Urbania or Z5 city centre lands, 55% of all types of uses are both welcomed and enjoyed.[1]

In Republika Suburbia a form of 'mixed-use cleansing' is enforced to the detriment of the vitality and sustainability of liveable neighbourhood integration. It's rare to be able to walk from home to work in Republika Suburbia. Republika Suburbia does not allow or tolerate 'Office' use, nor does it allow or tolerate 'Guesthouses' or 'Internet Cafés'. It is unusual, if not rare, to be able to walk to a cinema or a restaurant in 'Republika Suburbia'. 'Republika Suburbia' is controlling and limiting.

Dublin's Employment/Enterprise Zone (Z6) zoned lands, an unofficial 'Zone *Arbeitan*' is a close ideological cousin of the land of Republika Suburbia. Despite its name, it is not possible to work in 'Education' or in a 'Financial Institution' in 'Zone *Arbeitan*', neither is possible to work in a 'Motor Sales Room' or a 'Hostel'. It is, however, permissible to work in a 'Hotel' and a 'Funeral Home'.[2]

In Federation Urbania, on the other hand, offices, homes, hotels and shops and supermarkets happily exist side by side. It's interesting that Republika Suburbia coincides or corresponds with those parts of the city that are the least culturally cosmopolitan and ethnically diverse. It's not surprising, perhaps, but interesting nevertheless, that we find a remarkable spatial connection or correlation between our imaginary Federation Urbania (the very real Dublin City Council Z5 Central Area), a land-use zoning tolerant of a diversity of a mix of uses, and the concentrated presence of non-Irish or foreign-born citizens. Might this be a spatial coincidence or have we unwittingly stumbled upon a simple urban law governing the attraction of diversity to diversity?

Hi " Arc of Disadvantage "

Wish you were here. Weather
is so-so, but everything is
green. Beautiful mature trees
everywhere. Having a fabulous
time. Biodiversity never felt
so good. See you soon,
perhaps! Green kisses as
always. Your loving, publicly
subsidised ecological friends.

Leafy Privileged, Ballsbridge

A Green Urban Story
Open Space in the 'Arc of Disadvantage'

In Chapter 2 we introduced Dublin city's ARC OF DISADVANTAGE.[1] Amongst the many challenges facing the Arc of Disadvantage is an acute deficit of green, publicly accessible open space. The largest green space in the Arc of Disadvantage – the grounds of King's Inns – is neither a public park nor ordinarily opened to the public at weekends. Another significant green space, the Incorporated Law Society sports grounds at Blackhall Place, is practically invisible and not ordinarily accessible to the public at all. These two 'green spaces' account for nearly a quarter of all the open space in the Arc of Disadvantage. Just 3.5% of the total surface area of the Arc of Disadvantage is zoned open space by Dublin City Council. This compares to 25% of all zoned land for the city as a whole.[2]

A closer examination of density uncovers an even greater deficit. Some 43,000 people, or one in twelve (8.5%) of the city's population,[3] live in the Arc of Disadvantage. This 8.5% live on less than 4% of the land area of the city,[4] yet these high-density dwellers enjoy a mere 0.56% of all designated open space in the city.[5]

Looking at it from another perspective, there is approximately 2,500 hectares of (designated zoned) open space in Dublin city. With a total city population of 506,000, that's a density of 196 people per hectare of open space. This works out at 51m^2 of municipally designated, mostly green open space for every man, woman and child, the equivalent of a large one-bedroom-apartment-sized park for every citizen of the city. In the Arc of Disadvantage there are just 14.5 hectares of land zoned open space. With a population of 43,000, that works out at 2,965 people per hectare of open space, or just 3.4m^2 per person, the equivalent of a large dining table of green park per resident. That's a staggering fifteen times less open space per person in the Arc of Disadvantage than for the city as a whole.

This imbalance is all the more remarkable considering the additional demands on inner-urban areas that simply do not exist in the suburbs. These include the daily tidal arrival of office workers and the seasonal influx of tourists, and the fact that the local residents are much less likely to have access to private green space – a front or back garden – than their suburban cousins. In addition, people on lower incomes are much more likely to be reliant on public services and public goods. The availability and accessibility of quality public parks is an important public good.

The Arc of Disadvantage is not just disadvantaged relative to the entire city (essentially suburban Dublin); it also compares unfavourably with both the rest of the city centre and the inner-urban suburbs when calculating the relative presence of green spaces or parks. Within Dublin's Canal Ring (of which the Arc of Disadvantage makes up approximately a quarter), the density of population (8,165 persons per square kilometre) is comparable to that of the 'Arc' (10,400). The Canal Ring, however, has 77 hectares of green zoned open space, or a density of 1,341 people per hectare, which generates 7.5m^2 of open space per person. That is more than twice the open space per person than in the Arc of Disadvantage.[6]

The Arc of Disadvantage, when compared to the south-east quadrant of the city (Dublin 2 and 4 inside the Canal Ring)[7] is particularly disadvantaged when it comes to open-space provision. The south-east quadrant of the Canal Ring is home to some of the great green parks and squares of Dublin – St Stephen's Green, Iveagh Gardens, Merrion Square and Fitzwilliam Square. This significantly leafy and green part of the city has a population less than half that of the Arc of Disadvantage but accommodates two and a half times the amount of green open space, or 36 hectares. That works out at 17.6m^2 of open space per person, or 5.2 times more than the Arc of Disadvantage.

The presence of local parks or accessible public gardens does not tell the whole story. Trees on urban streets are important in how an area is perceived, how it perceives itself, and is generally enjoyed as a desirable place to walk around, live or work. The pruning and management of trees, and the removal of dead leaves is a direct, but rarely discussed public subsidy of affluent neighbourhoods. Perhaps not surprisingly, the Arc of Disadvantage fares particularly poor in this regard. Huge swathes of the 'Arc' are simply devoid of urban greenery of any kind. Compared to Dublin 2 and 4 or well-established, mature working-class suburbs, the Arc of Disadvantage is relatively barren of street trees. The lack of trees along the Luas Red Line, Summerhill, Seán McDermott Street or Cork Street is as telling as it is noticeable. Why is this so?

The proximity of significant green spaces such as the Phoenix Park or Memorial Gardens on the doorstep of the Arc of Disadvantage cannot be ignored in this urban green story. These are, of course, great urban assets, but it's the presence of quality pocket or local green spaces in the heart of a neighbourhood, particularly a high-density one, that is so important in determining the quality of life in that neighbourhood. These local parks and spaces allow young children, accompanied by an adult, to walk there from home. They provide local play space for 10- or 12-year-olds who can walk there in five minutes. They potentially unify a community, providing public space for new communities to meet.

While the Arc of Disadvantage is deficient in meaningful local green space, it is also the home of too many derelict 'brownfield' sites and 'pocket grey spaces'. Perhaps not surprisingly, the Arc of Disadvantage has more land occupied by brownfield derelicts sites than it has devoted to green open space.[8] The 'pocket grey spaces' are equally plentiful. They come in varying sizes and shapes. They are generally treeless and joyless slabs of grey cement. Their origins are varied, many of them left over from road-widening schemes. They are almost invisible but nevertheless invasive. You walk through them, sense their presence but never quite see them. The 'greening' of these grey spaces, the provision of a bench to sit on, a children's play area, the planting of a tree, could transform these destitute grey spaces to create an urban 'green necklace'. These 'green necklaces', thread through the city, would have the capacity to transform both the perception of the Arc of Disadvantage and the quality of the lives of those who live there. Now that would be a great green urban story.

GREEN THE 'ARC OF DISADVANTAGE'

Post-Zonism?

Land-use zonings are a bit like individual nation states with varying degrees of desired diversity, or 'use purity', with enforceable border controls, employing different hierarchies of 'use' acceptance. Permissible 'uses', not unlike visa-waiver schemes for certain types of travellers, have almost automatic right of entry or access to land-use zones. Uses 'open for consideration' are subject to stringent entrance criteria to any specific zone.[1]

and protected the health – indeed, the survival – of vulnerable citizens following the rise of a powerfully changed 19th and early 20th-century social and economic urban landscape. It was a rational response to the emergence of toxic industrial-scale challenges capable of destroying entire communities, endangering their health and general wellbeing. Separating belching factories and polluting steel mills from artisan cottages made sense in the 19th century. In a post-industrial world, in a

POST-ZONISM

Z5 or city centre (mixed-use) zoning, as the name suggests, is the most open-minded and tolerant of all the zoning nations. It's the natural home to 41 of all the conceivable categories of uses imagined by Dublin City Council. It also gives a flexible and case-by-case consideration to the possibility of a further seven. It is a babble of use tongues, though it does shut its doors to the remaining 36.

Z11 'Waterways Protection' is the least tolerant or most restrictive of the nation of zonings. It's the home of just two types of use, a kind of bi-federal state of 'Open Space' and 'Water-based activities'. It is open to the arrival of just two more uses.

Z1 'Residential' zoning is the largest of the family of zoning nations. It is also the home of the vast majority of the citizens of the city, but tolerates just sixteen of 84 possible uses. A further sixteen are allowed entry under certain circumstances. Refusal or rejection is almost guaranteed to 52 other use groups.

Zoning was heroic, necessary, and of its time. It defended the interests

mixed-use society, where few jobs are carried out in a toxic or polluting environment, is it not better to live closer to the office than the factory, to be able to walk to school from home, and to walk to the park or to the shops?

Post-Zonism doesn't romanticise the possibilities of city connectivity; it values it. In a more complex and increasingly environmentally challenging world, might the intentions of zoning and urban sustainability be better served by a more diverse, mixed-use form of settlement? Have we largely outgrown the need for such rigid segregation of complementary land-uses? Increasingly, cities are moving away from zoning segregation to vertical separation. Vertical separation at its simplest is putting the homes on the upper floors of a building, the offices below, and shops and restaurants at ground floor. An openness and tolerance to a diversity of neighbourly friendly uses subject to well-designed and well-behaved rules of civic engagement is Post-Zonist. Can Dublin become Post-Zonist?

Choking Urbanism

Apartment Apartheid

If an embryonic urbanism is to flourish in Dublin, if, against all the odds, it manages to withstand suburban indifference and latent ecological or creeping green 'ruralification' and actually survive, it faces an almost immediate assault at birth. 'Apartment Apartheid' is the sometimes obvious, sometimes hidden discrimination of apartment-dwellers in inner-city Dublin. Like most discrimination, it is quite subtle and often denied. 'Gated communities, 'transients' and 'gentrification' are just some of the accusations, slurs and assaults hurled at an emerging Dublin urban culture and lifestyle. The term 'gated community', if commonly misunderstood by many, is nevertheless widely used to describe inner-urban apartment blocks in Dublin city that surround a communal private open space, perhaps visible to, but secured from the public street. What is understood is that when the term 'gated community' is used, it is used as a pejorative. A more common and meaningful understanding of the term 'gated communities' is generally that of a neighbourhood or group of neighbourhoods surrounded by walls or fences, restricting access through the use of a manned guard station or electronically operated gate.

Gated communities are almost entirely suburban, not urban. They usually restrict access to a road network, however small or large. Few, if any, of the so-called 'gated communities' in inner-city Dublin restrict access to a vehicle road network. They merely restrict public access to private communal space. This private communal space is the equivalent of the front and back garden of the suburban home. It is often a space where the kitchen or bedroom windows of homes open directly onto a shared garden or courtyard accessible to all the residents who live there.

How many suburban Dublin homes allow their neighbours, let alone strangers, to wander pass their bedroom or kitchen windows? Suburbia, with its front and back garden – in effect, the exclusive demarcation of an entire community of little privatised green garden spaces – is the ultimate gated community. In addition, unlike the communally run spaces of many apartment developments, there are remarkably few examples of privately owned but communally managed green spaces in two-storey, semi-detached suburbia.

'Transients' is another term of intended abuse hurled at city apartment-dwellers. What is entirely natural in all cities – the coming and going of people, the natural recycling (renting or subletting) of homes, the vitality and energy of people visiting, studying, creating new urban lives, however temporary – is, for some peculiar reason, a threat to some observers of inner-city Dublin. 'Transients', the argument goes, do not connect to others in the local community, invariably the 'indigenous community'. They are 'unstable' elements that do not put down roots in that community. 'Transients' are criticised for failing to behave or act out their urban lives according to the rules of others.

Those others, almost without exception, have never 'chosen' to live (beyond, perhaps, a short-lived student life) in inner-city or urban Dublin. They may have been born there or may have chosen to work or socialise there, but few have actually chosen to live there. Those who actually choose to live in urban Dublin rarely, if ever, label their fellow urban neighbours as 'transients'. They use many other adjectives, friendly, unfriendly, noisy perhaps, anything but transient. Transient is artificial, it's detached, it's not convincing to the real experience of urban life. These so-called 'transients' are urbanites. They choose to be urbanites. They are Irish or foreign-born, who may live for short periods of time in a particular apartment in a particular part of a city. They choose their own friends and acquaintances like anybody else. They have multiple identities and move within multiple communities, family, friends, work, college, the gym, whatever.

This peculiar Dublin judgement of transients tends to confuse local roots and obligatory connections with proximity, density, tolerance and respect as the critical ingredients of successful and dynamic urban communities. It's a peculiar confusion of what differentiates the village from the city. Cities are not exploded or magnified villages. Villages are places where one knows one's place, where hierarchies and behaviour are generally known to all. Cities are fluid, relationships and behaviour potentially anonymous. 'Transients' are of the city. Criticism of so-called 'transients' is nothing more than a criticism or distaste of urbanism itself.

Another common assault on inner-urban apartment dwellers in Dublin is accusations that their arrival has lead to 'gentrification'. Gentrification can be defined as a process of renewal and rebuilding which accompanies the influx of middle-class or affluent people into disadvantaged areas that may displace earlier usually poorer residents. The potential displacement of economically disadvantaged communities as a result of a local rising property market is a genuine and legitimate concern when areas undergo a period of rapid regeneration.

There is, however, little evidence of gentrification having taken place in inner-city Dublin. Considerable areas of the inner city remain disadvantaged with extensive dereliction. Few areas of Dublin 1, 7 or 8 have witnessed local house-price inflation over and above average city increases. The local long-term resident population of inner-city social housing complexes may have witnessed the arrival of thousands of new apartment dwellers, but they themselves have not been displaced. The fear or dislike of gentrification in inner-city Dublin is fed less by any evidence of social displacement having occurred than by a dislike of social dilution or social change. It stems from a fear of the other, of newcomers, a fear of the dilution of the ideals or values of some pre-existing or endangered, perhaps romanticised, indigenous community. This fear is sometimes rational – a fear of losing political control over that local 'indigenous' community, and thus a monopoly on the authenticity of the voice of that community.

Dublin City Council itself often struggles sometimes to understand the complexity of urban residential social structures in the inner city. 'The community' is commonly understood as the original long-term residents of the local flat complexes. Apartment-dwellers are rarely engaged as citizens, let alone as a resource for the inner city. They are not understood as forming a 'natural' part of the local inner-city community. They are viewed as an ephemeral byproduct of tax-designated infill development, albeit a grudgingly welcome one.

Apartment-dwellers (alongside all other residents) don't pay domestic rates or a property tax to the local authority, a fact that perhaps reflects the ambivalent attitude of civic authorities to their net contribution to the city's economy. Apartment-dwellers, however, unlike the residents of houses on the same street, are not afforded equal City Council access to on-street car-parking. If an apartment scheme is greater than four units (most high-density schemes invariably are), the apartment-dweller cannot avail of the same entitlement to an on-street car-parking space. What seems entirely reasonable in Dublin – discrimination in the delivery of municipal services based on housing typology – would be viewed as simply odd in other cities.

Apartment Apartheid manifests itself in numerous other small ways, sometimes subtle, sometimes not, some more important than others. Apartment-dwellers are constantly berated for visibly dripdrying their clothes on balconies. This is not an uncommon criticism from planners and architects, who seem oblivious to their role in ensuring simple design

solutions such as naturally ventilated drying rooms, partially hidden by louvered screens. The fact that MUDs (multiple unit developments) has become a legislative acronym and an increasing municipal euphemism for people's homes, without any genuine recognition or understanding of the implied derisory message it communicates, demonstrates the depth of the deep-seated, almost unconscious, official antipathy to apartment-living in Dublin. One could be forgiven for thinking that the peddlers of MUDs (dirt, muck, mud huts, muddling through), with its implied suggestion of alien, filthy communal living, were deliberately or subliminally seeking to undermine the value of high-density urbanism itself.

Is the continuation of Apartment Apartheid inevitable? No. Dublin city has witnessed a transformation of its inner-urban areas over the past twenty years. The inner-city population has doubled. This doubling of population has injected a vitality and dynamism into its street life, culture and city economy. If Dublin city is to retain these new urban pioneers (they can opt to leave just as quickly as they choose to move there; many homeowners bought their apartment homes more than a decade ago, many more are renting) they need to be engaged and valued, their interests understood, their contribution to consolidating a vital and sustainable urban economy acknowledged and rewarded.

If potential new urban dwellers are to be attracted to the city and not 'lost' to distant towns and suburbs in Kildare, Meath or north county Dublin, a radical overhaul of the ambition and vision of what is possible in city-centre living needs to be communicated. Language is important. It communicates values and intent. Inappropriate and inaccurate acronyms such as MUDs, 'gentrification', 'transients' and 'gated communities' do little to convince that the city (in the broadest definition of the term) understands and values the potential transformative economic and environmentally sustainable role high-density apartment-living can and does play in the vitality and dynamism of Dublin city life.

Inner-City Urbanism

Getting it right on the community left

One of the biggest ironies of community politics in Dublin's disadvantaged inner city is the inexplicable misunderstanding on the part of many professional community activists of the potential importance of urban geography on effective political lobbying for significant city or state resources. Dublin's inner-urban disadvantaged communities matter hugely, but not in the way that many on the community left very often imagine or believe. The strongest argument for a significant shift in city priorities and economic resources for these impoverished or underprivileged areas is not a plea for social justice to alleviative real generational deprivation to ensure fair and equitable access to public goods or private opportunity. These political arguments are well rehearsed, and for the most part well received. An established city and national political consensus of their importance, however, does not necessarily translate into action. There is, we believe, a less 'just', but perhaps a more powerfully persuasive and effective rationale for prioritising the plight of Dublin's inner city. This line of reasoning is underplayed and misunderstood, or dismissed as diluting or contaminating the purity of the narrative of the local professional social community activist.

The Liberties and North Inner City are not Darndale, Cherry Orchard, Ballymun or Ballyfermot. No disrespect to these neighbourhoods, but Dublin's inner-urban neighbourhoods are strategically far more important to the future of the capital city than any or all of these working-class suburbs. Geography matters to cities. Cities matter to the economy. Dublin's inner city is intrinsically linked to the future success of Dublin's economy. The expansion of a successful city centre into an underperforming inner city is vital to that economy.

Put simply, inner-urban Dublin matters to both the image and the economy of Dublin. It is home to some of the State's largest tourist attractions, including Guinness, Collins Barracks and the Hugh Lane Gallery. It is host to diverse and dynamic communities. It sits right next door to the city centre. The success of Dublin's inner-urban neighbourhoods is increasingly recognised as intrinsically linked to the city's future success. They carry within them the seeds of enormous urban potential, unparalleled and untapped resources (scarce vacant inner-urban land), and exciting sustainable-living alternatives to suburban sprawl.

Ironically, many on the community left who claim to champion the cause of these inner-city neighbourhoods don't quite seem to see it that way. Instead of claiming a special and rightful place in the urban hierarchy of a capital city, and thus a special claim on state or city resources, what is very often demanded is a special place in the consciousness of city myth-making. 'Born and bred in the inner-city' becomes a badge of honour, an automatic and rightful entry to some undefined urban authenticity. With that myth-making comes demands for quasi-territorial independence and an economically perverse desire for decoupling or detachment from the vitality of the commerce of the city, including an inalienable right to demand a veto on any 'intrusive' developments that are not perceived to directly benefit the 'indigenous' locals.

Sadly, many decision-makers and influential opinion-formers, most of whom don't reside in these areas, are only too happy to oblige or indulge in this romantic charade. The romanticisation of an impoverished community not only serves to alleviate the social consciousness of suburban middle-class detachment, but reinforces an artificial and ultimately self-fulfilling division between the city centre and the inner city. It perpetuates a divisive 'them and us'. The inevitable result is a prolonged marginalisation and underperformance of an inner city, detached from the potential dynamism and sustainable vitality of the city centre, which ultimately is economically and socially detrimental to both.

Homeless Urbanism

What is 'homeless urbanism' and who are its advocates? 'Homeless urbanism' is a peculiar form of Dublin urbanism that professes an understanding, a love even, of cities, yet is almost entirely devoid of any interest in either the design or delivery of high-density urban homes. 'Homeless urbanism' occupies a kind of city limbo space between 'real urbanism' – an urbanism in all its varied complexity and possibilities – and a faux-urbanism or narrow suburban view of what makes cities work.

At it simplest, the advocates and followers of 'homeless urbanism' believe that urbanism begins and ends with how things look, not how they function. For the adherents of 'homeless urbanism', taller residential buildings are generally only assessed as three-dimensional forms to be viewed from the outside, usually the street below. Apartment sizes and layouts, being invisible from the street, are of marginal interest, and thus an irrelevance to the practitioners of 'homeless urbanism'. 'Homeless urbanism' adherents' dislike of taller residential buildings, in Dublin at least, is inherently linked to and inseparable from a past indifference to high-density apartment-living. Because the 'homeless urbanist' cannot see inside the six-storey apartment block, it was therefore of no importance. Because the 'homeless urbanist' can only see the tower, they can't imagine the housing possibilities it affords; therefore it's just a tower. The possibility of living in a 200m² apartment on the twentieth floor overlooking the city or the sea is unimaginable to the 'homeless urbanist'. Equally, the size of homes, or the size of other people's homes – the apartment-dweller – is of little interest.

Collectively, these shortsighted views of the importance and potential of quality housing in city-making are essentially informed by a particular understanding of urbanism. It's an urbanism that values, above all else, what can be seen as opposed to the hidden possibilities of what can be imagined, understood or, most importantly, enjoyed and lived.

In the world of 'homeless urbanism', urban grain, scale and permeability are exalted and elevated to the status of a triumphant trinity of urban theology. Housing choice and spacious living is either an abstraction or just, well, boring. Urban housing quality simply does not exist beyond a narrow interest in block height, block massing, external fenestration patterns and material finishes. In this way 'homeless urbanism' unwittingly both confuses and perverts urban design as the overarching discipline in city-making. This is a place of three-dimensional façades and stage sets, where 'negative space' – the spaces between and critically above buildings – rules supreme over the life-affirming possibilities of 'positive space' – the delightful volumetric interiors of, or the captivating and stunning panoramic city views from the living rooms of those who might live there.

'Homeless urbanism' is a city of boxes masquerading as a belief system in urbanism. In this 'box city', buildings are primarily to be viewed from the outside, not experienced from the inside. Physical architectural models become all-important in interpreting that unlived experience. The models themselves become apt metaphors for the extent of the detached observer, an observer hovering giant-like and unreal from above, a suburban Gulliver in an urban Lilliputian world of Legoland architecture of varying blocks and shapes.

If 'homeless urbanism' is indifferent to the importance of high-density quality housing design, it is inevitably blind to the potential transformative impact quality housing has on urban regeneration. In a city with extensive inner-urban underperforming and derelict areas, this is a significant lost opportunity for visionary city-making. Indifference to high-density quality housing inevitably means an indifference to past mistakes. In failing to acknowledge the delivery of poor-quality and small apartments in the last fifteen years, Dublin is potentially blind not only to its city-making of the past, but also to the possibilities of its urban future.

The ebb and flow of the 'TIDAL CITY' versus the beat and pulse of the 'LIVING CITY'

The 'tidal city', as it names suggests, ebbs and flows to the rise and fall of its visitors. The 'living city', as it names suggests, beats and pulsates primarily to the rhythm and energy of its inhabitants. The urban vision of the tidal city prioritises attracting the fleeting attention or visits of others. The urban vision of the living city prioritises the long-term attraction and retention of those who choose to live and work there.

The influx of the rush-hour commuter, out-of-town shopper and seasonal migratory overseas tourist all combine to generate a particular overlapping wave of energy and priority for the tidal city. The constant presence of tens of thousands of workers, producers, consumers, and colourful, diverse immigrant communities all combine to generate a particular dynamic in the living city.

The tidal city values and is dependent upon the spending power or income of the daily visitors who do not dwell among its inhabitants. The living city values and is dependent upon the innovation and entrepreneurial spirit of its own citizens. The tidal city prioritises the free flow of commercial traffic through the channels of its arteries. The lifeblood of the tidal city is vehicular movement. The living city prioritises the uninhibited flow of creativity and ideas. The lifeblood of the living city is its people.

The key urban decision-makers of the tidal city, like most of the rest of its workforce, commute home daily to a life outside their city. The key urban decision-makers of the living city, like most of the rest of its workforce, live out their daily lives on the streets and in the homes of their city.

The tidal city believes in the importance of centrally located, flagship public-domain projects to communicate a message of urban intent. The living city understands the importance and simplicity of an extensive network of green, clean and safe streets in sustaining a vital urban economy and quality of life for all.

The tidal city seeks to attract people to visit as opposed to attracting people to live. The living city seeks to attract people to live as opposed to attracting people to visit, and in so doing ensures the attraction of both. The tidal city sees the city as a static urban stage upon which the economy is played out. The living city values the city itself as a critical active player in driving forward the economy. The tidal city is, at its heart, a suburban space. The living city is, at its heart, an urban place.

Is Dublin a suburban tidal city or an urban living city?

Urban Suburban Hassle Paradox and Calculator

Urban Suburban Hassle Paradox

The 'urban suburban hassle paradox' is the inherently contradictory, but entirely understandable suburban desire to drive hassle-free to the city centre on weekdays, to then avail of free parking and, having parked the car, to finally enjoy a pedestrian-friendly, largely car-free city. Is it possible? Perhaps, if the city is small, but not if the city is the size of Dublin.

Understanding and managing this contradiction is critically important in trying to resolve not just the Urban Suburban Hassle Paradox, but in transforming the quality of the liveability of inner urban Dublin. A pedestrian-friendly and walkable city almost by definition enjoys near-unanimity of consensus as a desirable policy for any city. Translating that near unanimity into practicable policy is altogether more difficult.

Any municipal initiative to reduce vehicular speed limits, extend bus lanes, introduce pedestrian-friendly traffic-calming or widen footpaths will testify to the true appetite of the suburban motorist for a pedestrian-friendly inner city. The limited expansion in 2010 of an already existing 30km speed limit in the centre of Dublin city provoked near hysterical opposition. The fact that it was initially spun by some as an anti-car 'get-on-your-bike' policy rather than a potentially civilising pedestrian- and child-friendly initiative perhaps exacerbated the negative public reaction.

That particular hostile reaction and the wider suburban desire to drive hassle-free and avail of relatively free parking is inextricably bound up with a general reluctance of many Dublin middle-class suburban residents to use public transport. Conventional wisdom states that this reluctance to use public transport is primarily driven by factors such as reliability, convenience, and vehicle comfort. How often does the train or bus come? How far does one have to walk to get to it? How clean and comfortable is the ride?

There are other barriers, perhaps unspoken taboos, about travelling on public transport, at least on certain forms of public transport in certain areas or through certain parts of the city. This is the social intimacy factor, sometimes an 'edginess factor', the uncertain and unwelcome chance that one's family may encounter an uncomfortable moment of unsolicited or anti-social interaction with fellow public transport-users.

A reluctance to use or a dependency upon public transport generates two types of equivocal urbanists, the 'trapped urbanists' and the 'avoiding urbanists'. The 'trapped urbanists' are those who are 'forced' to make use of unsatisfactory public transport to commute to the city centre. Poor reliability, inconvenience, high cost or unwanted social interaction compounds the discomfort. Travel choices are limited for the 'trapped urbanist'. Free or low-cost parking in the city is unavailable, all-day city-centre commercial car-parking unaffordable.

The 'avoiding urbanists', as the term suggests, generally avoids the city altogether. They are the mirror reflection of the 'trapped urbanists'. They are, in effect, 'trapped suburbanists'. There are many reasons why the 'trapped suburbanist' chooses not to visit the city very often. We have touched upon a few of them already – the lack of free car-parking and the hassle of traffic restrictions. In addition to the perceived dangers of a relatively pedestrian-unfriendly city centre, the 'trapped suburbanist' tends to perceive the city centre or inner city as unsafe for their children. If the 'trapped suburbanist' occasionally visits the city, their young children rarely do.

The 'trapped suburbanist' fear of inappropriate behaviour is sufficient for many suburbanites to write-off the city centre as a potential regular opportunity for family recreation. This explains in part why many middle-income Dubliners with children reject urbanism, or an 'urban Dublin' to be more precise. A visit to the city, however, is not quite the same as living in the city. Living in the city is an altogether more challenging and largely rejected proposition.

Urban Suburban Hassle Calculator

Middle-income rejection of Dublin inner-city or city-centre living would appear to be a complex equation of a multitude of real tangible benefits and costs. It is, we believe, a rather simple equation. For those with children, the flight to the suburbs occurs when the cost of urban living to your child outweighs the benefits of city life for you. Whether it is intuitive or calculated, instinctive or laboured, many parents who wish to live in the city juggle with the costs and benefits of urban living. We call this the 'urban suburban hassle calculator'.

The benefits of city-living are many and varied. For young working parents it can perhaps be reduced to two. The first is the benefit of a possibly shorter, less stressful, less time-consuming commute, with the added attraction of perhaps walking to work. The actual financial costs of commuting are rarely calculated and are thus given short shrift in most people's 'suburban hassle calculator'.

The second benefit of city-living is the immediate access to the diversity of choice in culture, dining and shopping that urban living affords. Easy, hassle-free access to restaurants, cinemas, theatres, concerts and museums are all 'pull' factors for living in the city. For many suburban Dubliners there is an apparent insufficient 'pull' factor for living in the city. The city is small. The variety and diversity of choice is perhaps just not big enough to warrant the investment (smaller homes for the same price as houses in the suburbs) or the hassle of city-living.

Perhaps a corollary to the relatively weak city pull is that it is not so inconvenient to drive into Dublin city in order to take advantage of its urban attractions in the evening or at weekends. (Parking is free every day after 7pm and all day on Sundays.} Getting there isn't such a chore. The quality of most people's cars, the ease of driving further and further away on spanking new motorways, and the 'time out' alone in a comfortable, indeed, comforting private space are all downplayed as if taboo or embarrassingly out of touch with received wisdom or the green zeitgeist of our time. People like their cars.

The cost of city-living, a cost magnified when rearing a child, is the push factor away from the city. It is the real and perceived cost of traffic congestion, lack of green spaces, poor pedestrian priority, unsafe cycling and a lingering fear of crime and anti-social behaviour. The quality of schools is critically important. There is a belief that local (non-fee-paying) schools in the inner city are inadequate or underperforming. Perhaps there is also an unspoken fear that the children might 'adopt' the wrong friends or accent. Poor housing choice is also an important factor. The

past failure to deliver spacious, quality city-centre apartments in Dublin has played a significant role in reducing real housing choice for many. That failure has also had a devastating impact on a potential, emerging middle-income, child-friendly Dublin urbanism.

There is strong anecdotal evidence that Dublin's inner city, its urban core, fares particularly badly relative to the suburbs on many child-centred quality of life issues. There is recent hard evidence to suggest that the overall perceived quality of life in Dublin's inner city fares poorly relative to other north European cities of comparable size. In a survey of 75 European cities, Dublin ranked 26th in the perceived level of neighbourhood safety, with 76% of Dubliners stating that they always feel safe in their own neighbourhood. This compares to 91% for citizens of Munich, 85% for Copenhagen, and 78% for Amsterdam. The average across the 75 cities was 69%.

Dublin, however, fell to a lowly 57 in the ranking when its citizens were asked whether they felt safe in the city; just 41% did so. This compares to 76% for Munich, 65% for Amsterdam, and 67% for Copenhagen. Not surprisingly, cities that scored high on the perceived safety of their neighbourhoods score well on the overall perceived safety of the city. Similarly, cities that fared poorly in neighbourhood scores generally performed badly on a sense of safety in the city.

Dublin city, however, falls dramatically to 74 out of 75 cities in the gap in perceived safety between neighbourhood and city. The residents of all 75 surveyed cities perceived 'their neighbourhood' as safer than 'the city'. The average gap for all cities is just under 19%. The gap between the perceived safety of neighbourhood and city for Dublin is almost double the average, at 35%. Perhaps the fact that most Dubliners are suburban residents, with very few citizens (particularly middle-class families) actually living in the city's downtown or inner-city area, explains Dublin's ranking. Perhaps the city centre and inner city at certain times in certain places is just perceived as too edgy and unsafe for many Dubliners.

Do middle-class families choose not to live in the inner city because it feels unsafe, or is it simply the case that anti-social behaviour is prevalent in the inner city because of the concentration of poverty? Which comes first, a safe inner city or mixed-income inner-city neighbourhoods?

Introducing the Urban Tourist

Spotting the differences between 'touring urbanism' and 'urban tourism'

Spotting the difference between the 'touring urbanist' and the 'urban tourist' may be perceptively difficult and, at first glance, a trifle irrelevant. Should you persevere in grasping an insight into the critical differences, your reward is a keen understanding of the priorities of some key decision-makers in the murky and fashionable world of professional 'urbanism' – priorities, by the way, that affect your city and, thus, your daily life.

The 'touring urbanist' is, quite simply, an urbanist who tours cities in order to experience them, to explore and understand how they work, and, if they are lucky enough, to socially and culturally penetrate the local psyche. The 'urban tourist', on the other hand, is the short-hop weekend tourist or traveller who takes city breaks to various (invariably European) cities in order to taste and visually consume. The overlap, of course, is huge, the distinction exaggerated.

So what's the difference you might ask? Well none of real consequence if the person travelling is not directly involved in prioritising, implementing or informing urban policy. If, however, they are members of the 'city-making professions' – architects, urban designers, engineers, planners – and have real power to design and shape the future of your city, it matters hugely. The critical difference is that the 'urban tourist' tends to value what they can 'see' in a foreign city as opposed to what they can't. The price and design of boutique hotels are more important than the quality and spaciousness of local apartments; farmers' markets matter more than supermarkets; reading prices in the city is more important than understanding the economy of that city. The experience or quality of public space interests far more than how it's paid for or how and when it was delivered. Shop fronts are prized over convenient shopping. The form, height and fenestration pattern of office blocks and apartment buildings intrigue and are endlessly visually deconstructed, usually from the street below, whereas business needs, workable layouts, ventilation – including views from the building as opposed to views to the building – are either of secondary importance or of little or no interest. The list is surprisingly endless.

The 'urban tourist' is a keen enthusiast and observer of excellence in landscape design and the architecture of civic buildings, but has little interest in or knowledge of the quality or functionality of local children's playgrounds or schools. Municipal galleries, public museums and high-profile exhibitions delight the 'urban tourist'. Innovation and local creativity, being that much less tangible and harder to consume, are of marginal interest and comprehension. Water of any description, as long as it's visible, fascinates the 'urban tourist'. Docklands, quaysides, water features and fountains of any shape or size arouse curiosity and investigation. Water services, local municipal swimming pools, underground piping, water sources and flood risk are dismissed as somebody else's interest or responsibility.

The 'urban tourist' is captivated by the past and consumed by the present. The future is somewhat of an abstraction in the enjoyment or understanding of any city. Over valuing what you can see as opposed to what you cannot may be logical, inevitable, preferable, even essential for the experience of the tourist, but it's a fatal flaw with potentially disastrous consequences for the native city of the touring urban policy-maker. It is unfortunately an all-too-common ailment or infliction to be found amongst urban policy-makers, particularly amongst those with a self-professed heightened sense of discerning visual aesthetic. Engineers tend to suffer least from this infliction. They tend also – perhaps not surprisingly – to be more refreshing, lucid and economical in their employment of language. Its is important to state that what the 'urban tourist' values is not any less important than the 'touring urbanist'; it's simply the inability of the 'urban tourist' – oddly for the urban professional – to complete the circle or see the full picture.

URBAN TOURIST VERSUS TOURING URBANIST   BOUTIQUE HOTELS VERSUS
SPACIOUS APARTMENTS   TALL BUILDINGS VERSUS HOMES WITH A VIEW
LANDSCAPE   DESIGN   VERSUS   CHILDREN'S   PLAYGROUNDS
SHOPFRONTS VERSUS CONVENIENCE SHOPPING   FARMERS'
MARKETS VERSUS SUPERMARKETS   PRICES IN THE CITY VERSUS ECONOMY
OF THE CITY   PUBLIC SPACE VERSUS STREET CLEANSING   PUBLIC
GALLERIES VERSUS PRIVATE CREATIVITY   OFFICE BLOCKS VERSUS
BUSINESS NEEDS   A City's Past VERSUS The City's Future
URBAN   TOURISTS   VERSUS   CITY   DWELLERS   STREET
FURNITURE VERSUS STREET NIGHTLIFE   WATER FEATURES VERSUS WATER
SERVICES   HISTORIC CORES VERSUS SUBURBAN SPRAWL   BIN
DESIGN VERSUS RECYCLING   WATERFRONT COMMUNITY VERSUS SWIMMING POOLS
SIGNAGE VERSUS ADVERTISING   CIVIC BUILDINGS VERSUS SCHOOLS   METRO DESIGN
VERSUS MORNING RUSH HOUR   BUDGET HOTELS VERSUS CITY BUDGETS   CITY
MUSEUMS VERSUS CITY LIBRARIES   LANDSCAPES OF VALUE VERSUS
EXPERIENCE OF STREETS   FENESTRATION PATTERNS VERSUS ROOMS WITH A VIEW

Creeping Green

If the phrase 'rurban' is widely accepted as describing a rural area that has become urbanised – an area that now exhibits both urban and rural characteristics – how do we describe an urban area at risk of being ruralised? 'Urbal'? Somehow 'urbalisation' doesn't quite sound right. 'Creeping ruralbanisation' or 'creeping green' perhaps? Whatever it's called, it is a kind of rural-sanitisation or urban-cleansing.

'Creeping green' is only really dangerous when a city is vulnerable, when its urban immune system is weak. This only occurs when a city's urban value system has not been sufficiently and robustly established. In confident, demonstrably urban cities, the advocates of urban 'communal city allotments', 'wasteland bio-diversity', time-consuming and labour-intensive home-growing of vegetables in parks and pocket green spaces adds to an already rich texture of urban diversity. They are a potentially additional ecological layer of sustainability.

In vulnerable cities, however, cities with very weak urban structures, cities struggling to exploit urban economic comparative advantages (growing carrots is rarely an urban economic comparative advantage), an inappropriate infusion of green experimentation in the front yard of proto-urbanism can endanger or snuff-out real city-living. It can conveniently, for some, also detract from the real source of unsustainable settlement, car-born carbon-belching commuting.

It is perhaps telling that most 'green' city allotment initiatives in Dublin are to be found in either deprived working-class inner-city areas on derelict urban sites (underperforming urbanism) or in the rural foothills of the Wicklow or Dublin mountains, accessed by weekender middle class SUV-driving suburbanites (unsustainable sub-urbanism). It is somewhat ironic that in a suburban city, 'underperforming urbanism' or 'unsustainable sub-urbanism' should be lauded as examples of 21st 'green' sustainability.

Dublin allotments may appeal to individual pastimes or ideologies, encourage or reinforce communal leisure or identity, initiate an interest or awareness in healthy eating, or even reawaken a collective romanticised reconnection to land and nature. They rarely, if ever, provide an ecologically friendly alternative to the mass-production and distribution of food to ensure sustainable urban living. Sustainable urban food distribution is best served by ensuring that almost all city residents can walk five minutes to a plentiful and affordable supply of quality food produce. High-density apartment-living and a range of local supermarkets selling efficiently farmed produce not surprisingly combine to do this quite well.[1] Allotments may sustain many things, but confusing food self-sufficiency (growing your own food) with food sustainability (environmentally efficient and secure food distribution) is neither sustainable nor 'green'.

Suburban sprawl eats up potential farmland that otherwise might provide locally produced food? So why is it that the home patch of high-density inner-city dwellers, with their limited public space and restricted private balconies, and increasingly costly but communally sustained management committees, should become the laboratory of a kind of experimental green home economics, whilst many of sustainable food advocates live out their 'sustainable' semi-detached lives in the suburbs complete with front and back grassed lawns?

Making compact sustainable cities more attractive and affordable places to live remains one of the most obvious 'green' urban strategies for all cities. For Dublin, with extensive areas of inner-city dereliction and blighted communities, it continues to remain a significant challenge, yet one of unbounded opportunity.

'Real green' urbanism makes new city parks not city farms. 'Real green' urbanism plants boulevards of trees in disadvantaged city areas, as opposed to protecting the biodiversity of overgrown wastelands on derelict sites. 'Real green' urbanism promotes the construction of high-density, quality, energy-efficient, spacious urban homes (more and better inner-city apartment development, not less). 'Real green' urbanism, in order to consolidate high-density living, endeavours to maximise, not minimise residential views of urban parks and water. It celebrates views of the Phoenix Park and the city's coastline. 'Creeping green' on the other hand, endeavours to minimise access to and protect views of sustainable urban green assets.

In a recent ranking of urban 'green' credentials in Europe, Dublin did not fare too well, coming in at 21 out of 30 surveyed cities.[2] Notably, Dublin substantially trailed behind all of its north-west European competitors.

Dublin ranked particularly low on transport (ranked 30) and poorly on CO_2 outputs (ranked 19), both indicative of a pattern of settlement sprawl and a car-dependent suburban culture.

The 'green' criteria employed included quality-of-life indices such as urban living, the length (and width) of cycling lanes, the percentage of the working population travelling to work on public transport. These are the critical issues informing 'real green' urbanism. Growing your own food supply on the balcony or in the front garden was, unsurprisingly, absent.

'Real green' urbanism is being serious about urban living. 'Ruralbanisation' or 'creeping green' on the other hand, with its peculiar obsession with growing one's own food or its romantic attachment to the 'land', is not the rediscovering of nature in a city; it is going back to nature to replace a city. This desire to replace the city perhaps explains why so many of the advocates of 'creeping green' in Dublin are suspiciously suspect of the 'real green' value of sustainable high-density urban living.

Pigeon House chimneys, Poolbeg
– tallest structure in Ireland, 207 metres

'Turning Torso', Malmö, Sweden
– tallest residential building in Europe, 190 metres

What if it replaced the Pigeon House chimneys?

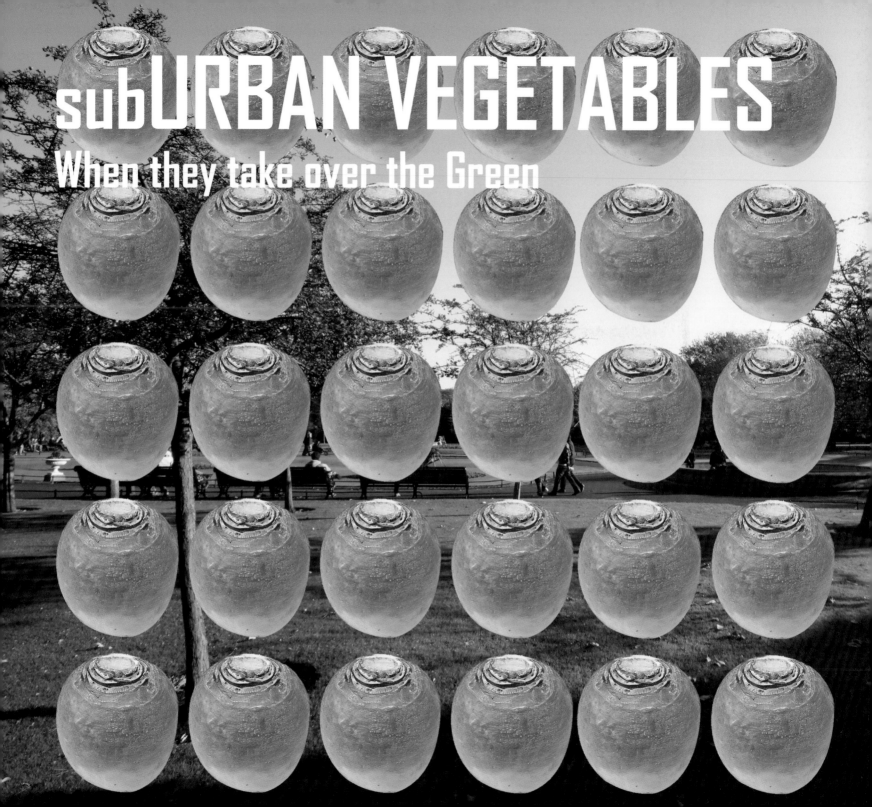

subURBAN VEGETABLES

When they take over the Green

'Loco' Green?

In LOCO GREEN we cast our mind's eye about to playfully expose and deconstruct some of the contradictory anti-urban 'green' thinking masquerading as green solutions to the challenges of environmentally sustainable living. In our Loco Green world – think local act loco – truly sustainable cities are increasingly under threat from morphological ecological extinction. In Loco Green, the advocates of science, density and innovation lose out to the guardians of supposition, consumption and taste.

loco

adj : informal or slang terms for mentally irregular
[syn: balmy, barmy, bats, batty, bonkers, buggy, cracked, crackers, daft, dotty, fruity, haywire, kooky, kookie, loony, loopy, nuts, nutty, wacky]

When planning policy and lifestyle choices combine to sustain a middle-class urbanism, where your car is almost as a big as

When you obsess about the energy rating of a single building,
but are indifferent to the environmental costs of suburban sprawl.

When you rail against the visibility of taller buildings, but are silent on the invisibility of poor-quality, high-density apartment design.

When you champion urban public transport
but distrust or dislike inner-city living.

When you promote turning off the lights in an entire city,
but remain indifferent to the ecological costs of rural living.

When you campaign against air-flown food,
but are unaware of the energy costs of local greenhouses.

What if ?

What if the State introduced a radical carbon tax on commuting 'lifestyles'?

Would residential densities inevitability rise in Dublin city? Would buildings heights go higher? Would policy makers encourage bigger apartments for families or smaller apartments for a denser, more compact city? Would prices rise for inner-city homes or fall as jobs left the city centre? Would investment in urban public transport necessarily follow? Would traffic congestion increase in the city core because of higher densities or fall as more people walked to work? Would urban living become more valued or jealousy resented? Would open spaces become increasingly threatened by inappropriate development or better utilised by residents of high-density living? Would the economy grow as CO2 outputs fell? Would inner Dublin become a more dynamic and diverse liveable space or an exclusive zone for the super rich? Would the city be a better place to live? Who's asking?

Not so Great?
Sustainable Housing in Greater Dublin

In a study of the oversupply of national housing stock, the National Institute for Regional and Spatial Analysis (NIRSA) lends gentle praise to 'the local authorities surrounding Dublin City (Fingal, Kildare, Meath, South Dublin, Wicklow) [for having] constructed housing approximately in line with demand'.[1] With an excess housing supply of 7.4%, Dublin City Council, by implication, is deemed to have erroneously assessed demand in constructing far too many homes (16,489 to be precise).[2]

Yet a cursory look at the 1999 Strategic Planning Guidelines for the Greater Dublin Area reveal an altogether more intriguing spatial picture. These government-issued sustainable strategic guidelines predicted that the respective population for each local authority for 2006 would be as follows: Dublin City Council, 509,655; Dun Laoghaire-Rathdown, 201,648; South Dublin, 235,992; Fingal, 187,213; Wicklow, 109,337; Meath, 116,192; Kildare, 150,772.[3]

The reality that emerged was somewhat different. The percentage difference between the population forecast in 1999 and what actually materialised in 2006 varied significantly between the six Greater Dublin Area local authorities.[4] The population of both the Dublin City Council area (-0.7%) and Dun Laoghaire-Rathdown (-3.9%) actually lagged behind anticipated growth. South Dublin (4.1%) grew marginally more than expected, with Fingal (22%), Wicklow (13.2%), Meath (28.3%) and Kildare (18.9%) all substantially 'over-shooting' their trend forecast.[5]

Combining all this competing and overlapping information suggests that the 'sprawl counties' of Fingal, Meath and Kildare would appear to have been building what people wanted – typical, and reasonably large suburban homes – in vastly greater numbers than the experts expected – a case of market-driven but unsustainable unplanned sprawl? Simultaneously, Dublin City Council, with an excess supply of housing more than seven times that of Co Meath, was clearly building what people didn't want, smaller than average apartment-style homes,[6] albeit in more sustainable urban locations. Vastly different housing strategies, yet both could equally lay a reasonable claim to Greater Dublin Area unsustainable development.

There are many losers in this sorry housing tale, a physical environment degraded by sprawl, traffic congestion, the loss of real housing choice for tens of thousands of people, and perhaps the least understood, an opportunity lost to consolidate a quality, high-density apartment urbanism for Dublin city.

How 'Green' is your Conscience?
Is it Sustainable?

So you recycle almost everything, eat fresh food only when it's in season, never eat red meat or fish, grow a significant proportion of your own food, the rest being both organic and locally produced. How low is your carbon footprint? Pretty low, if – and it's a big if – you don't drive or fly. All that recycling and dietary effort to be a virtuous green is offset by a single return flight to New York.[1] And the uncomfortable suburban fact remains that the most 'consciousness' of green lifestyles counts for little if you choose or have to drive to work.

The inner-urban dweller who does not drive and instead walks to work, and who, nevertheless, is unfashionably predominantly a red-meat eater, eats fresh food out of season, is indifferent to where their food comes from (indifferent to food air miles/km) and generally avoids recycling, generates less CO_2 waste than the most environmentally conscious individual on all of these issues if the latter drives just 4,000km a year.[2]

A car travelling some 16,000km a year generates three carbon tonnes annually.[3] The difference in carbon output, all other things being equal, between those who grow all their own food and those who are indifferent to where their food comes from is just 0.09 carbon tonnes.[4]

Long-distance public-transport commuters don't fare too well either in the carbon rankings. Suburbanites travelling on average 30km daily (60km round trip) generate 0.88 carbon tonnes per year.[5] Put another way, all things being equal (and the facts speak from themselves), urban living remains the ultimate 'green' choice. How 'green' is your conscience?

LEVEL + 1

Opening-Up Space

Sketching Spaces

In SKETCHING SPACES we open our minds to the possibility of opening space for others. We explore just a tiny fraction of some of the infinite urban possibilities of opening up new spaces for all Dubliners. Our 'opening-up spaces' are both public and private. Some are small, possibly hidden or unknown, others at a scale not easily imagined. Communicating dynamic visual possibilities, as opposed to 'drawing plans', is an important but largely untapped resource of the municipal architect, planner or city decision-maker.

In LEVEL+1 we compliment and celebrate the imaginative uses of higher roof levels, in this case the running track at Belvedere College in Dublin's north inner city. Green roofs, upper-floor gardens, a solitary decking refuge, a temporary event or party, private restaurants or public viewing platforms, whatever the use, Dublin needs to imaginatively re-imagine and reuse its empty roofs space.

In LEGALISE US ... UR-BAN US we champion the desire of Dublin's youth to inhabit, hangout and play in urban spaces. Inviting children and teenagers to occupy, engage, re-imagine or assist in designing our city streets is a necessary civic challenge in civilising and democratising our urban spaces. Successfully managing urban spaces for children manages spaces for everybody.

In AN URBAN CRIME SCENE we lament potentially one of the greatest urban spaces of Dublin city. What could be a flourishing, liveable and dynamically integrated sequence of public spaces is instead a partial surface car park.

The Office of Public Works site at Church Street in the north inner city, fenced by a blue-bordered barrier, has lain vacant for a decade in an area deficient of urban green open space. Might the OPW temporarily extend and re-imagine their role as custodians and guardians of the State's greatest parks and squares in furthering urban green regeneration?

'Legalise us ... ur-ban us'

An Urban Crime Scene

Dublin Castle – Special Branch Garda (police) headquarters

Under utilised inner city land vacant 2000-2010

Open Parks Working

Unlock a Park Gate

ACT ... *in the City*
Area Catalyst Task

An 'area catalyst task' is a simple intervention, usually a low-cost one, in your local street or neighbourhood that has the potential to yield dramatic, positive and real benefits to both you and your neighbours. The benefits gained are disproportionate to the initial outlay or effort.

An area catalyst task is a form of urban acupuncture, call it what you like. It's localised, relatively painless, but its impacts are seen and felt widely. It's the unlocking of a gate to a local park, removing an unsightly wall, planting a tree or two, installing a single bench in the right place, persuading the school board to allow local children to play on the school football pitch after the school has closed. It's about community confidence and local control. It sustains momentum in regeneration areas. Ultimately, it's about taking local control and responsibility for action in, or acting for, your local neighbourhood. Most importantly, it doesn't require a 'municipal plan' or a 'design professional', simply imagination, local co-ordination, ambition and a small but effective amount of political clout.

ACT-IN THE CITY is the positive, pro-active opposite of NIMBYism. It's about getting things done as opposed to stopping things happening in your neighbourhood.

What is the difference between 'Communal Allotments' and 'Public Parks',

and why it is so important to an emerging Dublin urbanism?

Communal allotments, as the term implies, are collective or community-driven and supported. They are also necessarily local and territorial. They require communal membership. Membership, no matter how loosely defined, requires approval of others, 'others' being self-appointed or collectively approved arbiters or guardians of what constitutes acceptable or approved community behaviour. The urban communal allotment is a form of communitarian village life – a quasi-private communal open space – grafted onto potential city or public space.

The public park, on the other hand, is about the freedom of the individual, made possible by collective thinking and organisation, the city or civic life. The distinction is subtle but hugely significant. It's possible to trespass onto an allotment. The city park is for everyone. You don't need the approval of others or membership to join or enter a public park. The only rule for entering and enjoying a public park is respect for the anonymous other.

Lord and Dame Stroll

Barcelona has one, Tel Aviv has one, many ordinary cities have one. It's familiar, popular, safe and casual. 'It' is the urban stroll. Does Dublin have one?

Whether it's the Ramblas or Rothschild, the urban boulevard is very often the symbolic heart and enjoyable civic artery of its host city. It's where people come to meander, to stroll, to see and be seen, to stop for coffee or ice-cream, dinner or drinks. The urban stroll is not to be confused with the Dublin Sunday afternoon perambulation up and down a windswept pier, the health-conscious brisk walk in the local park or the solitary constitution along empty seafronts. Enjoyable as these are, they are all suburban, ritualistic, and perhaps infused with an almost anti-urban sense of rediscovering or reconnecting to a rural idyll. They ultimately seek to escape from the city.

The urban stroll is thoroughly different, it's thoroughly social, thoroughly urban and distinctly pleasurable. It is an unashamedly city experience that seeks to nourish the mind and the body. The urban stroller enjoys, indeed needs the company, the visibility or the presence of others.

The urban stroll is played out on an urban boulevard. This urban boulevard can be a destination in its own right or it may simply form part of your journey elsewhere. It is both central to the city and civilising of that city.
It is an elongated civic square that is anchored at either end by something to do, somewhere to visit. The urban stroll seeks social pleasure. People wish to linger on the urban stroll.

Dublin city is peculiarly lacking in housing a single identifiable city boulevard, an urban stroll space. Neither O'Connell Street nor Grafton Street have the cafés or public seating. So can Dublin make a stroll space? And where can it happen? Why is it important at all?

There are many potential, exciting candidates for Dublin's first urban boulevard stroll. Some require greater imagination and change than others. The criteria for the urban boulevard are relatively simple. It should be centrally located within the city. It should be of a minimum length, at least 500m (a third of a mile). The urban stroll should be wide enough to accommodate a comfortable amount of space for pedestrians, kiosks and children's pocket play spaces. It should be green, preferably with a bountiful density of trees, and have plenty of seats along its entire length. It has a cycle path, but also allows for at least one lane of vehicular traffic.

This is not an exclusively pedestrianised street. It's visible to others passing alongside by car, providing the possibility of dropping someone off or simply cruising by. This type of vehicular traffic offers passive surveillance and the vitality of connected urban energy. The urban boulevard should be contained on at least one side by buildings with a reasonable supply, or potential supply, of restaurants and cafés. It houses people living in apartments overlooking it.

A re-imagined north Liffey quays, a traffic-calmed and greened Capel Street, or the George's Street / Aungier Street stretch are all possibilities. Our choice, however, is the Lord Edward Street / Dame Street axis. The imagined Lord and Dame Boulevard has one singular line of traffic moving west to east and a central median that is tree-planted. It can facilitate an urban stroll some 700m long. It's a boulevard that begins close to City Hall and ends at a new civic plaza at College Green. The Lord and Dame Boulevard has side-street access to both Dublin Castle and Temple Bar. It is already the home of many cafés and restaurants, and home to the Olympia, one of city's busiest theatres.

With a little imagination and ambition, and the redirection of traffic, it is possible to create a new urban stroll space, a new urban boulevard at the heart of the city. Creating new space is just the first step. Successful urban boulevards are fed and nourished by urban dwellers. These are the people that make city spaces work. Planners, architects or urban designers may provide the stage set for the city boulevard, but it is the local urban dweller that breathes life into and sustains them. It is urbanites of all ages that make the urban stroll safe. The presence of children and elderly people visible in the city, particularly at evening time, simply walking around, doing nothing extraordinary, demonstrates how far a city has evolved or needs to mature to be a truly great urban place. If the urban stroll is clean, safe and comfortable for the very young and the very old, both it and the immediate city centre, perhaps, will be clean, safe and comfortable for everybody.

Apartment Scrappage Scheme

Reimagining Liveable Urbanism

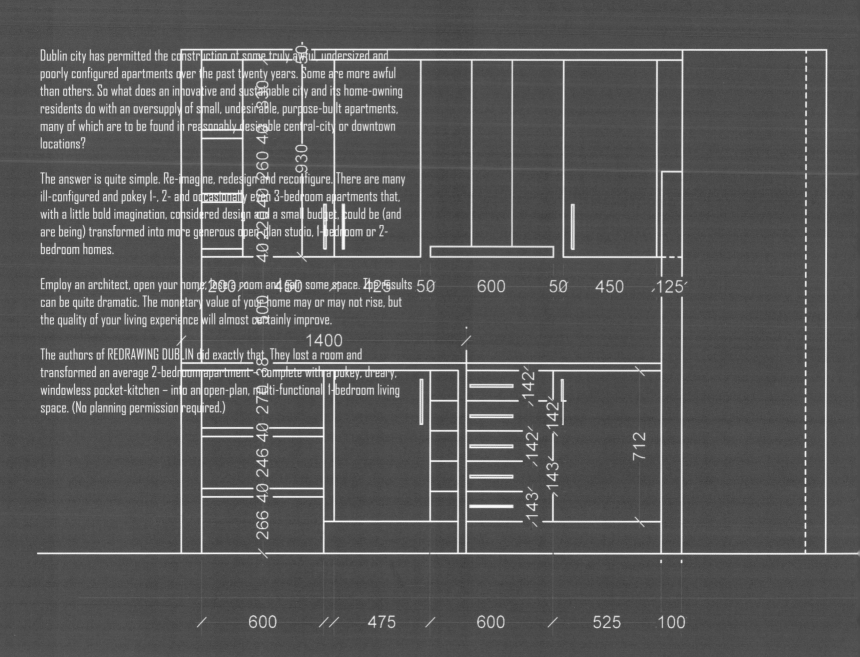

Dublin city has permitted the construction of some truly awful, undersized and poorly configured apartments over the past twenty years. Some are more awful than others. So what does an innovative and sustainable city and its home-owning residents do with an oversupply of small, undesirable, purpose-built apartments, many of which are to be found in reasonably desirable central-city or downtown locations?

The answer is quite simple. Re-imagine, redesign and reconfigure. There are many ill-configured and pokey 1-, 2- and occasionally even 3-bedroom apartments that, with a little bold imagination, considered design and a small budget, could be (and are being) transformed into more generous open-plan studio, 1-bedroom or 2-bedroom homes.

Employ an architect, open your home, lose a room and gain some space. The results can be quite dramatic. The monetary value of your home may or may not rise, but the quality of your living experience will almost certainly improve.

The authors of REDRAWING DUBLIN did exactly that. They lost a room and transformed an average 2-bedroom apartment – complete with a pokey, dreary, windowless pocket-kitchen – into an open-plan, multi-functional 1-bedroom living space. (No planning permission required.)

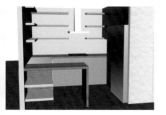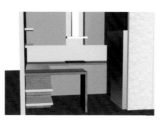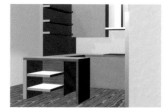

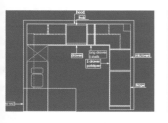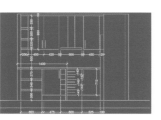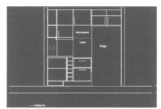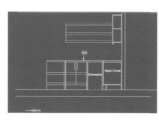

"VORTEX"

a photographic exhibition featuring the work of
Motti Ruimy and Paul Kearns

Vortex

In opening our minds to the possibility of realising newly imagined and public urban spaces for all, we should not lose sight of the many hidden or quasi-public places that only cities can and do provide for the pleasure of the few. Treasuring and valuing hidden city spaces, spaces that are unfamiliar, perhaps even forbidden, is necessary for an understanding of how cities really work, what they really offer. Hidden urbanism is no less urban or valuable because it's invisible to all but the very few. The urban sauna captures perfectly this hidden urbanism.

Hidden urbanism, because sometimes it is forbidden, is often lost forever when it physically disappears from the reality of city life. It vanishes into the folk memory of the very few. Recording examples of hidden urbanism before they are lost forever opens the space, visually or conceptually at least, to everyone. Whilst there is a long-established tradition amongst conservationists and architectural historians in archiving our historic built environment, much less attention is paid to recording the loss of more recent spaces, places perhaps on the margins of interest or acceptability.

In VORTEX we fuse both this urban archival tradition and concept of hidden urbanism, and present photographs of the former men-only sauna at Great Grand Street in Dublin I. The images capture the vacant ambience of the abandoned space, the emptiness of the once thriving four-storey labyrinth, evoking a sense of place and, in so doing, broadening interest and perhaps an understanding of alternative social life within the city .

The geography of the sauna building can be viewed as a microcosm mirroring the urban dynamic and language of the city itself. Messages and signage are posted to assist those negotiating the maze, where private and public space co-exists side by side competing and merging simultaneously. The corridor becomes the street, the rows of cubicles a terrace temporarily housing privatised space, and the 'glory hole' a purpose-built, dedicated public playground.

Just as successful public spaces thrive on choice, density, proximity and diversity, so too does hidden urbanism. Hidden urbanism, whether we care to look or acknowledge, understand or value, is very often nothing more than a testimony to the anonymity of the ordinariness of everyday life in ordinary buildings.

St Stephen's Greens

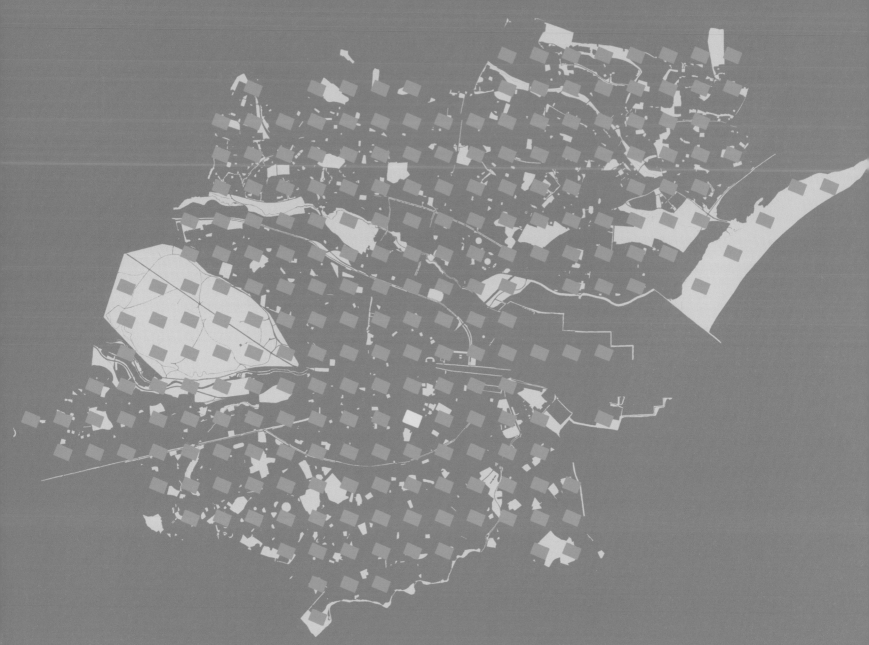

Garden City Revisited

The Irish psyche, it is argued (presumably the Dublin one is not much different), is deeply attached to living in a house with a front and back garden. City apartment-living is not for us, at least not right now and not here in Dublin, and certainly not for families with children, or at least not for 'our' children. An apartment in New York or Paris, a duplex in Marbella may be a different story.

There are many possible reasons for this antipathy to apartment-living. Perhaps it is the stigma associated with the past failed social experiment of Ballymun. Perhaps it's the failure in the recent past of the city to ensure the delivery of spacious and well-designed apartments. Perhaps, after fifteen years of a building-boom, planners and advocates of high-density apartment-living continue to find it difficult to identify many, if any, new, quality, high-density inner-urban residential neighbourhoods complete with new parks and spacious, roomy apartments. Maybe it is the fact that neither the real environmental or economic costs of low-density suburban sprawl are calculated or truly questioned, let alone priced or appropriately taxed. Perhaps it is because some of the real challenges of city-living – the need to keep high-density residential streets clean, parks safe and effectively manage drunken or drug-induced anti-social behaviour – are paid economic lip service or remain politically taboo. Perhaps it's because city decision-makers are not really convinced of the merits of inner-urban high-density apartment-living, or believe that Dublin's inner city, a historically socially disadvantaged area, can be truly transformed as a desirable place to live. Perhaps it's a mixture of all or some of these.

We will leave others to ponder these questions, and instead throw out some 'What if?' scenarios and present some 'green facts' to tell some untold urban building and design stories. What if everybody lived in well-designed and spacious apartments and, instead, all those front and back gardens of suburban Dublin – essentially private open space – were added together and magically converted into public parks. How many St Stephen's Greens could you 'make'? We estimate that all the front and rear gardens of Dublin city houses would combine to make 347 St Stephen's Greens.[1] That's nearly one to visit every day of the year. That's a total 3,054 hectares, or four times the size of the Phoenix Park. This would, of course, be in addition to the existing 2,500 hectares of green or zoned open space land that already exists in the city.[2]

If strategically placed across the entire city, it would mean that every resident, in theory, would be no more than a five-minute walk from his or her own local St Stephen's Green. If each were to specialise in one or two species of plant or flower, we could have a colourful urban seasonal mosaic, a horticultural diversity unsurpassed by any imaginable private garden. How many homes would delight in views overlooking such wonderful urban parks? Delighting in imagining the impossible makes possible the delights of other magical visions becoming real.

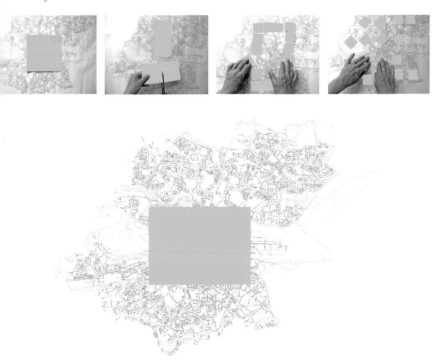

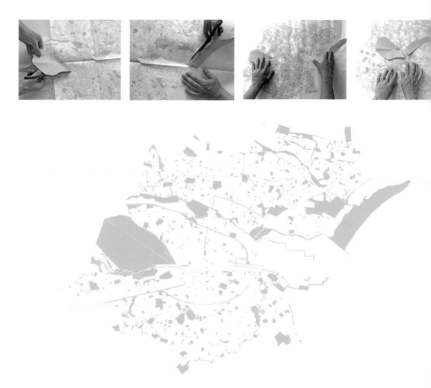

Garden Republic 'Yours', 'Theirs' and 'Ours'

Who cuts the grass and where?

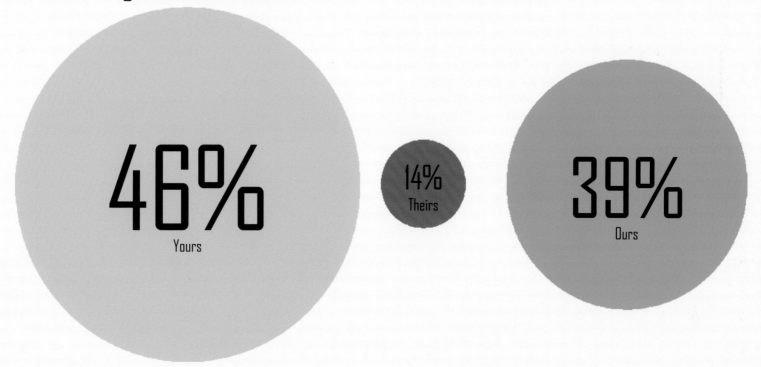

46%
Yours

14%
Theirs

39%
Ours

What type of city do we really live in? Private or public, urban or suburban? Perhaps the nature and ownership of 'our' green spaces tells us more about our city than we care to imagine or possibly know. In YOURS, THEIRS AND OURS we explore the concept and reveal the truth behind 'possession space', an analysis of how we access or experience green space in the city.

'Possession space' is a kind of 'green profiling' of the state of the city we live in. In YOURS, THEIRS AND OURS we calculate and compare the percentage of green space in Dublin city devoted to private front and back gardens ('Yours'), institutional green space or parkland which has a varied but somewhat detached and uncertain relationship to the public and public access ('Theirs'), and, finally, primarily publicly accessible zoned green open space ('Ours'). Our calculations reveals Dublin, despite the presence of Europe's largest urban walled park (the Phoenix Park) to

be a thoroughly private or 'Yours' green-space city, with 46% of all green open space in the hands or control of private households. A further 14% remains 'Theirs' (predominantly Catholic Church-controlled institutional lands), with just 39% of city green space devoted to public open space. ('Ours').[1] The Phoenix Park and Bull Island together account for just under half of all that zoned, public, open green space in the city.

Does any of this really matter? What is the ideal urban balance between 'Yours', 'Theirs' and 'Ours'? How does it compare to other cities? Perhaps before we can answer that we need to ask more probing questions. How does the balance between private and public space affect our enjoyment or experience of the city? Does our attachment to and preference for private space – the front and back garden – affect our attitude, perhaps even suppress our demand or expectations of quality public space?

The Green Lung #1
Croppy's Connection

If Dublin as a city straddles the 'green lung' of the Phoenix Park and the 'blue lung' of Dublin Bay, with the River Liffey the artery connecting them, why is it that the connection between park, city and river somehow just doesn't, well, connect.

Dublin's small and, perhaps, forgotten Croppy's Acre park occupies a unique position in that it physically if not mentally connects the green lung, river and blue lung. Sitting immediately west of the city-centre proper, but straddling the river and the Phoenix Park, this green space is a natural extension of the green lung of the Phoenix Park. The Croppy connection, if creatively re-imagined, could transform an existing poor linkage between city and park. In CROPPY'S CONNECTION we explore and exploit those potential urban connections.

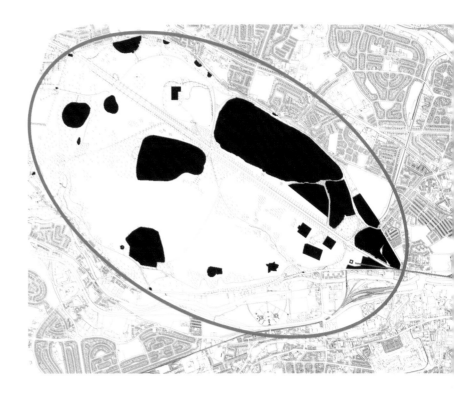

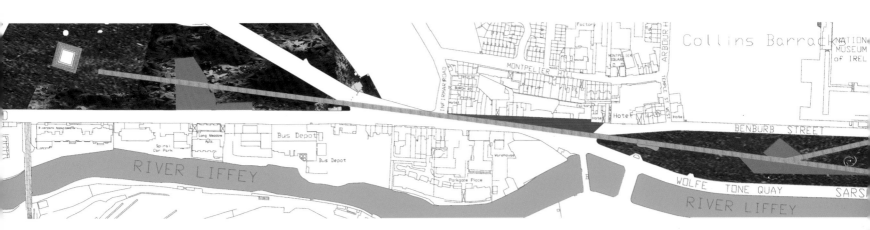

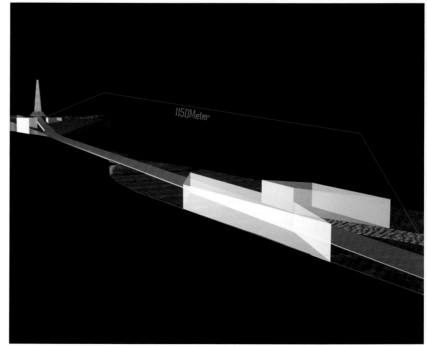

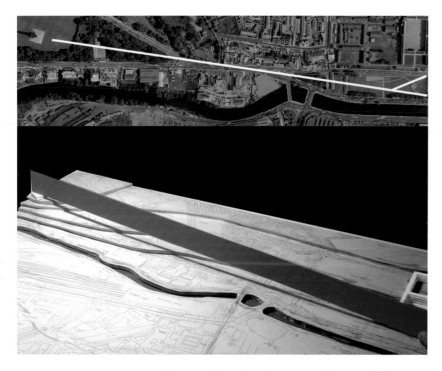

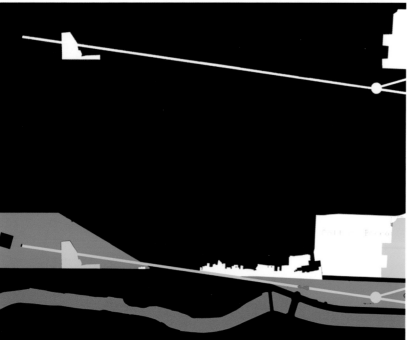

The Green Lung #2
Guinness Draft

One of the most oddly evocative urban experiences in Dublin city is the drive southward along Chesterfield Avenue in the Phoenix Park. It is odd in that the drive is along a seemingly endless, often empty two-lane, four-kilometre carriageway surrounded on either side by the vastness and emptiness of the green grass of the park. Perhaps it's not so odd. Central Park in New York, Hyde Park in London and Dublin's St Stephen's Green are all intimately and profoundly urban spaces. But the Phoenix Park is surely different? It may be the largest urban walled park in Europe, but it's a relatively empty place, more a rural refuge than an urban park, a historic green wilderness dotted with the odd jogger and free-roaming deer.

Perhaps the drive southward along Chesterfield Avenue is not so much an urban experience as it is an urban expectation. The grandeur and scale of the Park, the solemnity of the straight axis, the hint of the city as it comes into view with the industrial 'towers' of the Guinness brewery at St James's Gate. For a very brief moment, one expects or senses this grand journey, with its increasingly exciting and emerging urban vista, to open out, to reveal an even more impressive city boulevard, a boulevard that might lead through the Guinness lands straight to the heart of the city, perhaps terminating somewhere close to St Stephen's Green.

Instead, one comes to a shuddering halt in front of a wall of miniaturised, forlorn-looking semi-derelict Georgian buildings. Turning left brings glimpses of a new possible city – the drama and scale of the new courts building – a sharp right and you exit urban Dublin. What if we could extend this unique axis into the core of the city? It would provide an instantaneous urban vista, a potential pedestrian eco-boulevard, and a possible 5km cycle route from the heart of the urban core to the heart of the Park. It would, simultaneously, give added rationale to 'opening up' the lands of the Guinness brewery, provide a living urban linear magnet, drawing people from the city through a somewhat down-at-heel Thomas Street. It would also act as a potential 'eco-catalyst' capable of transforming the underperforming lands of the historic Liberties. This new boulevard would immediately provide direct access along a potential civic processional route linking Áras an Uachtaráin in the Park, the historic home of the Irish president, with the seat of national government in Kildare Street, a 21st-century interpretation of the Wide Streets Commissioners, an eco-democratic Park Avenue.

In time, it might become an urban architectural laboratory of excellence attracting foreign embassies along its green axis. The seeds are already there and germinating further. The existing US ambassador's residence is already secure in the Park. Sometimes good urban planning requires delicate interventions. It may be the unlocking of a gate or unblocking of a laneway, the creation of a new link or pedestrian walk, a kind of urban acupuncture. Sometimes, however, it requires grand ambitions of the imagination and the will to see them through.

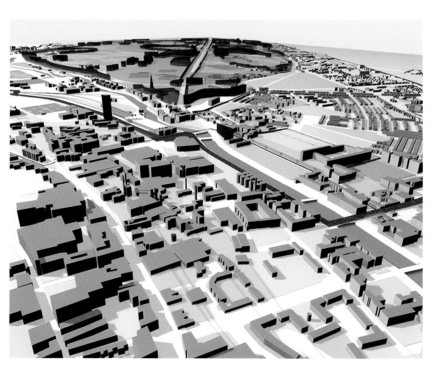

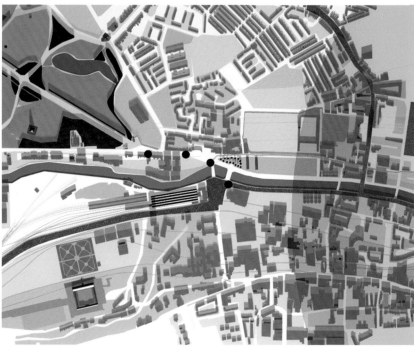

Lattice Connection

Boulevard as a living organism

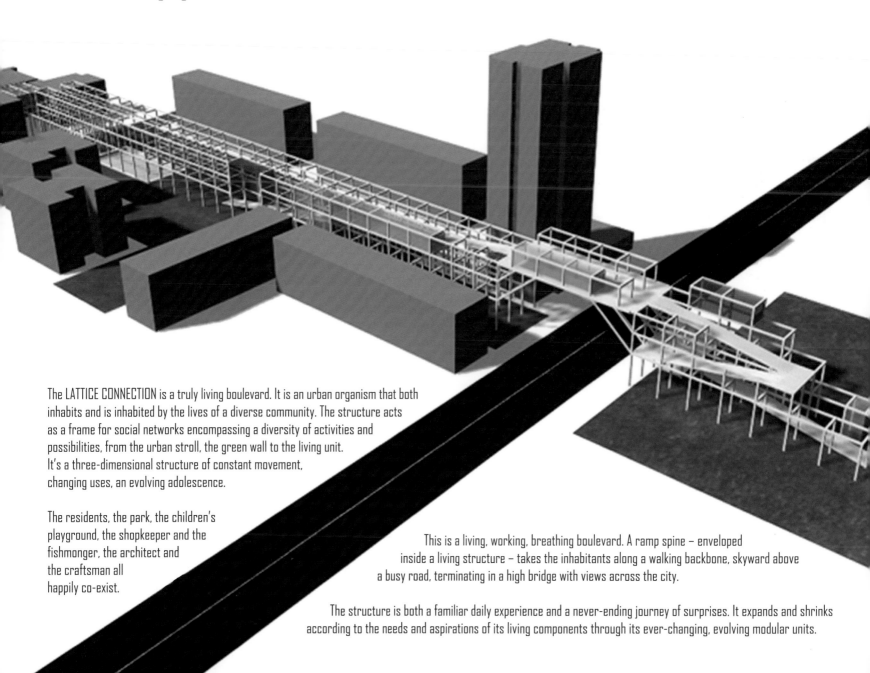

The LATTICE CONNECTION is a truly living boulevard. It is an urban organism that both inhabits and is inhabited by the lives of a diverse community. The structure acts as a frame for social networks encompassing a diversity of activities and possibilities, from the urban stroll, the green wall to the living unit. It's a three-dimensional structure of constant movement, changing uses, an evolving adolescence.

The residents, the park, the children's playground, the shopkeeper and the fishmonger, the architect and the craftsman all happily co-exist.

This is a living, working, breathing boulevard. A ramp spine – enveloped inside a living structure – takes the inhabitants along a walking backbone, skyward above a busy road, terminating in a high bridge with views across the city.

The structure is both a familiar daily experience and a never-ending journey of surprises. It expands and shrinks according to the needs and aspirations of its living components through its ever-changing, evolving modular units.

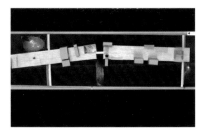

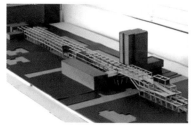
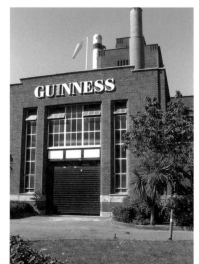

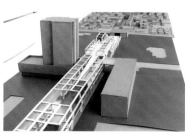
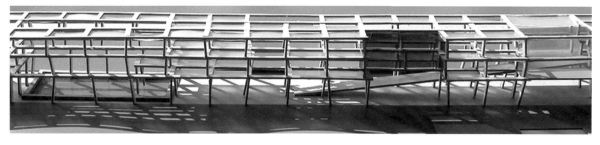
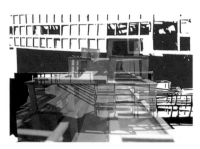

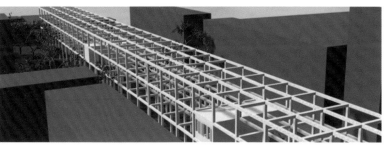

World Parks

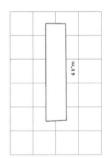

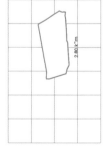

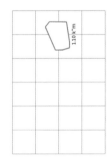

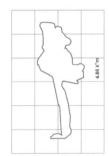

San Diego
Balboa Park
490ha

Mexico City
Chapultepec
600ha

New York
Central Park
340ha

Dublin
Phoenix Park
712ha

London
Hyde Park
142ha

Paris
Parc de la Villette
55ha

Tel Aviv
HaYarkon
350ha

The Green Lung #3
The Phoenix Park Project

Dublin is often described as a city straddling the 'green lung' of the Phoenix Park and the 'blue lung' of Dublin Bay, with the River Liffey the artery connecting them. However it's imagined, the Phoenix Park occupies a special place in the consciousness of Dublin and Dubliners. The facts are powerful. Most Dublin children can tell you this is the largest walled urban park in Europe. At 712 hectares, the Phoenix Park is twice the size of Central Park in New York City, and more than five times the size of Hyde Park in London. It is the home of Irish president, the United States ambassador and the State's number one tourist attraction, Dublin Zoo. This is clearly no ordinary city park; in fact, it is not a city park at all. Dublin City Council has no direct responsibility for its management; instead the Phoenix Park is run by the Office of Public Works (OPW) and defined as a National Historic Park.

Who manages the Park is not an irrelevant or arcane administrative detail. The management ethos fundamentally informs everything, from what sports may or not be played right through to its long-term vision and relationship to the city. As a National Historic Park, the Phoenix Park sits somewhat aloof from the city, physically slightly raised, emotionally almost detached. This is a park that is viewed and cherished by many Dubliners as an escape, almost a rural refuge from the city. Surrounded on almost all sides by swathes of two-storey suburban housing, there is a strong consensus in the city that physical development of almost any kind should not be visible from inside the Park.

Daily commuters flow into and out of the city through the Phoenix Park, pouring through an hourglass bottleneck at Parkgate Street. The hourglass flips each morning and evening.

Designated as a National Historic Park and eulogised as a rural escape, it is perhaps not surprising that one of the weakest links to the city beyond – for the pedestrian at least – is the very short walk from the Park along Parkgate Street to the walled quays of the River Liffey and the city proper. It's as if both city and state authorities subliminally collude in the Park's splendid isolation and detachment from direct and immediate inner-city or urban contamination, and, in so doing, ensures proximity without touching, visibility but segregation, a rural refuge, safe and pure.

In the PHOENIX PARK PROJECT we visually deconstruct the park's history, its current geography, and contemplate and sketch, perhaps, its urban future. The project ponders and muses 'What if?' scenarios, analyses morphology, maps a 'grid system', identifies 'zones' and 'layered surfaces' of assembled uses. THE PHOENIX PARK PROJECT proposes a resolution to the ongoing ambiguous relationship between the city and its largest green open space. The project concludes with a proposal for 'mini-parks' of intensive recreation on the outer fringes, whilst simultaneously retaining a vehicle-free zone at the heart of the National Historic Park, consisting of approximately 75% of the Park's land area. The duality of a proposed peaceful co-existence of an intensive outer-urban recreation zone surrounding an inner passive green wilderness supports choice, and in so doing ensures respect for those who view the park as either an urban opportunity or an escape from city life.

City Axis

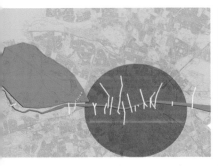

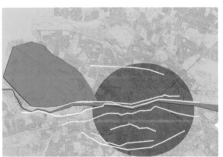

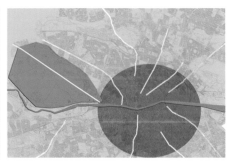

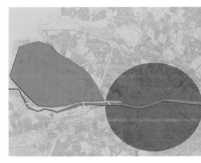

North-South Axis – bridges crossing the river
The Park relative to the City

East-West Axis

Radial Axis

Access to the Park

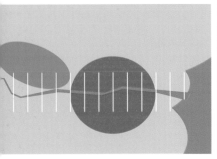

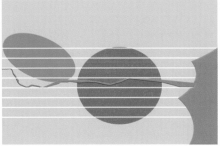

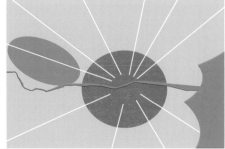

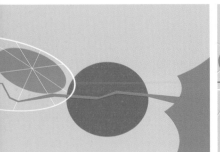

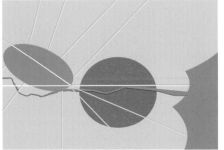

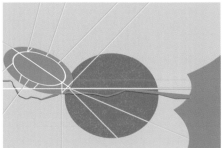

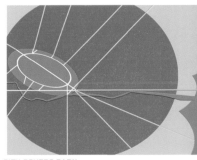

Radial Axis from the Park

Today the Park is surrounded by suburbs, and its south-western edge is tangential to the city centre

The Keys to reveal an URBAN PARK

CITY CENTRE PARK
2020 ?

Onion Analysis

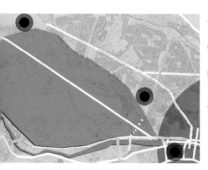

Analysis – Today, the park surrounded by underutilised areas.

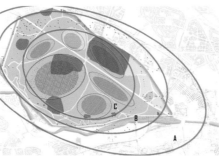

Analysis – The park acts as an onion, from its inner core to an outer belt, sliced by key routes

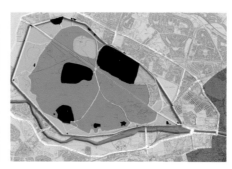

Proposal – Zones with an urban park ring

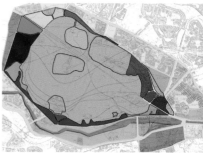

Proposal – The different colours represent different activities

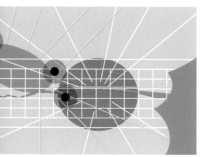

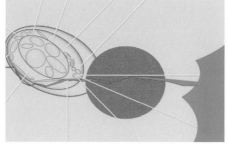

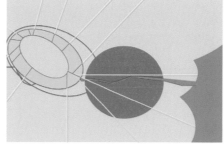

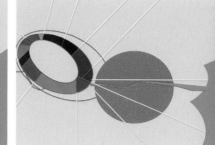

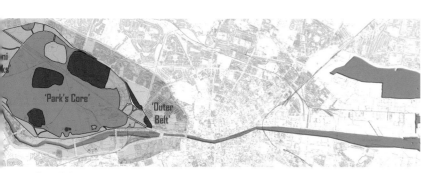

Zone Definition

Parcelling

Analysis Definition of the Existing

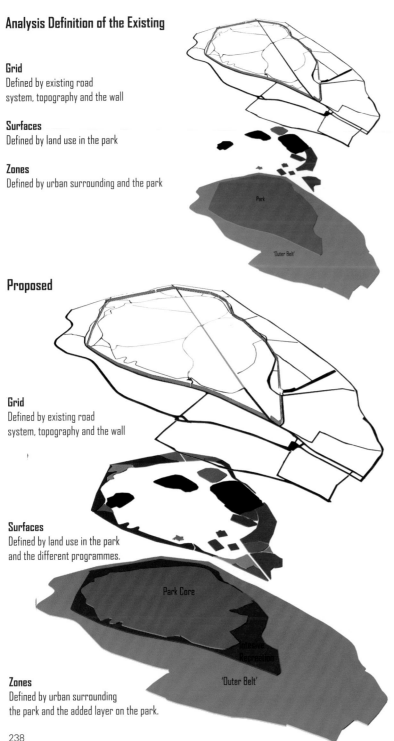

Grid
Defined by existing road system, topography and the wall

Surfaces
Defined by land use in the park

Zones
Defined by urban surrounding and the park

Proposed

Grid
Defined by existing road system, topography and the wall

Surfaces
Defined by land use in the park and the different programmes.

Zones
Defined by urban surrounding the park and the added layer on the park.

'Ciúnas' – A Rural Refuge or an Urban Gaelic Zen?

In the book *l'Empire des signs* by Roland Barthes,[1] in a chapter entitled 'City-centre, Empty-centre', he writes *"…quadrangular, reticular cities (Los Angeles, for example), the emotions they elicit or produce and perhaps what we might call a profound sense of uneasiness. They challenge our cenesthetic perception of the city, which demands that every urban space should have a centre, a place we can go to and come back from, a compact place to dream about .A place to which we are led to and from which we can distance ourselves: in short, a place where we can invent ourselves.*[1]

For a number of reasons (historical, economic, religious, military), the 'West' has absorbed this rule of spatial man-making all too well. All its cities are concentric. Moreover, infused with a Western philosophy, which views each centre as the seat of all truth, our town centres are always full. They are the places where the values of civilization are collected and condensed: values of spirituality (churches), power (offices), money (banks), goods (department stores) and words (the 'agora': cafes and walks). Going downtown means encountering social 'truth', taking part in the sublime richness of 'reality'.

The city I'm referring to [Tokyo] presents an amazing paradox: it does have a centre, but this centre is empty. The whole city resolves around a place that is both forbidden and indifferent, an abode masked by vegetation, protected by moats, inhabited by an emperor whom no one ever sees, literally, no one knows who does ever see him. Everyday, with their rapid, forceful motion, taxis speed like bullets, avoiding this ring, whose low rooftops, visible forms of invisible, conceal its sacred nothingness. One of the two most powerful cities in the modern world is therefore built around an opaque ring of walls, water, roofs, and trees. Its centre is no more than an evaporated ideal whose existence is not meant to radiate any kind of power, but to offer its own empty centre to all urban movement as a form of support by forcing perpetual traffic detours. Thus it appears as an image that unfurls again and again in endless circles, around an empty core."

The 'silence' or, more importantly, this desire for silence at the heart of Tokyo is a unique example that arguably has a parallel in Dublin, the desire to seek silence in order to replicate or recreate a longing for lost space, a kind of 'rural refuge or escape from the city'. The desire to escape from the city within the city, however fleetingly, reflects a particular Irish psyche among many of the capital city's residents. Like the Japanese Zen, the spatial equivalent of a 'silence of the mind', the Phoenix Park could simultaneously pulsate with an active urban fringe whilst embracing a comparable Gaelic Zen or 'Ciúnas' at its core.

Analysis and Zones Definitions

A grid, defined by the existing road axis and the Park's wall, defines the zones. The inner-park area becomes a protected conservation core. Chesterfield Avenue, the axial road crossing the Park, is partially rerouted underground to allow for a greater sense of central 'rural refuge'. The 'outer belt' becomes a new intensive recreation zone.

What if? scenarios

What if? scenario. What if the Park is pierced and dissected by pockets of alternative private but communal accessible uses and spaces, such as more restaurants, museums and sports grounds?

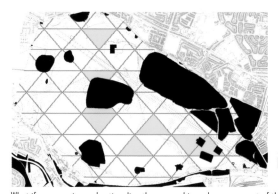 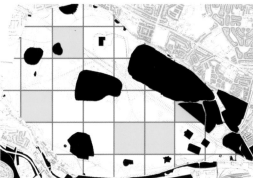 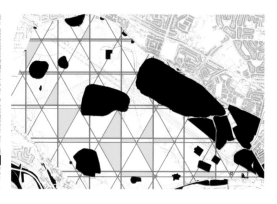

What if we organise and rationalise the ownership and management of the Park through a semi-autonomous grid system?

1 – Reinforcing the historic wall through intensification of adjoining public domain

2 – Intensifying the Chesterfield Axis, the most utilised, visited and trafficked corridor of the Park

3 – Adjoining residential density patterns envelope the Park

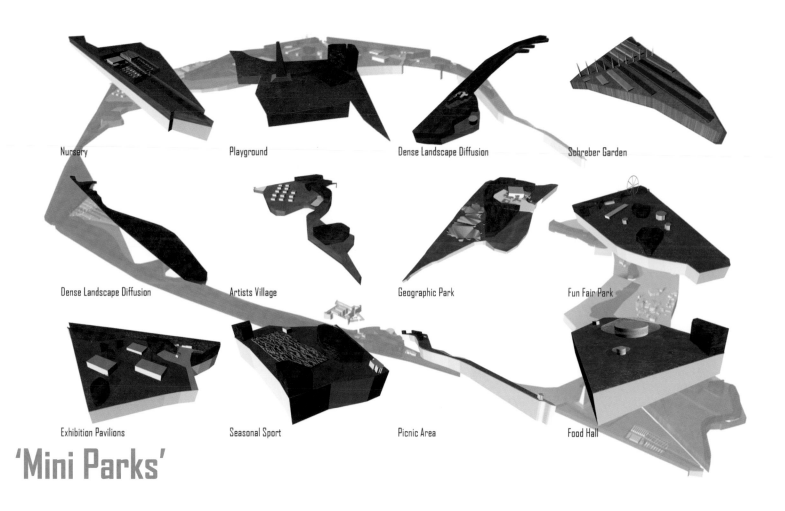

Nursery

Playground

Dense Landscape Diffusion

Schreber Garden

Dense Landscape Diffusion

Artists Village

Geographic Park

Fun Fair Park

Exhibition Pavilions

Seasonal Sport

Picnic Area

Food Hall

'Mini Parks'

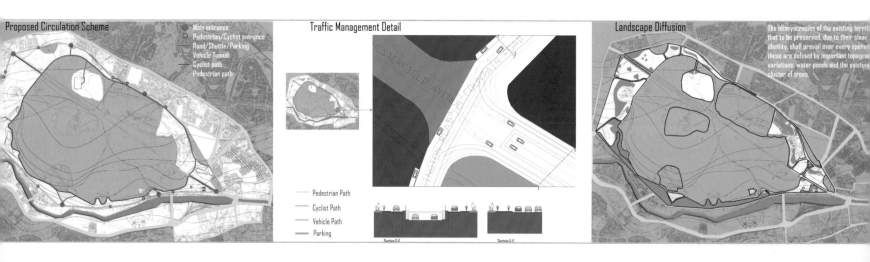

Proposed Circulation Scheme

Main entrance
Pedestrian/Cyclist entrance
Road/Shuttle/Parking
Vehicle Tunnel
Cyclist path
Pedestrian path

Traffic Management Detail

Pedestrian Path

Cyclist Path

Vehicle Path

Parking

Landscape Diffusion

The idiosyncrasies of the existing territ
that to be preserved, due to their cleac
identity, shall prevail over every opera
these are defined by important topogra
variations, water ponds and the existin
cluster of trees.

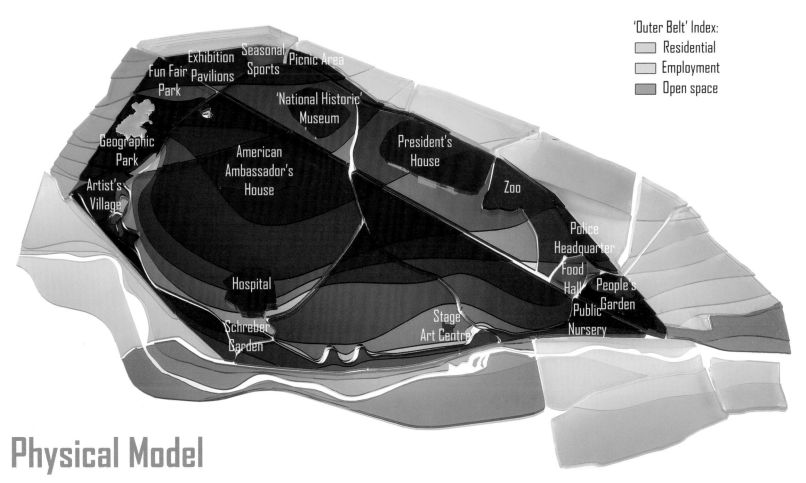

Exhibition Pavilions

Seasonal Sports

Picnic Area

Fun Fair Park

'National Historic' Museum

Geographic Park

President's House

American Ambassador's House

Zoo

Artist's Village

Police Headquarter

Food Hall

People's Garden

Hospital

Public Nursery

Schreber Garden

Stage Art Centre

'Outer Belt' Index:
- Residential
- Employment
- Open space

Physical Model

Programme Distribution

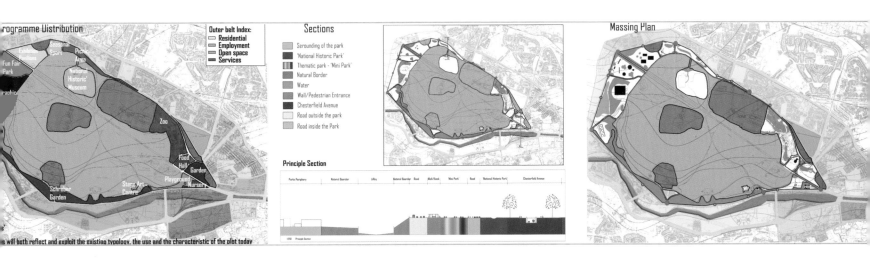

rogramme Distribution

Outer belt Index:
- Residential
- Employment
- Open space
- Services

Seasonal Sport

Picnic Area

Fun Fair Park

Exhibition Pavilions

National Historic Museum

Geographic

Zoo

Food Hall

Garden

Stage Art Centre

Playground

Nursery

Schreber Garden

Sections

- Serounding of the park
- 'National Historic Park'
- Thematic park - 'Mini Park'
- Natural Border
- Water
- Wall/Pedestrian Entrance
- Chesterfield Avenue
- Road outside the park
- Road inside the Park

Principle Section

Parks Periphery | Natural Boarder | Liffey | Natural Boarder | Road | Mall/Kiosk | Woo Park | Road | 'National Historic Park' | Chesterfield Avenue

Massing Plan

s will both reflect and exploit the existing typology, the use and the characteristic of the plot today

NEW YORK CITY

area: 786m²
population: 8.4 million
density: 10,500 people per km²

CONTIGUOUS METROPOLITAN DUBLIN

area: 797m²
population: 1.25 million
density: 1,500 people per km²

Density Rediscovered

In the Thick of It

Dublin city has a population of approximately half-a-million people, spread, somewhat unevenly, over 114 square kilometres. That generates a density of population of 4,400 people per square kilometre.[1] How does that density compare with other European cities, cities that many of our leading urban planners and architects tend to most admire?

The 'city' of Barcelona has a population of 1.6 million concentrated in an area of 100.8 square kilometres, an area slightly less than the size of the Dublin City Council area. This generates a remarkable high density of 15,800 people per square kilometre, nearly four times higher than Dublin city.[2] How can Barcelona sustain such a high density of population? The city has few tall buildings and a generous amount of well-designed pubic open space. The answer is quite simple, 97% of the residents of Barcelona live in high-density apartment-style residential developments, a housing type that may explain its dynamic and busy street life.[3]

The 'city' of Copenhagen is the home to 510,000 people, almost identical to Dublin city, but those people are spread over just 88 square kilometres.[4] The Danish capital thus has a density of population of 5,800 people per square kilometre, approximately 30% higher than the Irish capital. Lyon, the second largest city in France, is regularly cited as a model of urbanism that Dublin should, if not exactly emulate, learn from. This city has a comparable population (470,000) to Dublin city but occupies just half the land area.[5] Lyon has a population density of 9,800 people per square kilometre, twice that of Dublin city.

It is evident from the above that Dublin city has a reasonably low density of population compared to other attractive and successful European cities, cities that Dublin is both encouraged and prodded to flatter and imitate. This simply reflects the reality that Dublin is essentially a city of two-storey housing estates. Increasing the density of population is widely accepted as desirable. It provides for a more environmentally sustainable compact city, reduces commuting times and supports an efficient public-transport system. It also facilitates an intense and dynamic urban street life, a driver of cultural and economic innovation.

High densities also support the delivery of efficient local services – libraries, swimming pools, local parks – that otherwise might be simply too costly to deliver.

So how can Dublin increase its urban density? The mass demolition of two-storey housing estates seems neither politically practicable nor necessarily desirable. The construction of new dwellings on existing parks or open space is, by common consensus, wholly undesirable. There is, however, a third alternative. There is a surprisingly extensive amount of undeveloped land in Dublin city, perhaps more than most people imagine. Dublin City Council estimates that there are 480 hectares (1,186 acres) of zoned land in the city that could be developed for residential use.[6] This amounts 4.7% of all zoned land in the city.[7] The Council, however, states that only a 'portion' of this land will be available for development at any given time.

This estimate of potentially available land, we believe, is somewhat conservative. A detailed analysis of the fifteen land-use zones in the city would suggest that the figure is somewhere within the range of 700 to 1200 hectares, perhaps more if lands zoned Z6 (effectively single-storey warehouses in industrial estates) became mixed-use residential areas. For the purposes of our density exercise, we have chosen the upper figure of 1,200 hectares. This amounts to 11.9% of all zoned land in the city.[8] Our 1,200 hectares assumes that a third of institutional zoned land in the city (Z12 and Z15) would become available for residential development, in addition to 80% of all existing zoned inner-urban regeneration land (Z10 and Z14). Our 1,200 developable hectares also assumes Dublin Port moving north of the city and Guinness lands at St James's Gate becoming available. Armed with this 1,200 hectares of 'new urban' or 'spare' housing capacity, how would Dublin fare in the density comparisons?

If Dublin city were to achieve the overall densities of the 'city' of Copenhagen, it would require an additional 153,000 people. If these additional 153,000 new Dubliners were accommodated on our 'new urban' 1,200 hectares of land identified above, it would result in a density of 12,750 people per square kilometre on these new lands. The density on these new urban lands would thus be slightly greater than that of New York City (10,500).[9] It is worth noting that the density of population within the canals in Dublin is already over 8,000 per square kilometre, just below the density of Lyon.[10]

The equivalent figures if Dublin city as a whole were to achieve Lyon densities are ambitious. Our 1,200 hectares of new urban lands would have to accommodate 617,000 additional Dubliners. That would result in an exceptional density of 51,400 people per square kilometre, or twice that of the island of Manhattan (27,500 people per km^2).[11] The figures for comparable Barcelona densities are more dramatic. If Dublin city was to achieve the overall urban densities of Barcelona, our 1,200 hectares of developable land would have to accommodate 1.3 million people. That would be an astonishing 108,166 people per square kilometre. This is more than twice that of Kowloon (45,000 people per km^2), one the most densely populated urban districts of Hong Kong, which is, itself, one of the most densely populated cities in the world.[12]

Assuming reasonably well-designed and spacious apartments with quality private and public open space – all compliant with Dublin City Council's own development plans standards – building heights would inevitably have to rise. So how high would building heights have to go on these new mixed-use residential 1,200 hectares if Dublin city was to achieve overall the density of population of the city of Barcelona?

The maths isn't too complicated. Accommodating the additional 1.3 million to enjoy comparable Barcelona densities would require approximately 520,000 new homes. This assumes housing occupancy (the number of persons per home) remains reasonably static, which is currently 2.5 people per dwelling in Dublin city compared to a national average of 2.8.[13] In our calculations we have reduced Dublin city occupancy rates to 2.35 in line with the expected continued downward trend which has taken place over recent years.[14] This would generate a need for 552,000 dwellings. With average size homes of 90m^2 and allowing for 20m^2 per home for internal communal circulation space, and an additional 50m^2 per residential unit for local shops, schools, offices and services, 552,000 homes would generate over 88.4 million square metres of development.

Leaving aside a slump in demand for new housing, temporary or otherwise, this quantum of development would generate an overall plot ratio of (7.3:1) on our 1,200 hectares of new urban residential lands. Allowing for public parks, private communal space, gardens, building circulation, cycle paths and public roadways (approximately 70% of overall site coverage), this quantum of development would require every single building to rise to over 24 storeys high. The density may be comparable to Barcelona, but the skyline would not. Something obviously has to give. And if it's not an exciting, perhaps dystopian, but challenging explosion in height, the wholesale demolition of Crumlin or Templeogue, or the building of new homes in the heart of St Anne's Park

or the Phoenix Park, perhaps we should be more careful in invoking muddled or misunderstood inappropriate urban comparisons. With density, be careful what you wish for. The facts speak for themselves.

So it would appear that Dublin as a city cannot achieve the densities of Barcelona without significantly altering its skyline or demolishing vast tracts of two-storey housing. Perhaps it doesn't need to do either. It can achieve significant increases in densities on underperforming and undeveloped land, densities that would consolidate an urbanism beyond a tiny city core. The density of population within the Canal Ring is already 8,000 people per square kilometre (this with considerable remaining derelict sites). A number of inner-city wards already have a density twice this figure.[15] Turning the equation around, what population could Dublin city sustain if it chose not to demolish vast tracts of two-storey suburbia but instead built high-density mixed-use developments with an average building height of five storeys, a plentiful supply of parks and open space, and adequate community and social services.

Using our earlier breakdown of site development mix which includes 70% of the site devoted to open space, roadway and circulation, with new homes averaging 90m^2, a mixed-use development with an average of five-storey building height would generate a plot ratio of 1.5 across the 1,200 hectares of developable residential lands, and would provide an additional 112,500 homes. That would accommodate an extra 263,000 people. Dublin city could, therefore, in theory, secure a high-density, 'low-rise' sustainable urban future by accommodating an additional quarter-of-a-million people, or a 52% increase in its population.

Despite a net outflow in population since late 2007, the ESRI (Economic and Social Research Institute) predicted in late 2009 that the overall population of Ireland would increase by 860,000 over the next decade.[16] Should Dublin city aspire to capturing 30% of this figure it could increase its population by a quarter of a million, or 258,000 to be exact. It is interesting to note that the increase in population between 1991 and 2006 in the 'exurban' counties surrounding Dublin city – Kildare, Meath Wicklow and Fingal – was a not too dissimilar at 235,000 people.[17] Much of that growth occurred not in towns, but in sprawling new two-storey housing estates.

To accommodate that additional 258,000 people, the density of population on our new urban lands would rise to 21,500 people per square kilometre (258,000 persons on 1,200 hectares). Interestingly, six of the ten Barcelona urban districts have residential densities in excess of 20,000 people per square kilometre.[18] In accommodating 258,000 additional Dubliners, the density for the entire city, however, would rise from 4,400 people per square kilometre to just 6,700 people per square kilometre, a density somewhat above Copenhagen (5,800) and still considerably below that of Lyon (9,800).

MANHATTAN

area: 59km^2
population: 1.6 million
density: 27,500 people per km^2

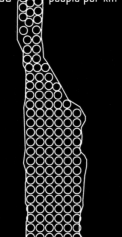

BARCELONA

area: 100km^2
population: 1.6 million
density: 15,800 people per km^2

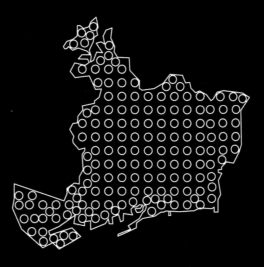

LYON

area: 48km^2
population: 0.47 million
density: 9,800 people per km^2

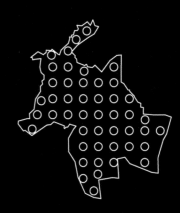

COPENHAGEN

area: 88km^2
population: 0.5 million
density: 5,800 people per km^2

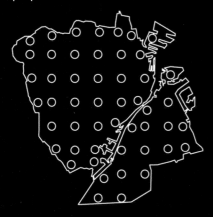

DUBLIN

area: 114km^2
population: 0.5 million
density: 4,400 people per km^2

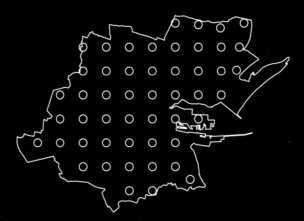

Neighbourhood Density

How dense is your neighbourhood? Perhaps before endeavouring to answer that question, it is important to know what measure one is employing, and useful to have overall comparative densities for Dublin city as a whole.

There are many measures of density. Population per square kilometre, bed-spaces per hectare, and housing units per hectare are three of the most commonly used by planners and architects. We have chosen to examine housing units per hectare. With 190,711 units, and an area of 114km^2 (11,400 hectares), the overall density of homes in Dublin city is 16.7 housing units per hectare. Is this high or low? It depends on the comparison.

In the neighbouring, largely suburban, local authority area of Dun Laoghaire-Rathdown, the figure falls to 5.4 housing units per hectare. The Dublin City Council Draft Development Plan 2011-2016, however, aspires to build densities of 135 units per hectare on inner-urban, mixed-use residential sites. On many existing inner-city apartment development schemes the density exceeds 250 units per hectare.

It is, of course, unfair to compare density policy for a theoretical, small site and the density of an entire municipality. In NEIGHBOURHOOD DENSITY we compare the density of housing units per hectare of six diverse Dublin city neighbourhoods or suburbs. Taking six maps at the same scale, each approximately thirty hectares in area, we have calculated the density of housing units per hectare. The lowest density is the Shrewsbury Road / Ailesbury Road area of Ballsbridge with just four housing units per hectare. The density of housing units in the Seafield Road area of Clontarf is 10 units per hectare, with a similarly low density of 14 units per hectare in the Lough Conn area of Ballyfermot. All three are well below the average density of 16.7 housing units per hectare in Dublin.

The density in Marino is 30 units per hectare, three times higher than neighbouring Clontarf and almost twice that of the city. In Stoneybatter, perhaps surprisingly the most dense area of all, the density rises to 40 units per hectare. If we excluded the inaccessible Arbour Hill prison and St Brican's hospital (the relatively empty areas in the south-west corner of the Stoneybatter map), the overall density would rise to just 55 units per hectare.

Interestingly, the Department of the Environment considers an urban density less than 50 units per hectare as unsustainably low. If, however, we were to exclude all the lower-density areas to the north-east and south-west of the Stoneybatter map, and instead retain only those areas traditionally understood as characteristically residential Stoneybatter (those areas with a visibly higher density), the density would rise to 76 units per hectare. A density of 76 units per hectare with almost no public space and minimum private garden space (most homes have only a small rear yard) would be widely accepted, in an urban context as a middling but underperforming density.

Stoneybatter
40 units per hectare

Clontarf
10 units per hectare

Ranelagh
30 units per hectare

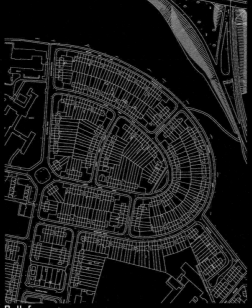

Marino
30 units per hectare

Ballyfermot
14 units per hectare

Ballsbridge
4 units per hectare

Does Density Matter in Stoneybatter?

This is a Dublin residential community with a population of fewer than 3,000 people, the equivalent of a small Irish town – greater than Claremorris and Skibbereen, but less than Kilcock or Carrick-on-Shannon.[1] It has a population density of over 11,000 people per square kilometre. This is almost two-and-a-half times the density of Dublin city (4,403), and closer to the density of the city of Barcelona (15,800) or Lyon (9,800).[2] This neighbourhood has a density of approximately (depending on exact boundaries) 55 homes per hectare, more than three times the Dublin citywide average of 16.7 homes per hectare.[3] Over half of all the households who live in this neighbourhood 'own' their own homes, compared to less than one in three or just 30% in the rest of Dublin city's inner suburbs and inner city.[4] Half of all those who own their own homes own them outright – that is, they have no outstanding mortgage. Just one in ten householders inside Dublin's Canal Ring own their homes outright. This is a community of comfortable homeowners.[5]

Over 30% of all adult residents who live here are classified as belonging to the 'managerial' or 'professional 'class. This is higher than for the city as a whole. This is obviously an affluent community.[6] Almost half of the people (44%) who reside here walk or cycle to school, college or work. This would appear to be a 'green' or ecological neighbourhood. It is an area that is generally recognised as a desirable place to live, romanticised even. It has a strong identity and, anecdotally at least, a cohesive sense of community. Have we unwittingly stumbled upon Dublin's perfect picture postcard of a high-density, comfortable, 21st-century sustainable urbanism? Perhaps.

There is, however, something not quite right with this place. You can sense it walking around the area. The neighbourhood is almost exclusively made up of single or two-storey cottages. This is a residential community devoid of almost of any public open space. It hangs together through an extensive network of tarmacadam public roadway. This public roadway and pavement makes up over 30% of the surface area of the entire area or more than fifteen times the amount devoted to publicly accessible green open space. Put another way, 95% of all publicly accessible walkable areas in this neighbourhood are either hard concrete pavement or tarmac roadway. You are potentially never more than two or three metres away from a parked or moving car. The public 'open space' here is either roadway or surface car-parking. There are no municipal

children's playgrounds. There are few tree-lined streets.

Homes in this neighbourhood have minimal private open space. Few houses have a front garden. Most have a small concrete rear pocket-yard. Average home sizes are smaller than the rest of the city. If the 1,300 homes in this community were being built today, the city planners would require (applying Dublin City Council Development Plan standards) approximately 26,000m² to 41,600m² of public open space. That is a public park, or collection of parks, averaging 3.4 hectares (or 8.3 acres),[8] just over two-thirds the size of Merrion Square or twice as big as Fitzwilliam Square.[9] The homes in this neighbourhood would be unlikely to be granted planning permission today. They are simply too small, built too close together, have no quality gardens or balconies and little public-park or green amenity space.

Built as artisan cottages in a bygone industrial era, this inner-city redbrick neighbourhood now occupies a kind of schizophrenic place in the mental map of contemporary Dublin residential living. It is trapped, largely unnoticed, between the perception of most locals and a few outsiders who view the area through the prism of rose-tinted suburban spectacles and others, primarily outsiders, who view it through the prying magnifying glass of a detached urban analyst. Is this neighbourhood a romanticised rural cottage idyll or an underperforming inner-urban housing reality? Perhaps both. The plot ratio is low (0.5:1).[10] The density of homes at 55 homes per hectare is also low by urban standards.[11]

So does the plot ratio or the numbers of units per hectare tell us anything about the quality of housing in this community? Put another way, does density actually matter in Stoneybatter?

SIZE DOES MATTER

FROM MATCH BOXES TO LIVEABLE HOMES? THE VISUAL DIARY OF DUBLIN APARTMENT EVOLUTION IN THE MODERN ERA

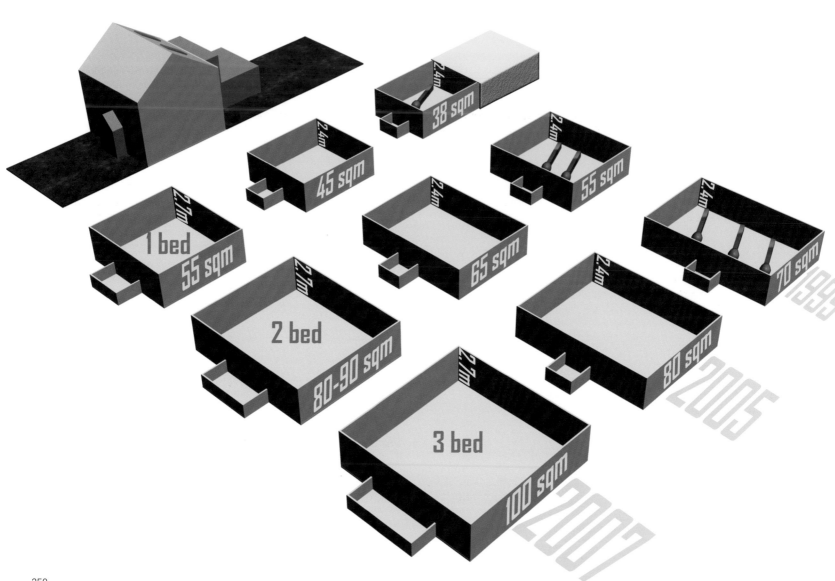

Size Does Matter

Dublin city boasts, by contemporary western European housing standards, a considerable number of very small single-storey cottages at the centre of its urban area. They are visible almost everywhere across the inner city. These dwellings have, until recently, fetched extraordinarily high prices for properties with little or no private open space, many with purpose-built floor areas of less than 40m². The paucity of a reasonable supply of large, affordable, well-designed city-centre urban alternatives was probably not an insignificant factor in this price-inflated cottage housing market. The failure over a fifteen-year building boom to deliver centrally located high-density homes of 100m² or 150m² (real alternatives to suburban living) led to a scenario whereby, at the height of the Irish property boom, the real housing choice for a young Dublin family was a either a spacious but distant house in a suburb in Meath, Kildare or Fingal, or a centrally located but absurdly priced single-storey 'cottage' with a footprint of 40m² or 50m² (this despite the continued presence of vast underperforming sites in Dublin's inner city).

How did this happen? What were the forces that had led to a housing scenario, whereby a 40m² or 50m² redbrick single-storey cottage with no garden and poor aspect had become the 'fashionable' default 'choice' for the young middle class seeking a spacious urban townhouse? This is the urban story of apartment building in Dublin, specifically the story of apartment sizes.

Dublin city, throughout the 1990s and beyond, was simply not building enough spacious, attractive, well-designed, high-density apartment homes close to the centre of the city to provide a real alternative housing choice to the urban 'cottage' or the suburban house. Why was it that generously sized, airy, spacious apartment-living proved unattainable for so many for so long?

The generously size, airy spaciousness and delightful light-filled volumes of any home are generally and unremarkably considered important factors in their attractiveness. It's an instinctive recognition; one doesn't need an architect or a planner to tell you so, to interpret mathematical rules or deconstruct delightful space. It is remarkable, then, that a Dublin City Council policy initiative to increase the minimum size of apartments in 2007, a policy that was eventually adopted, should have elicited such suspicion, opposition and derision, not from developers or builders (they

had their fair share of detractors), but from a not insignificant proportion of the building design profession, including planners and architects.[1]

What was it about championing quality spacious apartments that many design professionals found so challenging? The motivation to oppose, delay or complicate the delivery of sustainable, spacious, high-density living is difficult to comprehend. We suspect it probably had a lot less to do with an understanding of housing economics, future city-making or city-living than it had with professional institutional control, individual personal housing choices, or a desire on the part of many urban professionals to distance themselves from past architectural designs or planning decisions.

Whatever the motivation, in the TEN COMMANDMENTS OF THOU SHALT NOT INCREASE SIZE we endeavour to summarise and debunk the ten strongest 'arguments' against increasing the size of apartments in Dublin city. These arguments are well rehearsed. They are familiar to those close to the discussion. They may surprise those interested in city-making but not privy to municipal or academic debate on home sizes. The urban tale of evolving apartment sizes in Dublin is a peculiarly fascinating one. It captures, probably like no other urban story, the hidden subconscious or deep-seated antipathy to real urban living in the capital city.

Between 1999 and 2004, the city of Dublin continued to permit apartments of 38m² in developments where 50% of all the proposed apartments had just one bedroom. These were probably the smallest new homes mass-built since the foundation of the State.[2] By 2005 the city had increased those minimums. The minimum size for one-bedroom apartment homes was increased from 38m² to 45m², two-bedroom apartment homes from 55m² to 65m², and three-bedroom homes from 70m² to 80m².[3]

By 2007 many of the more forward-thinking and astute developers had begun to understand that the market was beginning to outgrow the aspirations of the policy-makers. A more sophisticated Dublin consumer expected more. A small but growing number of inhabitants of the city had grown comfortable with the possibility of city living as the city centre was rapidly undergoing a physical and cultural renaissance. Many Dubliners, including newly arrived immigrants, had first-hand experience of apartment-living abroad and were tiring and increasingly critical of what was on offer in Dublin city.

In hindsight, it is neither unreasonable nor unfair to say many urban decision-makers for too long, with a few notable exceptions, were failing to lead. It's not that apartment design was not the constant subject of discussion, but rather that it was narrowly focussed. Much of that discussion, including earlier 'architectural' criticism of apartment-building, tended to be framed around apartment façades as opposed to the experience or substance of real apartment-living. Apartment criticism had become increasingly reduced to commenting on pastiche designs, jarring fenestration patterns, poor brick detailing, or the inappropriate use of white pvc and reconstituted stone. Planning assessments tended to focus on the impact these high-density developments had on adjoining residents, the height of proposed blocks and the application of various mathematical abstractions, including applying minimum suburban distances between opposing block windows.

Interesting and important as some of these issues were or are, the actual size and airiness of apartment homes, their internal configuration, the experience of actually living in them generated little interest for planners. There are many possible and varied explanations for this disinterest in apartment design, some more convincing than others. They can, however, perhaps be reduced to a very simple one, a kind of 'Occam's razor' urban law, which states that of several acceptable explanations for a phenomenon, the simplest is preferable, provided that it takes all circumstances into account.

Our explanation as to why the city permitted the mass-construction of small apartments for so long is a rather simple but perhaps provocative one. The decision-makers, and the friends and colleagues of key decision-makers, simply didn't live in apartments. Few were likely to ever have stayed overnight in a Dublin apartment, let alone had a desire or an opportunity to do so. Understanding the challenges of storage, the importance of cross-ventilation, the attractiveness of workable layouts, the height of ceilings, or the charmlessness of windowless micro-kitchens were all somehow abstract and detached. Rules and guidelines were minimal, but apparently sufficient, for most of those entrusted with the power to enforce them. Spaciousness or the lack of it was rarely questioned. Wider urban or civic interest in the quality-control or output of high-density apartment schemes was similarly delayed. It is one of biggest ironies of the Celtic Tiger boom that some of the most objectionable apartment developments that were built in the early 1990s generated the least number of planning objections from the public. This is perhaps because the significant majority of these developments were four or five stories or less, and thus generated little or no interest from the conservation lobby, whose primary interest had moved from inappropriate demolition to 'inappropriate' height.

Inner-city communities were also ill-equipped at the time to engage in an informed debate about the quality of new high-density homes. Perhaps ill-advised, their efforts in engaging with the planning process tended to focus on trying to stop development as opposed to seeking to extract the maximum amount in development levies for ring-fenced publicly funded local projects for their community.

A consensus has since emerged that the fault of all this inappropriate development was foisted upon an unwitting city by greedy or unprincipled developers, facilitated by indifferent administrators and compliant politicians, conveniently abdicating all responsibility from the city-making design professions. The reality is that most developers did what they legally could (the early apartment trailblazers undertook significant investment risks in a largely derelict city) and most regulators and planners did what they readily understood. That level of understanding was, as many blocks across the city testify, clearly insufficient. The result was tax-subsidised regeneration that permitted the construction of poor-quality but policy-compliant apartment developments.

An even more peculiar, if not perverse, strand of thinking has since emerged, brought about in part by the collapse of house prices since 2008, that the whole exercise in apartment-building was a faddish novelty that somehow went awry, and that it can all be tossed aside in favour of a reinvention or reworking of high-density, back-to-back, artisan, own-door cottages. This growing anti-apartment sentiment is fed, ironically, by the very failure of many in the urban-design professions to take responsibility for the delivery of quality and spacious apartments in the first place. The irony somehow seems lost on those closest to the subject. Yet despite the extensive presence of exceptionally small homes in inner-city Dublin, there remains concerted pressure on the city, partly under the guise of diversity and flexibility, to introduce studio bedsits of 25m² or less. In the interest of housing choice and diversity, there may be a case for allowing, but strictly geographically ring-fencing, studios of 25m² in Ballsbridge or other affluent suburbs with a substantial number of larger homes. Dublin's inner city critically requires a further variety of diverse investments, but an additional supply of small homes is not one of them.

Today in many parts of Dublin's inner city, more than half of all homes have two rooms or less – in effect, one-bedroom apartments. Most of these homes are 38m² in size (the statutory minimum standard for a one-bedroom apartment according to the Dublin City Development Plan 1999-2005). In the heart of Dublin's north-west inner city, in an area extending north-south from the North Circular Road to the River Liffey, and east-west from Amiens Street to Dorset Street, over 40% of all homes have just one bedroom or less. Most of these homes were built over the past fifteen years. The combined population of this area is just over 17,000 people, the equivalent of Sligo town.[4]

There are many disparate losers in this sorry early tale of apartment-building. These include the environment (sprawl), reduced choice for tens of thousands of housing consumers, diminished urban regeneration and, critically, a quality urban future if not denied, then certainly delayed, for much of Dublin city. The unavailability of quality, spacious, family-friendly, high-density homes in inner-urban Dublin has significantly reduced housing choice for many potential but ultimately 'lost' urban residents. Choice isn't simply choosing between what's available; it is the art of making possible real but unimagined possibilities. If people 'choose' small back-to-back homes in cluster developments, is it because they really want them or because they haven't been offered the choice of light-filled, airy, 140m^2 apartment homes with cityscape views?

It is entirely reasonable to conclude this reduced urban-housing choice is likely to have been a significant factor in suburban sprawl. What is perhaps less understood or accepted is the impact arising from the construction of extensive blocks of one-bedroom homes in disadvantaged area in the inner city. That failure to deliver affordable, spacious homes attractive to middle-income families massively increases the risks of permanently consolidating Dublin's inner-urban 'neighbourhoods' as a housing trap for the poor, shutting out the possibility of real mixed-income urban neighbourhoods. It also risked permanently damaging the broader image or brand of apartment-living for Dubliners.

Reimagining what Dublin's inner city could have become rather than trying to 'fix' it, 'stitching' in some curtain-wall infill, performing a kind of urban dentistry by filling in the missing gaps, was probably the biggest lost planning opportunity of the Celtic Tiger building boom. Despite these setbacks, one of the greatest challenges for Dublin city in 2010 and beyond is the not-too-dissimilar challenge it faced twenty years ago to broaden the housing choice for middle- and working-class families by providing high-density attractive apartment-style homes close to the heart of the city.

The Ten Commandments
of 'Thou Shalt Not Increase Apartment Size'

Debunking the arguments that delayed the delivery of quality apartment homes in Dublin city.

01 | Single people need or want only small one-bedroom apartments

The argument here confuses affordability and the entry point to the housing market with the actual size of an apartment. The former is a critically important issue for those starting out on the housing ladder. The factors affecting the price or affordability (distinctly different) of apartments are as complex as they are multifaceted, and include issues as diverse as density and design, interest rates and mortgage-lending, salary and employment levels, population growth and family sizes, land-values and labour-costs, city and national planning policy, immigration and emigration, speculation and expectation. The list is endless. It is, ultimately, an interaction between those critical factors determining supply and demand.

Apartments, however, can be both spacious and affordable. What's more, they can be spacious and affordable and environmentally sustainable. Spacious, affordable and sustainable apartments are to be found elsewhere in the world, so why not in Dublin? There is also an assumption here that single people automatically imply reduced income-power. Why would single people earning a middle or high income want, never mind need, a 25m² or 35m² one-bedroom apartment?

Finally, people – including single people – usually seek to buy the largest home they can afford in the area they wish or choose to live in.

02 | It's all about design. It is possible to design bespoke beautiful small apartments.

Yes, of course it is possible to design bespoke beautiful small apartments. But this argument misses the point entirely. It is also possible to design bespoke beautiful spacious apartments. This baffling and intriguing obsession with the design challenges of miniaturised apartment-living we term 'nano-apartment architecture'. Greater size and better design are not mutually exclusive.

03 | The neighbourhood and immediate street environment are more important than the size of your home

The neighbourhood and immediate street environment are critically important to quality of life. However, improving the spaciousness and attractiveness of well-designed homes is a critical factor in attracting middle-income earners to any area. Mixed-income neighbourhoods thrive best. They generate diversity, support local businesses through increased spending power, and provide political capital to effect positive change, including a bigger tax income base to deliver public goods. Spacious, well-designed apartments and quality neighbourhoods are not mutually exclusive. They are, in fact, very often inextricably linked. It is somewhat ironic, but not uncommon, that those who argue that the design of your urban neighbourhood is more important than the size of your urban home are very often the least interested in the challenges of managing clean and safe streets in urban neighbourhoods.

04 | It will collapse the housing construction market

As stated in °1 above, the factors affecting the price or affordability of apartments are as complex as they are multifaceted. There is little, if any, economic evidence, all things being equal, that an increase of 10m² or 15m² in the floor area of an apartment materially impacts on deliverability of housing supply.

05 | Household sizes continue to fall so families need smaller not larger urban homes

This is a variation of °1, but is infused with quite a deal of unchallenged social snobbery or uniformed social-housing knowledge masked or confused as urban sustainability. A great many working-class Dublin families, families of seven or eight or more, grew up in purpose-built social housing estates with average floor areas of 60m^2 or 70m^2. Most of these homes had three bedrooms; a significant minority however had just two. That often worked out at less than 10m^2 per person.

It is entirely reasonable that the children of the children who grew up in Ballyfermot or Marino, Crumlin or Cabra, or the family of four who may have moved in to these areas, might have greatly increased housing expectations in a wealthier society in the 21st century. Why shouldn't they aspire to larger and more spacious homes? In addition, Dublin suburban houses, whatever their size, can be and usually are extended. Apartments, on the other hand, almost universally cannot. The assumption that falling household sizes should automatically result in falling home size is rather simplistic. How many of those advocating smaller homes actually propose to live in them?

06 The 'market' doesn't want them. There is no demand for three-bedroom apartments.

The 'market' is simply the interaction of supply and demand, and its sets a price. People do not 'not want' larger, spacious, well-designed homes. They usually desire the best homes they can afford, and pay a price accordingly. The assertion that people don't want large apartments is often confused with a very different phenomena entirely, namely a weak demand for over-priced, poorly designed or ill-configured large apartments in cheaply built blocks in areas where anti-social behaviour is threatening, locals schools are underperforming, and there is a perception rightly or wrongly that the local quality of life is challenging.

07 It's not the business of planning or planners to involve themselves directly in the complex workings of the apartment 'market', a market they don't understand.

This is a code for 'it's not the business of planners or public officials to involve themselves in the design, layout, attractiveness and functionality of high-density housing supply'. We would argue that if it is not the responsibility of public policy or the city planner, then whose responsibility is it? Furthermore, we would argue, as evidenced by too many poor-quality apartments in many parts of Dublin 1, 7 and 8, it was a responsibility that perhaps was given insufficient attention in the past.

08 Families don't want to live in apartments. You are imposing unwanted 'cultural tastes'.

This is classic 'bigotry of low expectations'. It is a peculiar form of 'it is because it is' logic. What is accepted and experienced as attractive abroad in cities as diverse and far apart as Stockholm or Auckland somehow wouldn't work in Dublin for apparently no other reason then we haven't actually built it. It is not an unreasonable assumption that because in the recent past the city permitted the construction of thousands of small, ill-configured, poorly ventilated apartments in socially marginal areas that we may have suppressed a demand for what quickly became perceived as a tainted product.

How many Dublin families would reject a Parisian Haussmann-style apartment? How many decision-makers have walked into, let alone lived in a spacious, airy, Bauhauss-designed apartment?

09 Regulation inhibits innovation

The relationship between regulation and innovation is complex and not a one-way street. Appropriate or environmentally smart regulation can stimulate innovation, and is generally accepted as an important factor in driving forward design and technology. Sensible rules governing generous space are more likely to stimulate, not inhibit, a diversity of delightful design solutions. It is also interesting, if not somewhat peculiar, that those least keen on 'regulation' of the size of apartments are generally, without exception, the most ardent supporters of the regulation of their height.

010 The city doesn't need larger apartments. There exists an underutilisation of existing larger-sized 'empty nester' housing stock in the suburbs.

This argument is flawed on two accounts. Firstly, it is not possible to simply displace people from their homes, to transfer larger families to large homes, or aging couples to smaller ones. It is politically and economically impractical, and may not even be socially desirable. People generally prefer to stay in their own communities when they 'downsize' or 'trade-up'.

Secondly, perhaps more interestingly, it exposes an implicit suburban assumption. A large five-bedroom outer-suburban house is not necessarily the first preference housing choice of all; for the real urbanist, it rarely is. The provision of quality spacious homes in the city is a reasonable and sustainable housing objective for any city. Why should Dublin be so different?

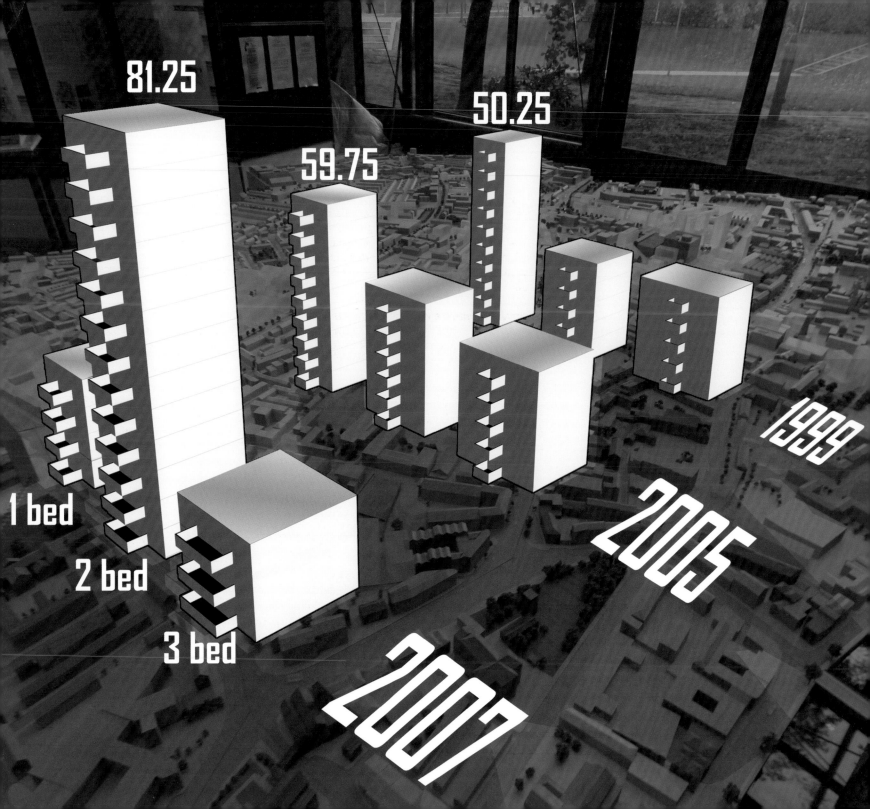

The Minimum Apartment Mix

In MINIMUM APARTMENT MIX we metaphorically 'build' the legal minimum combination of apartment sizes permissible under a progressively evolving city apartment policy. Our one-, two- and three-bedroom towers of varying sizes demonstrate what it was possible to build in Dublin city over time in any given larger apartment scheme. As late as 2004 it was legally possible and politically acceptable for a developer to build an apartment development in Dublin city whereby 50% of all the new homes proposed had just one bedroom. The City Council required that these one-bedroom homes should have a minimum floor area of just 38m².

These minimum-size standards and bedroom-mix requirements (one- versus two- or three-bedroom units – a proxy for size) changed substantially three years later. In 2007 the minimum permissible floor area of one-bedroom units was increased to 55m², and the maximum number of one-bedroom homes in any development was reduced to 20%.[1]

It is, therefore, possible to calculate the change over time of the legally permissible, overall average minimum floor area of the homes in an apartment development. This has risen from 50.25m² in 1999-2004 to 59.75m² in 2005 and 81.25m² in 2007. A civic understanding and an urban belief in the importance of the provision of quality, spacious, well-designed apartment homes is the necessary first step in convincing a sceptical public of the desirability of high-density apartment-living.

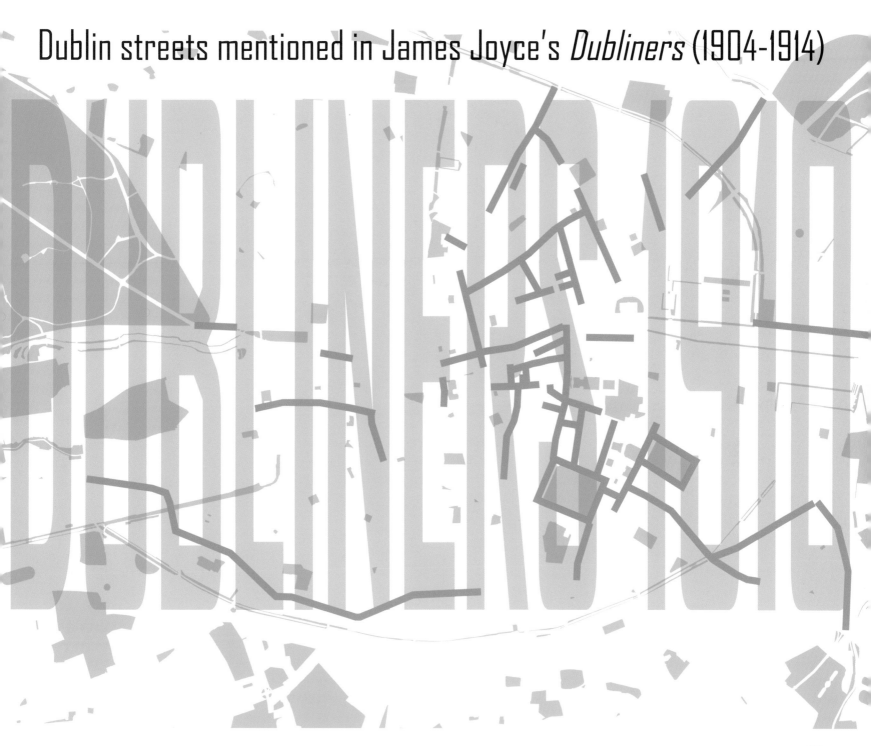

Dublin streets mentioned in James Joyce's *Dubliners* (1904-1914)

...Spar, Joyce or Literary Convenience

Density of Convenience and 'Shopfrontantiurbansuburbanism'

What is it about urban convenience shopping that so many Dublin architects and planners find so visually inconvenient? What is it about popular shopping outlets that the adherents of urban branding find so unfashionable to shop in? Why exactly does Spar, Centra or an equivalent invoke such equivocal reactions?

It can't possibly be a simple dislike of signage or colour? Perhaps it's simply lamenting the loss of the local inner-city corner shop (a shop that rarely provided choice or value), or the received wisdom that dictates a dislike of certain international brands that are ubiquitous and very popular.

It couldn't be the increased food choice for impoverished communities, the additional employment-generation or the often multi-cultural or multi-ethnic colour such convenience shopping adds to a local urban community.

Perhaps it is simply the inability of the 'tidal' city visitor or commuter to comprehend that those living in an urban area appreciate having to walk five minutes or less to buy fresh bread or milk, and that the density of branded convenience shops on almost every inner-city street is, well, just simply convenient to urban living. And why is it assumed by predominantly middle-class consumers that all local 'independent' and 'family-run' grocery shops automatically implies greater choice, quality, cleanliness, service and hospitality?

Tasting the Architecture of the Urban Brownie

TASTING THE ARCHITECTURE OF THE URBAN BROWNIE is a metaphor for the celebration and exploration of choice and diversity inherent in all great cities. Urbanism has historically provided the stage for the potential playful or delightful experiences and opportunities afforded to the curious and adventurous individual. Great urbanism has always had, at its core, a desire for and a celebration of pleasure and consumption, pleasures often forbidden or denied in the village or suburb. Great urbanism has always been at the forefront of creativity and knowledge.

In an environmentally challenged world, consumption and pleasure are increasingly frowned upon by a particular strand of puritan thinking that is interested less in saving the planet, promoting sustainable urban living or celebrating new technologies than in saving our consuming souls. In 'Tasting the architecture of the urban brownie' we quantify and celebrate consumption; we advocate the quality rather than qualify the limits of urban pleasure.

Leon
Airy, smells of chocolate icing
price: €4
weight: 130 grams
cost per gram: 3.1 cents
dimensions: 2 x 10 x 9 cm
volume: 180cm³
density: 1.38

Butler's
Rich, buttery, soft, melty
price: €2.60
weight: 124 grams
cost per gram: 2.1 cents
dimensions: 2 x 7.5 x 7.5 cm
volume: 112cm³
density: 0.91

Fallon & Byrne
Smells of Easter eggs, crumbly moist, nutty, chocolatey
price: €2
weight: 100 grams
cost per gram: 2 cents
dimensions: 3.5 x 7.5 x 6.5 cm (height x length x depth)
volume: 170cm³ (height x length x depth)
density: 1.7 (vol/weight)

Avoca
Whole Macadamia nuts, quality chocolate, moist, crumbly. A winner.
price: €2.70
weight: 140 grams
cost per gram: 1.9 cents
dimensions: 3.5 x 8 x 7 cm
volume: 196cm³
density: 1.4

Queen of Tarts
Small amount of broken nuts, crumbly and soft. Lovely sweet meal.
price: €3.50
weight: 138 grams
cost per gram: 2.5 cents
dimensions: 2.5 x 10 x 7.5 cm
volume: 188cm³
density: 1.36

ABORTED SKYLINE

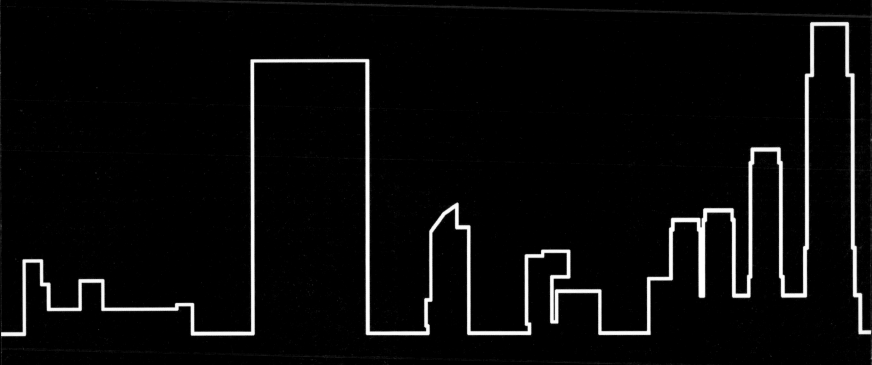

School Street   Spencer Dock hotel   Parnell Street   Bridgefoot Street   Digital Hub, Liberties

Building Sights

'The City That Never Was'

Architects are usually judged by the buildings they have designed or may have built, urban designers and landscape architects on their ability to deliver and sustain quality new spaces. Planners are judged on the realisation of a vision that may reveal itself in our towns or cities. How do we judge the judges or executioners of the city that never was?

When we talk about the city landscape, most of us, for obvious, reasons invariably concentrate or elaborate on its existing or current condition and form. Some specialise in the recent or distant past, whilst others concentrate on the possibilities for the immediate or distant future. In effect – the city that is, the city that was and the city that might be.

There is a fourth city. This is a city that might have been or the city that never was. It is a deliberately lost city. It is not simply a city made up of those sketches and designs of buildings and spaces that, for whatever reason, never left the drawing board or never came into being. This is a systematically rejected city, rejected by the appointed judges or arbiters of urban taste and acceptability.

This is a city of the imagination, but the imagination of the past passing into the memory of what might have been. It's an unborn city made up of aborted skylines. For some, it is a city mosaic made up of little lost pieces of different dreams, visions and ambitions. For others it's an unopened urban Pandora's box, a terrifying but prevented city dystopia.

We have chosen a few images of a few pieces of this twilight city. We make no judgement now. We do, however, through selected extracts from publicly accessible reports, reveal the judgement of others.

Jury's Ballsbridge

project: Mixed-use development incl. 536 apartments and 91,000m² of commercial, recreational, retail and leisure space

floor area: 188,102m²
site area: 2.8 hectares
plot ratio: 6.7:1
max height: 136.3m or 37 storeys
location: Ballsbridge, Dublin 4
architects: RKD Architects

The Planner...

"For some, the introduction of a tall building to this part of Dublin will have a positive impact as it will add interest to the skyline, provide a landmark for Ballsbridge to help orientate both visitors and city residents, and symbolise the ambitions of Dublin in the 21st century. For others, the presence of a tall building will constitute a negative impact. For some, the visual impact of the taller building as viewed, for example on axis from Pembroke Road, will be a disturbing shock; for others it will be exciting. In the words of Séamus Heaney, it could 'catch the heart off guard and blow it open'."

The Inspector...

"The architect for the proposal, Mr Raysse, described the scheme as a complete book, a novel. While it may be possible to make the chapters thinner or thicker, one could not take out a chapter without impacting on the entire scheme, he said. I agree."

The Bord...

"Notwithstanding the high quality of the architectural treatment of individual buildings ... would constitute an inappropriate response to the existing context of the site, making a radical change in the urban form of the area, at odds with the established character of Ballsbridge."

Digital Hub South

project: Mixed-use development including
38,400m² of office space, 360-bedroom hotel and
125 apartments

floor area: 81,179m²
site area: 1.1 hectares
plot ratio: 7.4:1
max height: 171.9m or 53 storeys
location: Thomas Street, Dublin 8
architects: de Blacam & Meagher

The Planner...

"The unprecedented height of the buildings and their effects on the city's skyline could be described as haphazard and unplanned. Considered as pieces of architecture in themselves, they are slim and elegant."

The Inspector...

"The raised podium, by its very nature, will not be enjoyed as a public space along a city route; in effect it is a cul-de-sac. So, while the space is intended as a dramatic public area, it could result in a physically non-integrated development with the effect of marginalising existing communities"

The Bord...

"The proposed development, notwithstanding the high quality of design of the buildings, would not represent an appropriate redevelopment of this area or a form of development that is sufficiently sympathetic to its historic character."

Digital Hub North

project: Mixed-use development incl. 268 apartments, 13,000m² of office space, 2,800m² of retail

floor area: 45,785m²

site area: 1.29 hectares

plot ratio: 3.5:1

max height: 67.3m or16 storeys

location: Thomas Street, Dublin 8

architects: HKR Architects

The Planner...

"In this area we see the continuous evolution, often radical, of the city skyline with each new landmark, reflecting the age, the technology and the economy in which it is built. The proposed taller building is a confident and proper continuation of this heritage of taller interventions in this area..."

The Inspector...

"...the scale and height of block A [16 storeys] would not be in keeping with the streetscape on Thomas Street/James's Street, and would dominate it. The site is already possessed of a landmark building [the windmill]. The appearance of this slim tower is attractive, but its proportions are wrong for this site."

The Bord...

"...it is considered that the proposed development would not represent an appropriate redevelopment of this area or a form of development that is sufficiently sympathetic to its historic character or that is, as a whole, of a sufficiently high standard."

School Street

project: Mixed-use development incl. 82
apartments and public car park

floor area: 18343m²
site area: 0.55 hectares
plot ratio: 3.3:1
max height: 12 storeys
location: School St, The Liberties, Dublin 8
architects: Mitchell & Associates

The Planner...

"...a 21st-century positive contribution to an evolving robust architectural grain ... The potential drama of the urban views of many of the units is a critical factor in adding to the overall diversity and quality of the housing stock in the immediate area."

The Inspector...

"The scheme is imaginatively planned and the design gives evidence of architectural coherence. Essentially the layout, height size and scale would be appropriate in its context and would make a positive contribution to the urban environment."

The Bord...

"...the proposed development would be an inappropriate form of introverted development ... and would fail to integrate with or enhance the social and physical fabric of the neighbourhood."

Bridgefoot Street

project: Mixed-use development incl. 41 apartments

floor area: 8,835m^2

site area: 0.14 hectares

plot ratio: 4.2:1

max height: 13 storeys

location: Bridgefoot Street, Dublin 8

architects: Mitchell & Associates

The Planner...

"The delightful architecture including the dramatic cantilevered element is a significant gain for the area ... will provide a local landmark creating a sense of place in an amorphous area characterised by dereliction and a partly implemented road-widening line."

The Inspector...

"The impact of the development would be positive, it would improve its visual character and ameliorate the impression of urban decay and underutilisation which persists there. It would provide a high standard of residential amenity for its occupants and would have a positive impact on the character of the area."

The Bord...

"...the proposed development would not seriously injure the amenities of the area (subject to the condition that) ... the top six floors of the proposed tower in the south-east corner of the site shall be omitted."

Spencer Dock

project: Hotel
floor area: 59,220m²
site area: 0.176 hectares
plot ratio: 33.7:1
max height: 152m or 35 storeys
location: Spencer Dock, Dublin 1
architects: Shay Cleary

The Planner...

"...the 35th floor public viewing area will provide spectacular views over the city from all sides of the building resulting in a significant planning gain. Dublin is currently bereft of such amenities; the proposed 35th viewing space would constitute a significant addition to family friendly civic amenities in the city.

The Inspector...

"Notwithstanding the strategic significance of the development concept and the high-quality architectural treatment and the location of the site at a major public transportation infrastructure node ... the proposed development by reason of its slab-form shape, scale, massing and height would be highly visually obtrusive."

The Bord...

"the erection of a high-rise building of the scale of the proposed development at this location ... it is considered that, by reason of its height and massing, this 35-storey development would be visually obtrusive and at odds with the morphology of the immediate area..."

A 'Tall' story

A tale or two of too many storeys for some, perhaps even a story too many for others

A Tall Story

No city-making subject has probably generated more heat and less light, more discussion and less height than the Celtic Tiger-boom story of tall buildings in Dublin city. From the language of 'shoulder heights' and 'maximum governors'[1] to a proposed 53-storey digital hub, from Zaha Hadid to Norman Foster to visions of a 'crystalline' 37-storey residential tower in the heart of Ballsbridge, the story of tall buildings has been an emotional and physical roller coaster of decision-making, construction and demolition over the past fifteen years.

Dublin city's tallest building in the early 1990s, on the eve of the Celtic Tiger boom, was the 16-storey, 60m high Liberty Hall, built in 1965. Dublin city's tallest building in 2010, at the eclipse of the Celtic Tiger boom, remains the same 16-storey Liberty Hall. It is, perhaps, ironic that after fifteen years of proposals to build higher, there is a greater chance that this building will be demolished rather than surpassed in height by the construction of a taller building elsewhere in the city. With the demolition of the high-rise flats in Ballymun, the city appears to be going down not up.

For the outsider, occasional visitor or casual observer of the city's skyline, this stasis in building height may appear unremarkable, almost unobservable. The relatively stable Dublin skyline does, however, mask a remarkable fifteen-year period within which the city and citizen, in the broadest definition of those terms, solicited, entertained, discussed, occasionally permitted, mostly rejected 'skyscrapers' of all shapes, heights and sizes, few of which ever received eventual official sanction, none of which has been built. For good or ill, this civic dialogue or debate, sometimes conversational, sometimes intensely emotional, occasionally aggressive and accusatory, ultimately preserved the building height status quo. Dublin remains a low-rise city and it is unlikely to witness a mid- or high-rise district or quarter anytime soon.

Did we save the soul of the historic city and thus escape the worst excesses of developer avarice, or did we throw away the greatest opportunity to re-imagine underperforming areas and transform housing choice for tens of thousands of potential urban Dubliners?

Definitions of what actually constitutes a tall or high building are important. Dublin City Council definitions are derived from a study the authority itself commissioned in 2000, *Managing Intensification and Change*, and which forms part of overall planning guidance on height. This study defines mid-rise as 5m to 50m, or up to twelve storeys, high-rise as 50m to 150m, and super high-rise as buildings greater than 150m.[2] The tallest building permitted by Dublin City Council, but not built, is the 117m high, 32-storey Heuston Gate residential tower, commissioned by the Office of Public Works and designed by Paul Keogh Architects. The Dublin Docklands Development Authority permitted a 120m high Scott Tallon Walker-designed Watch Tower, which has been temporarily abandoned following the completion of its three-storey basement in 2009. Another irony, perhaps, is that the tallest building to ever commence construction is halted three storeys underground.

One of the tallest buildings built in Dublin during the boom is the 16-storey, 51m high residential Alto Vetro building in Dublin 2. The building was completed in 2006. Technically Dublin City Council categorises this building (above 50m) as high-rise. The tallest building built in Dublin during the boom period was No. 1 George's Quay Plaza (59m). Constructed in 2002, the impact of its height is somewhat diminished as it forms part of a group of buildings. The tallest building rejected by the City Council was the spectacular 53-storey, 172m high mixed-use tower incorporating podium gardens, which formed the centre feature of a cluster of towers designed by De Blacam & Meagher Architects for Manor Park Homes at the Digital Hub site, adjacent to the Guinness Brewery on Thomas Street, Dublin 8. Some of the other rejected or refused high-rise high-profile projects include Seán Dunne's proposal for a 37-storey residential tower in Ballsbridge, Dublin 4, and the Treasury Holdings proposal for a 35-storey hotel designed by Shay Cleary Architects at Spencer Dock, Dublin 1.

Dublin's tallest built structure, as opposed to the tallest accessible or occupied building, are the Pigeon House chimneys at Poolbeg. These twin towers rise some 207m. Interestingly, they are also scheduled for demolition. The Dublin Spire, erected in 2003, is the tallest structure in the heart of the city at 120m. The spire of St Augustine's Church on Thomas Street in Dublin 8 reaches 70m. This structure, completed in 1895, has therefore a reasonable claim to the title of tallest building in the city.

Can't see the Scale of it

Architects, urban designers and planners increasingly talk about 'scale' or, more importantly, 'appropriate scale' in city-making. Understanding what is an 'appropriate scale' for a development on your street, your block or your city is apparently a magical formula for unearthing a critical component in successful city-making. Get the scale right and you're more than half-way to best practise in the design and management of successful and attractive urban spaces.

Scale is important in city-making. It is the building blocks of form, determining positive and negative space, the places we inhabit and the places we walk through. Pinning down what constitutes 'appropriate scale' is altogether more difficult. Definitions are somewhat elusive.

Appropriate scale seems just that, obviously appropriate. Can imaginative, transformative, altered, or daring scales ever be 'appropriate', delightful, inspiring even? Who decides?

The experts or arbiters of appropriate scale seem to find this pretty instinctive. While one city obviously differs from the next, the appropriate scale for each city, and each district in that city, seems somehow intuitive or unconsciously understood for the arbiters of appropriate scale.

Appropriate scale, in the context discussed above, is instinctively understood to mean the height or massing of a single building or group of buildings relative to another building or group of buildings in a city block, and its relationship to the width and length of the adjoining patterns of streets and public spaces. We suspect, however, that the insightful invocation of 'appropriate scale' is fed less by either an astute understanding of mathematical volumetric relations, or an innate aesthetic sense or insight into universal laws of geometrical beauty, but by the rather simple but acute awareness of what we call the 'reality of the now' – in other words, a knowledge of what currently exists on or near the site in question.

Is it possible that the staunch advocates of 'appropriate scale' tend to confuse bad architecture with radical change of scale? For many they are simply one and the same thing. Perhaps that is understandable. There is a lot of average architecture around, and increased scale only magnifies its mediocrity.

There is, however, nothing more disturbing or dislocating to the mind of those who fastidiously adhere to the received wisdom of 'appropriate scale' than there may, in fact, be a multiplicity of answers to what is 'appropriate scale'. It's simply disturbing to accept that an infinite spectrum of possibilities exists, a kind of 'relativism of scale', informed by and dependent upon excellence in design and execution, each with a terrifyingly different but equally aesthetically and functionally satisfying answer to the question of 'what is the appropriate scale?'.

If 'appropriate scale' is to be reduced to a kind of architectural moral relativism, then all sorts of delightful urban architectural designs are, in theory at least, imaginable. For the adherents or proponents of 'appropriate scale', however, this is nothing short of a vision of urban dystopia, a potential uncontrollable Pandora's box of built possibilities, a form of perverse abnormal urban expression that is uncensorable or uncontrollable.

It is somewhat intriguing that many of those who most eloquently dissect the language and extol the virtues of the importance of appropriate scale in city-making – in Dublin at least – rarely extend their use of the word beyond a narrow range of certain urban scales. It is interesting that the passionate interest and defence of the appropriate scale of individual buildings rarely extends to a discussion of either the macro, urban city scale (how big our city should be) or the micro, liveable urban scale (how big our apartment home should be).

Somehow the importance of the appropriate scale of a building is instinctively understood in designing attractive sustainable urbanism, whilst the scale of the city itself or the scale of the homes within it are either of marginal interest or somebody else's responsibility. We suspect the reason for this is rather simple. Just as the wisdom of appropriate scale is dependent on the pedestrian observation of the now, the size of somebody else's apartment (it is invariably somebody else's) or the size

of the city is not as easily imagined or visually consumed, and thus is of little interest. Yet designers of real urbanism require an understanding or at least an informed opinion of the very large and very small scales at which effective city-making takes place. City-makers need to ask the intriguingly and increasingly more important question: how big should our city be? Should we plan to double the population or keep it stable? Reduce it or half it? Would doubling the population of Dublin city over the next twenty years significantly reduce Ireland's CO_2 output if, over that same period, the overall population of the State only marginally increased?

Similarly, there is an urgent need for a robust debate on the role the provision of spacious apartments would play in consolidating urban living and a compact city? Would providing high-density, family-friendly apartment homes, akin to suburban houses in counties Meath or Kildare affect consumer housing choice and potentially CO_2 output?

If Dublin is to understand the importance of scale in designing for its future, if scale is not to be interpreted as narrowly as how many floors are acceptable in a particular building, the city needs to broaden its understanding of the importance of scale, a scale that is both really experienced and economically and environmentally understood, and not just one that is simply casually observed or seen.

STILETTO ARCHITECTURE

There is a general consensus in Dublin, particularly amongst city decision-makers, that significant progress has been made in the delivery of 'quality' apartment homes in recent years. This consensus rightly acknowledges the notable and visible increase in the quality of material finishes being used in newer developments. Whether it is external or internal, marble versus formica, stone versus render, it is not too difficult to recognise the difference in the quality of appearance between those apartment blocks built in the late 1980s and early 1990s and those built in more recent years. Yet despite this progress, perhaps even because of it, significant deficiencies remain in overall quality of apartment design.

The majority of new purpose-built apartments remain either relatively small, poorly configured or both. What is taken for granted in a typical newly built Dublin house (and in many foreign city apartments) – a naturally ventilated bathroom, a decent-sized kitchen, a dedicated dining area or a third or fourth bedroom – generally continue to remain elusive in most Dublin apartments.

Few Dubliners aspire to living long-term in an apartment. Apartments are generally viewed as either starter homes or airily dismissed as a housing choice more appropriate for 'others', others being 'renters', students, single people or retirees. In STILETTO ARCHITECTURE we have endeavoured to capture much of the lauded but superficial progress in apartment material finishes, a progress that celebrates appearance over function, material finishes over spaciousness, marble countertops over liveability.

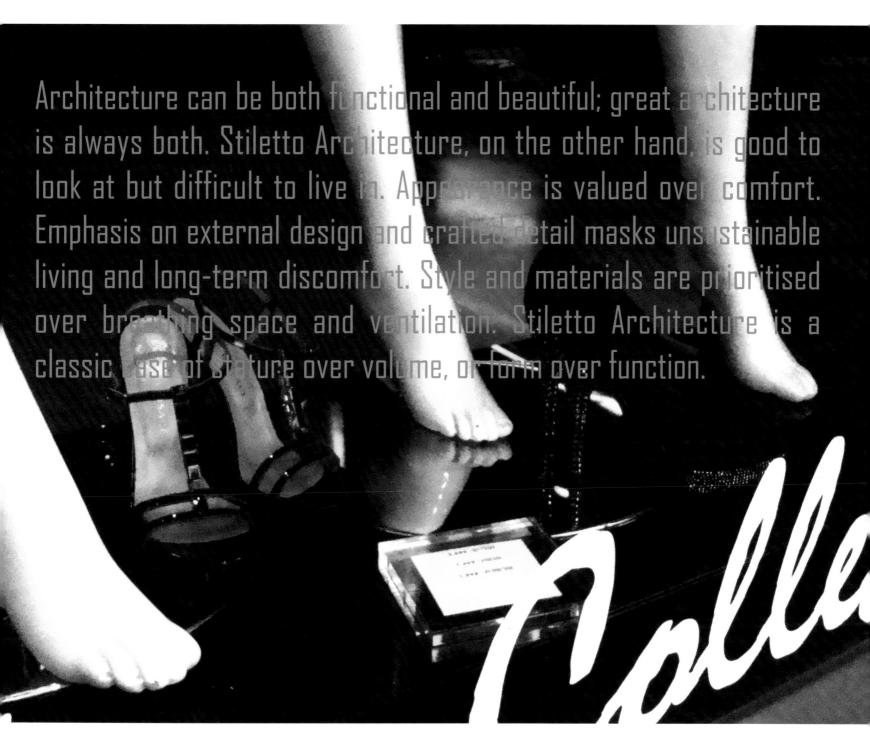

Architecture can be both functional and beautiful; great architecture is always both. Stiletto Architecture, on the other hand, is good to look at but difficult to live in. Appearance is valued over comfort. Emphasis on external design and crafted detail masks unsustainable living and long-term discomfort. Style and materials are prioritised over breathing space and ventilation. Stiletto Architecture is a classic case of stature over volume, or form over function.

DUBLIN
BILBUN
NUBLLD
UBIDNL
UBIDNL
ILDNUB
UNBLID
UNBLID
LUBDIN

N U B I L D

Captures a particular flavour of built or urban Dublin. This is a somewhat recent urban face of the city that is neither celebrated nor acknowledged.

BUMPARKS

Local parks with no seating, presumably to deter homeless people from loitering ... instead they deter everybody else from visiting and sitting down.

SQUINTING FAÇADES

Buildings that appear to squint back at you with their odd window patterns ... or any building that makes you squint if you catch a glimpse of it as you walk by.

BLIND-SPOTS

'Big Land-Islands of Non-Development' that nobody sees anymore ... vacant or derelict sites that become such a part of the urban fabric that any proposal to redevelop them invokes local outrage.

BODYBUILDERS

Buildings that seem to amass more and more inappropriate bulk ... with ever-diminishing visual returns.

NODDY CORNERS

What should be small, innocuous buildings, often at inconsequential corners ... stand out like sore thumbs with clumsily designed corners and upper-floor 'hats'.

BLOCKSHOPS

High-street convenience stores on the ground floors of new apartment blocks ... usually with blanked out windows.

Urban Bio-Diversity or City Dereliction or both? Who decides?

N   A   M   A

NAMA

NATIONAL ASSET MANAGEMENT AGENCY

NAMA meaning in Hebrew:

f.v.' to drowse', 'slumber', 'doze', 'take a nap'. Nam, Nama, Lanoom, Lenamnem.

URBAN LENS

Going Global

What's up with Dublin?

In an international survey of over 198 countries in 2005, the *Economist* magazine ranked Ireland as the nation with the highest quality of life in the world.[1] In the same year, Mercer Consulting ranked Dublin the 22nd best city in the world in which to live.[2] The criteria employed by the *Economist* and Mercer are as varied as they are numerous.

Ireland has since fallen a little in the *Economist* international comparative rankings. In 2010 it was eclipsed by Norway, Australia and Iceland.[3] In 2010 the United Nations ranked Ireland fifth for quality of life in its annual Human Development Index (HDI). Norway and Australia once again outperformed Ireland; New Zealand came in third, and USA fourth.[4] With enormous economic challenges and financial strains, Ireland may fall a little further in the years ahead. Whether it is first, fourth or fifth, Ireland's relative rise in the global rankings of quality of life is remarkable. As recently as 1998, Ireland ranked 18th in the global table in the HDI; in 1985, it ranked 22nd. If Ireland is a recent star performer, is Dublin, its capital city, lagging somewhat behind?

In 2010 Mercer ranked Dublin joint 26th in its quality-of-life survey.[5] A ranking of 26th perhaps is not too bad considering Mercer evaluates local living conditions in 215 cities worldwide. Dublin has, however, slipped three places on its 2005 position. The *Economist* also ranked Dublin joint 26th in 2010.[6] A more meaningful evaluation, perhaps, is to compare where Dublin ranks as a city relative to equally affluent nations. Canada and Australia, including the major cities of Ottawa, Toronto, Vancouver, Sydney, Melbourne and Perth, are all ranked above Ireland and Dublin as more desirable places to live. Interestingly, of the 25 cities ranked higher than Dublin in Mercer's 2010 urban quality-of-life table, no fewer than nineteen are to be found in countries ranked lower than Ireland in both the 2009 *Economist* and 2009 United Nations national quality-of-life surveys. These nineteen cities include, among others, Copenhagen, Amsterdam, Vienna, Munich, Berlin, Geneva, Wellington and Auckland. With the exception of Wellington and Auckland, all are near neighbours of Dublin in north-western Europe. Eleven of the nineteen cities are either to be found in Scandinavia or are German-speaking cities.

So why is Ireland outperforming Dublin, or Dublin underperforming relative to Ireland? What exactly is up with Dublin? A possible clue is that Dublin is ranked 58th when it comes to infrastructure, a broad list that includes public-transport provision. Climate, interestingly enough, is also a factor in the Mercer ranking, a factor perhaps that detracts from Dublin's appeal as a desirable city to live in.

EUROGOOGLE CITY HITS – In 'EuroGoogle' we uncover probably the most popular, accessible and perhaps the most honest test at a given moment in time of international city recognition – the relative number of 'EuroGoogle' urban web-hits. So how often does Dublin appear on the Google search engine relative to other European cities? Surprisingly, for an English-language-only search of cities, it languishes mid-table.

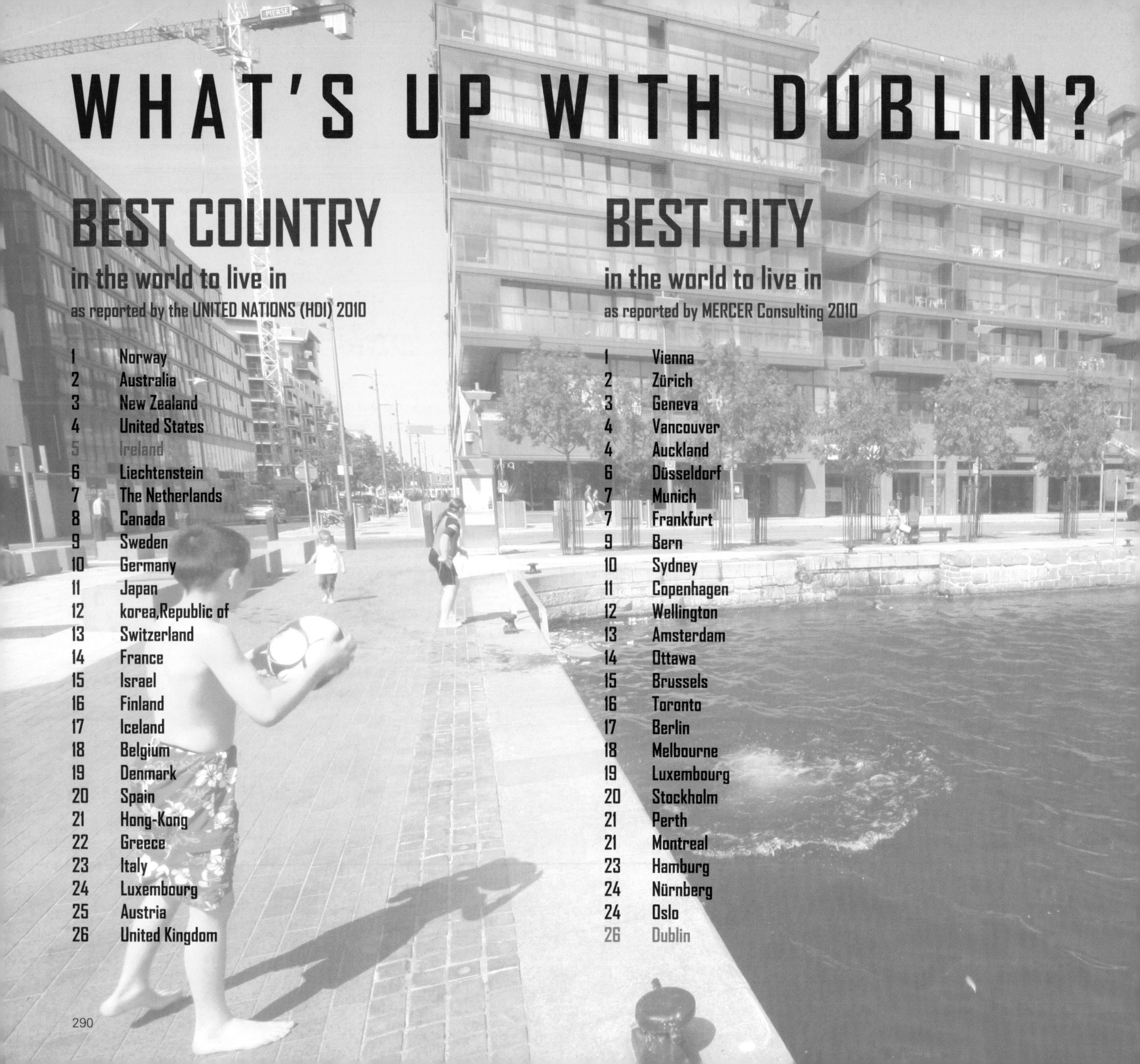

WHAT'S UP WITH DUBLIN?

BEST COUNTRY

in the world to live in

as reported by the UNITED NATIONS (HDI) 2010

1   Norway
2   Australia
3   New Zealand
4   United States
5   Ireland
6   Liechtenstein
7   The Netherlands
8   Canada
9   Sweden
10 Germany
11 Japan
12 korea,Republic of
13 Switzerland
14 France
15 Israel
16 Finland
17 Iceland
18 Belgium
19 Denmark
20 Spain
21 Hong-Kong
22 Greece
23 Italy
24 Luxembourg
25 Austria
26 United Kingdom

BEST CITY

in the world to live in

as reported by MERCER Consulting 2010

1   Vienna
2   Zürich
3   Geneva
4   Vancouver
4   Auckland
6   Düsseldorf
7   Munich
7   Frankfurt
9   Bern
10 Sydney
11 Copenhagen
12 Wellington
13 Amsterdam
14 Ottawa
15 Brussels
16 Toronto
17 Berlin
18 Melbourne
19 Luxembourg
20 Stockholm
21 Perth
21 Montreal
23 Hamburg
24 Nürnberg
24 Oslo
26 Dublin

WHAT'S THE WEATHER LIKE?

According to the EU Urban Audit, Dublin is the rainiest capital city in the European Union, as measured by the number of days it rains per year,[1] with an average of 246 rainy days a year (that's two out of every three days). London, our nearest neighbour, has more dry days than rainy days (163 rainy days). In Helsinki, more than two out of three days (115) are rain-free.

If Dublin is rainy, it is perhaps not surprising that it is also not very sunny. The same Urban Audit ranks Dublin the least sunny capital city in Europe as measured by the average number of hours of sunshine per day over the year.[2] Dublin has an average of just four hours of sun per day. Nicosia is the sunniest, with just less than nine hours of sunshine on average per day. Copenhagen, despite its more northerly latitude than Dublin, is remarkably 35% sunnier then the Irish capital, with on average 5.4 hours of sun per day per year. Madrid, Lisbon and Athens all have over seven hours of sun per day, with Athens the driest capital city of Europe.

Dublin, however, is not the coolest capital city in the summer. The average temperature of its warmest month is 19° Celsius. The coolest capital (temperature-wise at least) is Helsinki, with the average temperature of its warmest month just 17°C. Rome sizzles to the top of the summer table with average temperatures of 32°C.

Dublin, however, is positively Mediterranean in the winter, with only Valetta, Lisbon, Nicosia and Athens, alongside Dublin, having temperatures above 8°C on average for it coldest month. This compares to a shivering −5°C and −7°C for Riga and Vilnius.

SUPERCITY

$$SC = (BI*8 + BS*0.25 + R*0.5 + C10)/6$$

Tired of sifting through those endless rankings and lists of the biggest, the best, the richest, the most expensive or least expensive cities in the world? The academic literature on the comparative rankings of 'Global Cities', 'Emerging Cities', 'Alpha and Beta Cities' appears endless, bewildering and often contradictory. The lists of authoritative, subjective quality-of-life city rankings seem to exponentially increase year after year, simultaneously fascinating urban junkies but potentially paralysing city decision-makers.

In a thoroughly subjective, but nevertheless scientific exercise of ranking the world's top cities, we bring you the ultimate, definitive ranking of all rankings, SuperCity.

SUPERCITY (SC) is itself, however, a composite and complex highly calibrated formula

$$SC = (BI*8 + BS*0.25 + R*0.5 + C10)/6$$

BI=Biggest City, **BS**=Best City, **R**=Richest City and **C**=Connected City

'SUPERCITY' is a formula using four separate and distinct criteria, each of which are drawn from international research and/or academic literature.

BI=Biggest City is probably the most straightforward. It's simply an objective ranking of the world's metropolitan regions by population size. Greater Tokyo, with a population of 35 million, tops the list. Mexico DF comes in second. Eleven of the top twenty cities are Asian, four are in Latin America.[1]

BS=Best City is altogether more subjective. Our source, however, is Mercer Consulting city quality-of-life rankings, widely recognised as one of the more authoritative. The top three ranked cities, headed by Zurich, are all European and all German-speaking. Fourteen of the top eighteen cities have English or German as their mother tongue. Australian, Canadian and north European cities all rank high. Singapore, at 28th, is the highest-ranked Asian or 'non-western city'. Dublin comes in at joint 26th.[2]

R=Richest City is subject to wildly different calculations. Currency fluctuations, booms and busts, and the exact chosen boundary of a city are some of the factors that can produce radically different rankings. We have employed a UBS 2009 survey of 73 international cities, which ranked Dublin as the tenth richest city (per capita) in the world.[3] Dublin was ranked second in 2008. Copenhagen tops the list. New York is ranked fourth.

C=Connected City* is by far the most complex and arguably the most important criterion. It endeavours to capture the power of cities, their influence, to some degree their wealth-generating capacities – fundamentally, the extent to which they are plugged into the global financial and political economy and, ultimately, authors of their own destiny. We have used the 'alpha', 'beta', 'gamma' rankings of the GaWC (Globalization and World Cities Research Network).[4]

SUPERCITY Rankings

The relative weighting of each of our four categories is entirely subjective. Perhaps not surprisingly, New York is our No.1 SuperCity. Tokyo, however, beats London to take the second slot. Mexico City, the world's second largest metropolitan region, comes in at No.8. Three of the top ten SuperCities are located in 'developing countries' or 'emerging market' economies.

SUPERCITY

1	NEW YORK	11	SINGAPORE	21	MOSCOW	31	GENEVA
2	TOKYO	12	MILAN	22	AMSTERDAM	32	STOCKHOLM
3	LONDON	13	SAN FRANCISCO	23	TAIPEI	33	OSAKA
4	PARIS	14	FRANKFURT	24	BUENOS AIRES	34	MANILA
5	LOS ANGELES	15	SEOUL	25	SHANGHAI	35	CARACAS
6	CHICAGO	15	TORONTO	26	BANGKOK	36	CAIRO
7	HONG KONG	17	SYDNEY	27	BEIJING	37	ISTANBUL
8	MEXICO CITY	18	ZÜRICH	28	DELHI	38	KUALA LUMPUR
9	SÃO PAULO	19	MADRID	29	MUMBAI	39	BARCELONA
10	JAKARTA	20	BRUSSELS	30	BOSTON	40	DUBLIN

SUPERCITY the formula:
SUPERCITY = (BI*8+ BS*0.25+R*0.5+C10)/6

EUROZONE

CAPITAL CITY

ENGLISH SPEAKING

MONTREAL

AMSTERDAM
BILBAO   ANTWERP   MADRID
MILAN   MUNICH   PARIS
TURIN   FRANKFURT   ATHENS
HAMBURG   BERLIN   VIENNA
LYON   HELSINKI   BRUSSELS
VALENCIA   ROME   LISBON
MARSEILLE
BARCELONA
ROTTERDAM
BORDEAUX   CORK
GALWAY
WATERFORD
LIMERICK   DUNDALK
MANCHESTER   SYDNEY
MIAMI   JOHANNESBURG
ATLANTA   CAPETOWN
TORONTO
NEW YORK   MELBOURNE
CHICAGO

TOKYO   TEHRAN
MEXICO CITY
MOSCOW   JERUSALEM
COPENHAGAN
BRASILIA   JAKARTA
CAIRO   STOCKHOLM
BUENOS AIRES
TAIPEI
LAGOS   BEIJING
KINGSTON   SEOUL
OTTAWA
PRETORIA
WELLINGTON
LONDON
SINGAPORE
AUCKLAND
VANCOUVER
HOUSTON
LOS ANGELES

DUBLIN

SAO PAULO

RIO

SHANGHAI

TEL AVIV

CASABLANCA

Dublin is uniquely placed as the world's only English-speaking capital city within the euro zone. This allows the city to capitalise on its power as a seat of government to make decisions quickly, to connect internationally as an English-speaking city whilst simultaneously and beneficially being locked into the currency and monetary stability of the euro zone – the world's largest trading bloc. Might this unique multiplicity of political, linguistic and economic connectivity give Dublin its 'brand'? Dublin is ranked 12th in Europe in terms of brand strength, higher than Edinburgh but lower than Naples and Antwerp. (source: Saffron Brand Consultants, European City Brand Barometer, 2008)

BRAND DUBLIN

The global branding, marketing or packaging of cities is big business and increasingly fashionable for civic decision-makers. The capacity for any city to project a positive image (Dublin is no exception) is important to sustainable tourism and potential investment, and may even contribute to a confident sense of self or civic pride for local citizens.

The branding of Dublin is inextricably bound up with its people, pub culture, buzz and energy. Dublin has also traditionally focused on its past, its Georgian architecture, literary heritage and historic association with Guinness. Marrying these characterisations is sometimes complementary, sometimes problematic, but often slips into corny cliché, occasionally becoming smug and self-satisfied.

Cities have many customers. Striking an appropriate balance between the interests and needs of them all is sensible and necessary. A city like Dublin, which is, in effect, a 'tidal' city – dependent on the daily and seasonal inflow of commuters, shoppers and tourists – is at risk of overvaluing the brand that attracts those same commuters, suburban shoppers and tourists at the expense of its existing urban residents, or, more importantly, its potential urban residents. Dublin city, we believe, should focus more on what makes urban life attractive and liveable for those who live there. Remedying the shortfall in quality inner-urban housing, providing safe, walkable and pleasant green streets, prioritising the pedestrian resident over car-borne visitors, dealing with edgy anti-social behaviour, are all likely to significantly affect the brand image of Dublin for the better.

Some of the best global cities seem to blend this marketing and everyday urbanism effortlessly. Barcelona, Copenhagen, Sydney and New York have all achieved excellence in global brands; they are also highly desirable urban places to live. The dynamism and liveability of these cities, including the quality of inner-urban residential neighbourhoods, attracts others. Like Dublin, their biggest tourist attractions are to be found in their city centres. Unlike Dublin, however, all have vastly larger liveable urban cores that embrace an urbanism beyond the branding of a 'heritage' downtown.

If creatively considered, Dublin's existing top tourist destinations afford enormous opportunities to re-brand and re-imagine the city as a great urban place to live. The cultural and literary heritage has the potential to breath life into and 'oxygenate' a contemporary Joycean appreciation of the vitality of Dublin street life. Interestingly, eleven of the top fourteen tourist attractions in Dublin city (including three of the top ten state tourist attractions) are located either in or directly adjacent Dublin's Arc of Disadvantage, or Dublin's inner city, as opposed to Dublin's city centre. Whilst all are walkable from the heart of the city core, most require a relatively unpleasant journey by foot. These include the Guinness Brewery, Dublin Zoo, IMMA (Irish Museum of Modern Art) and the National Museum at Collins Barracks.[1] The primary pedestrian routes to these top tourist attractions, the Red Luas Line, Benburb Street and Thomas Street, are generally characterised by a poor public domain, potential anti-social behaviour, challenging pedestrian barriers, and a significant levels of vacancy and dereliction. As key pedestrian tourist routes, and ultimately urban economic routes, they do little to communicate positive city-branding. This is highly unusual for any city, particularly for one dependent upon an already well-recognised global tourist brand. Making these places work, improving the safety and the quality of the pedestrian experience for local urban residents, is of direct benefit to the 'transient' visitor or overseas tourist and critical for building upon and consolidating Dublin's brand image. Attracting and impressing the 'transient' visitor to the city is of paramount importance to the branding of Dublin.

It is somewhat ironic that many of those who choose to live in the heart of the city (as opposed to the suburbs) are themselves very often labelled 'transients' – a very much intended pejorative term – by those who choose to live in the suburbs and who themselves, along with tourists, are the 'transient' visitors to the city. It is a branding irony that oddly seems lost on many, including the branders themselves. Just as form follows function, perhaps branding should follow function, or a functioning urbanism, to be precise.

Post-European

In GOING GLOBAL we briefly explore the urban tales of unexpected places or 'post-European' lessons from afar. Tokyo, Tel Aviv, Mexico City and São Paulo do not readily spring to mind for most Dubliners when searching for lessons or best practises in everyday urbanism. These are cities that are perceived by many, in particular the advocates of an Anglo- and Euro-centric 'new urbanism' as forbidden metropolises. They are shunned as being either too exotic, politically incorrect, polluted, overcrowded, dangerous, over-scaled, or just downright inappropriate models of urban living.

Dublin has plenty to learn from these and other great cities that rarely register on the Euro-centric radar. Open your mind and you'll be delightfully surprised by cities that happily exist outside the 'bubble' of received wisdom. We have chosen just a sample, a taste of what most impresses us most about Tokyo, Tel Aviv, São Paulo and Mexico City.

What Dublin can learn from Tokyo

Attention to detailed design.
An ability to simultaneously combine a seemingly chaotic urban energy with an acute appreciation and understanding of the importance of civic cleanliness and public order.
A capacity to successfully marry and merge the very old and the very new, the very big and the very small, often in close proximity.
An appreciation, as a capital city of an island nation, of the pleasure and benefits of a great central fish market.
A delightful, almost childlike appetite for new technology.
A playful and civic awareness of city sounds: cars hardly beep their horns; people rarely raise their voices on the street; machines, doors and sometimes even public toilets sing and talk.

What Dublin can learn from São Paulo

An obvious love of and ability to deliver 'temples' to modern architecture.
High-density urban living that effortlessly includes apartment lobby entrances unseen and unimagined in Dublin.

The energy and pleasure of recreational and urban views from above.
24-hour living; nothing ever closes.
An insatiable appetite for fun and partying that doesn't include falling over drunk or urinating in the street.
Big-city brashness, hip sense of style combined with a charming, unaffected friendly modesty.
Pulsating embracement of urban values, density, scale, change, pleasure and enterprise.

What Dublin can learn from Tel Aviv

A long and continuously evolving history of understanding modern apartment design and living.
Civilising green and central urban boulevards with plentiful inner-urban tree-lined streets.
High-profile, energetic city mayor with real political powers.
Children's play spaces dotted along major boulevards in the heart of the city.
Flip-flop informality and a pared-back lifestyle.
A capacity to sustain a 24-hour social city with some of the coolest bars and best nightlife in the world, and yet maintain 'edgy'-free streets.
A thoroughly urban appreciation in both winter and summer of the local beach.

What Dublin can learn from Mexico City

How to design and sustain one of the greatest, most efficient and beautiful urban metro transport systems.
Dedicated bus corridors akin to an urban light-rail system
Effective and imaginative use of one of world's largest and greatest city parks (Chapultepec).
Sustainable, liveable inner-urban residential districts that support innovation in apartment design.
Passion for colour in the urban landscape.
Urban boulevards that frequently double-up as outdoor public art galleries.
Weekly family-friendly civic celebrations and festivals in the city centre.

Reading Chaos

All about Shopping

Games

Constant Change

Tokyo Cool

Eating Fish

At Night

Wired

Everydayliness

Manga

São Paulo

Brasilian Urban Bio-Diversity

City Scape   Difference

Bossa Nova Design   24 Hours

Parks and Architecture

Hall Door   Modernism

SkyBar   Skycraper

TEL AVIV

Food

Beach

24 Hrs.

Melting Pot

Boulevards

Apartments

Flip Flop

Informality

Bauhaus

Coffee Culture

ciudad de mexico

Festivals

Chapultepec

Sky-Lines

DF Taxi

Metropolis Ciudad

Metro

Their Apartment

Colour

Mexican

Busyness

THE WAY WE LIVE

Delusional Dublin

Domestic Space
of City Decision-Makers

It is perhaps stating the obvious that the most influential or wealthiest decision-makers in any city, usually those with power affecting the future direction of that city, are likely to choose to live in the most desirable (however that is defined locally or individually) neighbourhood or area of the city they inhabit. Influential 'trendsetters' may not value exactly the same urban space as other influential policy-makers. The wealthiest may prefer a different choice of home than the politically powerful. The powerful or influential young may seek different residential options from their powerful or influential elders. But no matter how, or who, we define as the 'movers and shakers' or 'city-makers' in any city, a knowledge of where the wealthy and the powerful choose to live gives us an invaluable insight into the 'urban' values of that city. Dublin is no exception.

Put simply, do where our 'city-makers' choose to live affect the 'making' of our city? Or does the making of our city affect their choice of where to live? Extracting meaningful conclusions is fraught with danger, the conclusions or logic potentially circular. Interpretations are subjective, so therefore we let the data speak for itself.

We asked 59 key decision-makers three simple questions: Where do you live? What type of home do you live in? And how do you travel to work? It is important to state we didn't choose our 59 decision-makers; they were chosen for us. Those chosen decision-makers were identified by Dublin City Council as having the most influence on the future development of the capital city.[1] They include leading figures in government, public administration, business, education, academia, journalism and the arts. We are grateful to those who agreed to participate. The spatial pattern of their collective responses, whilst not surprising, is nevertheless strikingly revealing.

Of those who were identified by the city authority as exerting the most influence on the future direction of Dublin city, less than half (42.2%)

actually reside within the municipal boundary of the city itself, with just 17.8% living within Dublin's Canal Ring or inner-urban suburbs. It's worth noting that the functional area of Dublin City Council is home to 500,000 people and accommodates a vast and diverse housing stock. It is home to some of the richest and poorest neighbourhoods in the Greater Dublin region. The urban area within the Canal Ring, where more one in five of municipal Dubliners live, is also home to the some of the largest detached homes and the smallest flats and studios in the State. Urban housing choice in the city would thus appear, superficially at least, to be wide and varied. One in three of our Dublin city decision-makers (33.3%) lives outside the city in the affluent but decidedly suburban adjoining municipality of Dun Laoghaire-Rathdown. Almost one in eleven live outside of Co Dublin itself, in the adjacent 'exurban' counties of Kildare, Meath and Wicklow.[2] Do the key city decision-makers of Paris, New York, London, Copenhagen or Barcelona live outside their city? It's doubtful.

There are two further important distinct but interrelated urban questions that should be asked here: Why do Dublin city decision-makers forsake their city? And does where they choose to live affect the policy priorities of Dublin city?

The first question, why our 'city' decision-makers prefer a 'suburban' as opposed to 'urban' lifestyle, has potentially multiple and overlapping answers. What might deter Dublin's movers and shakers from city-living? Is it the quality of the schools in inner-urban Dublin? Is it the shortage or availability of spacious, well-designed, high-density homes? Is it the grittier, more challenging side of Dublin urban life? The traffic maybe? Perhaps the city – Dublin's inner city and city centre – is simply not an attractive place to live. Perhaps Dublin city decision-makers have made rational decisions on the basis of an urban reality on offer, or perhaps in their hearts they are simply enthusiastic suburbanites. Whether the preference of key decision-makers to live in the suburbs affects their policy priorities for the city is probably impossible to answer for no other reason than very few would probably dare to admit it.

There are, perhaps, some telling urban clues from the type of home our decision-makers choose to live in. Nearly a third (31%) of our decision-makers live in detached homes.[3] Less than 5% or just one in twenty of all Dublin city homes are detached dwellings.[4] Over 30% of Dubliners live

The Arc of Comfort
or the Arc of Low Expectation?

in purpose-built apartments or flats, compared to just 4% of its decision-makers.[5] Might the civic understanding of the design needs of apartment-living have suffered because of that detachment? Dublin has made enormous progress in the last decade or so in playing catch-up in its output of quality-designed, high-density homes. It has, however, by common consensus, made some mistakes in the not-so-recent past in allowing poorly designed, ill-configured and very small apartments to be built.

What has been taken for granted for decades in cities as diverse as Lyon, Tel Aviv or Stockholm – how to design and deliver quality high-density homes – has been for Dublin city a very steep and short learning curve. That steep curve is in danger of going into reverse as a peculiar anti-apartment mood takes hold amongst many of our urban-design professionals. It is precisely because the spacious and well-designed homes of our key decision-makers in suburban Dublin are so attractive that Dublin's inner city needs to compensate and compete by building exceptionally attractive, spacious and visionary apartment homes at its urban centre.

Why is it that Dubliners most enjoy visiting decidedly urban parts of foreign cities yet don't aspire either to live in or create similar environments in their home town of Dublin? Dubliners delight in meandering through Haussmann's Paris and the Marais, New York's Central Park, downtown 20th-century Barcelona and historic Rome. These areas, diverse as they are beautiful, enchant and fascinate us because they are all successful urban places. Yet, despite this apparent urge to visit foreign cities, most Dubliners live out their lives in two-storey semi-detached suburbia, for the most part detached from daily urban life. Why this detachment?

Does suburban Dublin really believe that Ballinteer or Rathfarnham, Dundrum or Stillorgan, or any other mass-built south county Dublin suburb is anything but residentially rather repetitious and aesthetically quite dull? These suburbs, after all, compare poorly with the lush, leafy, green, open-garden detached homes of the best of suburban America. So why is it that, as citizens of Dublin city, we have elevated vast tracts of mediocre semi-detached suburbia to the near-exalted status of 'most desirable place to live' for middle-class Dubliners?

Is it because we, as Dubliners, just don't believe we can do great urbanism here – a kind of bigotry of low expectation? Is it because these suburbs are simply safe? Safe in the broadest sense. This is where most of us are conditioned to believe we are supposed to choose to live. It's where our parents live and expect us to choose to live, choices that are comfortable and low-risk, choices that manage to somehow simultaneously reflect high status yet low expectation. Is it because the Marais or the Upper West Side is simply not available here? Which comes first for suburban middle-income Dubliners – the perceived or real lack of urban choice or the decision not to choose to be urban?

Almost **1 in 3 (31%)** of the Decision Makers' homes are **detached**

just under **2 in 5 (36%)** are **semi-detached**

25% of their homes are **terraced**

4% are purpose-built **apartments or flats 4%** are defined as **mews**

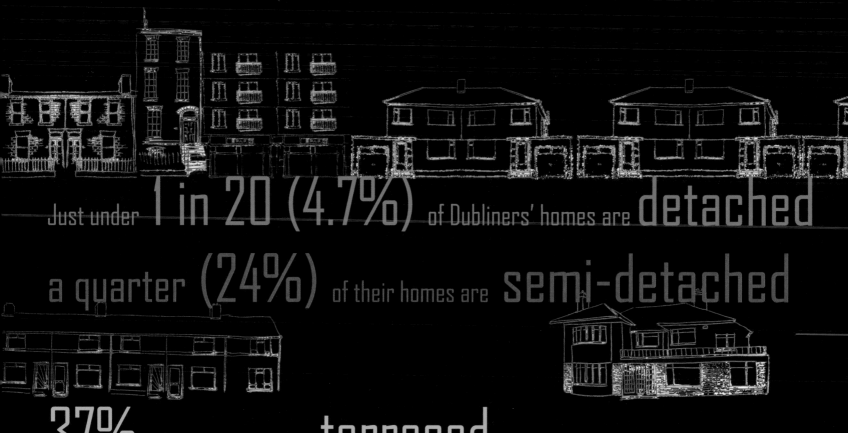

Just under **1 in 20 (4.7%)** of Dubliners' homes are **detached**

(24%) of their homes are **semi-detached**

37% of their homes are **terraced**

more than a fifth **(22.6%)** are purpose-built **apartments or flats**

2.5% of all Dubliners' homes are defined as **bedsits**

Just over **1 in 4 (26%)** of the Architects' homes are detached

1 in 14 (7%) of their homes are semi-detached

37% of their homes are terraced

approx **1 in 10** are purpose-built apartments or flats

approx **1 in 7** of te Architects' homes are defined as mews

I'm a

SuperGrouper

From **Group**91 to Suburban-**Super**Rural

paulkeoghrachaelchidlowsiobhannieanaighyvonnefarrellvaleriemulvinshaneotoolemichael
mcgarryderektynansheilaodonnellshelleymcnamaraniallmcculloughshayclearyjohntuomey
tomdepaormartinhenchiondavidosheadominicstevensdarellodonoghuekarenmcevoymerrittbucholzpetercodyroisinheneghan
dermotboydshifupengantoinmacgabhanntarlamacgabhannpaulkellymichellefagangarylysaghtciaranogaorashaneotoole

SuperGrouper: the DNA of an Irish architect

Does it matter where our brightest and best architects live? Is it interesting to know, beyond causal curiosity, what type of home they choose to live in? Are they trendsetters or trend-followers in housing design? Does their personal housing choice differ much from other comparable earning and influential decision-makers in other professions?

Perhaps the factors influencing the decision of where to live are no different for the leading lights in the field of Irish architecture than they are for the rest of the population. It's simply everything from family connection, job location, personal preferences, affordability, the quality and availability of housing choice, perhaps even wider society's idea of how or where it is fashionable to live. Does it really matter where our leading architects choose to live or what they choose to live in?

We believe it actually does matter. Architects, like planners and urban designers, are somewhat different from the rest of the populace. They are hardwired to value the importance that good design, a sense of place, liveable spaces and sustainable living all have on the quality of our daily lives. It is in their DNA to understand and translate this for others. The architect's job, after all, is to convince clients and developers, to persuade politicians and policy-makers of the critical importance that quality architecture and liveable neighbourhoods can and do have on personal wellbeing, social cohesion and sustainable economic prosperity. It is therefore reasonable and legitimate to ask the question: Where do our leading architects actually live? And what type of homes and living environments do they really value?

So can we gauge anything from residential choice of the Irish architectural elite that may give us insight into what they or we as citizens value in residential living? Does it tell us anything about what type of country or city we really live in or, indeed, the type of city or country the design professional actually wants the rest of us to live in? For the purpose of our small study we asked thirty leading Irish architects where they lived, how they commute to work, and what type of home they live in.

In the interest of simplicity, we reduced almost all imaginable housing typology, all infinite design possibilities to just six different categories of domestic residence, as follows: apartment; mews; Georgian, Edwardian or Victorian terrace; other terrace; semi-detached house; detached house. We drew our shortlist of architects from two prestigious lists, those who made up Group 91 and those involved in the exhibition and publication *SubUrban to SuperRural*. The members of Group 91 Architects, authors of Dublin's award-winning Temple Bar architectural framework plan in early 1990s, remain leading lights in Irish architecture today. *SubUrban to SuperRural* was Ireland's submission for the 10th International Architecture Exhibition at the Venice Biennale in 2006. We have called our new group of prestigious architects 'SuperGroupers'. Three out of four of our SuperGroupers responded to our survey. On the basis of their responses, we playfully recreate a kind of urban domestic street of how our architects live, affectionately called 'Architects Town'. It is simply a composite image of housing typology and transportation modes statistically representative of the total answers received.

So can unearthing the personal domestic choices of our design professionals tell us anything about the interests or priorities of Irish architects? As is the case with our key Dublin city decision-makers, extracting meaningful conclusions is fraught with danger, as interpretations are potentially very subjective. We will instead let the data speak for themselves: 11% of our SuperGroupers live in apartments, 15% in purpose-built mews, and 37% live in a Victorian or Georgian terrace. Three in five (63%) of our SuperGroupers live in the postal code area of Dublin 2, 4 or 6. But perhaps surprisingly for a profession at the forefront of building sustainability, 26% live in detached houses in rural Ireland.

A spatial pattern of public patronage or private privilege?

So where exactly was the best of Irish architecture built at the height of the property boom?

Can a spatial analysis of the last decade of RIAI (Royal Institute of the Architects of Ireland) annual architectural awards in Dublin city tell us anything about the nature of city-making, public sponsorship or private support in the pursuit of excellence in Irish architectural design?

We have mapped out all of the RIAI award-winners over the past ten years in Dublin city to create our own GEOGRAPHY OF COOL, each brick a building block in the construction of a city of architectural quality.

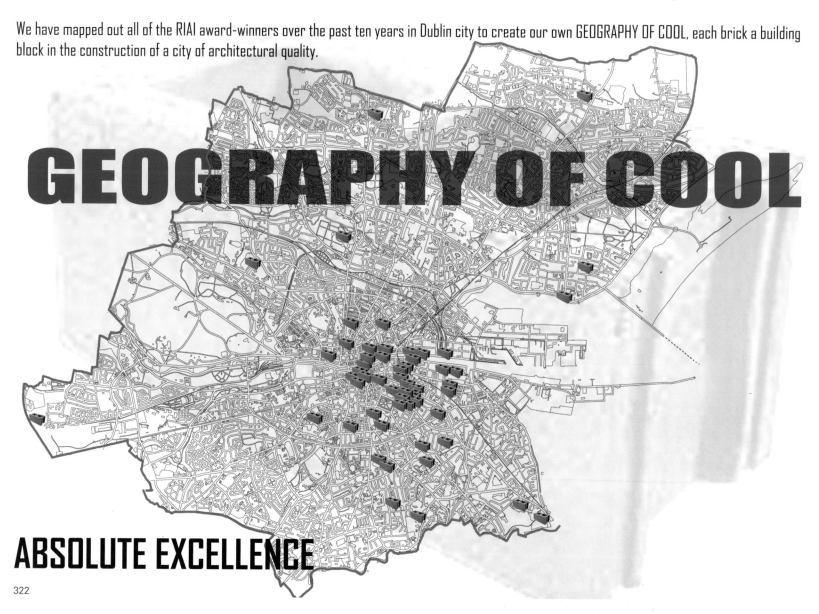

GEOGRAPHY OF COOL

ABSOLUTE EXCELLENCE

What if ?

What if the city required all municipal workers earning over €50,000 to live within the city's municipal boundary?

Would those workers currently living outside the city municipality leave their jobs or move their homes? Would it matter much to the city if they choose to move or stay? Would the City Council attract a more appropriate workforce? Would it reward more knowledgeable local decision-making or generate greater local conflicts of interest? Would those workers who objected to moving object because of personal inconvenience or inadequate and reduced housing or school choices? Would inadequate and reduced housing or school choices become greater policy priorities for those key decision-makers who chose to move to the city to retain their jobs? Would such policy choices reflect personal interest or simply a greater understanding of living in the city? Would other city-living concerns, such as anti-social behaviour, street-cleansing, the width of pavements or the speed of traffic, become a greater priority? Would the prioritisation of these urban issues directly benefit these workers, the city or both? Would the city's workforce be happier? Would the city be a better place to live?

Urban Dublin Monopoly

What does Monopoly, the world's most popular board game, tell us about 'urban Dublin'? Shrewsbury Road and Ailesbury Road are the most expensive addresses on the original Irish Monopoly board. Both are in Dublin city, both are in Ballsbridge, both are decidedly suburban. The most prestigious city addresses in Dublin have two-storey semi-detached houses. There are no restaurants or coffee shops on Shrewsbury Road or Ailesbury Road; there are no art galleries or museums, no designer stores.

Mayfair and Park Lane are the two most prestigious addresses on the London Monopoly board. Both Mayfair and Park Lane are thoroughly urban. Park Lane has a plentiful supply of fashionable and expensive hotels, bars and restaurants. Many of the buildings along this street are eight storeys tall, or more; many of the homes are apartments. The most prestigious address on the New York Monopoly board is Central Park. There are few two-storey, semi-detached houses overlooking Central Park.

Do the preferences of the rich drive local urban culture or does local urban culture drive the preference of the rich? If it is the former, how do you influence the preferences of the rich to deliver a successful city? Should urban regeneration in a suburban city with underperforming residential urbanism perhaps also focus on the urban needs and desires of the very rich? Achieving sustainable mixed-income areas is, after all, an important goal in any successful urban regeneration.

SHREWSBURY ROAD
SEMI-D

Taps and Things in 'Dubh Linn' and the Blue Lung

The city of Dublin, its policy-makers and inhabitants, have a somewhat peculiar, very often uncomfortable, and certainly ambiguous relationship with water. This is a city whose citizens were casually indifferent until very recently to the reality that it actually doesn't have enough of the 'right type' of water. It is hard, after all, to convince the citizens of the rainiest capital city in Europe, notwithstanding leaky Victorian pipes and a growing population, that municipal water charges are both economically and environmentally necessary to ensure continued uninterrupted flowing taps and flushing toilets.

Yet this is also a city that can be curiously blind to the fact that very often it has too much of the 'wrong type' of water. What other coastal city that endures rainfall on two out of every three days (summers included) would mimic landlocked and altogether sunnier Mexico City and Paris and organise a week-long artificial urban outdoor beach? The Dublin Docklands Development Authority (DDDA) despite a plentiful supply of accessible, local beaches, oddly did so.

In TAPS AND THINGS IN DUBH LINN we briefly reflect upon some of the watery peculiarities of Dublin city. Whether misunderstanding the realities or opportunities of rainfall, an apparent public indifference to the absence of municipal street-hosing and public toilets, or a tolerance of separate hot and cold and vanishing shop canopies, Dublin city would appear to be both confusing and confused in its embracement and rejection of water. It is perhaps ironic, perhaps a historical coincidence, that the depth of this somewhat schizophrenic, dark, mysterious, almost surreal relationship with water should manifest itself in a city called 'Dublin', the Hiberno-English derivative of the Irish *Dubh Linn*, commonly translated as 'Black Pool'.

Showers

In 'Black Pool' or *Dubh Linn*, the actual amount of rain falling on Dublin may be more than its residents desire but it less than many people imagine, particularly for those who have never visited the city. Total annual rainfall in the city is estimated at approximately 740mm. This compares favourably with Dallas, Boston, Rome, Lisbon, Sydney and

Beirut, all of which surprisingly have a higher average annual rainfall. Unlike the rain in many other cities, average hourly rainfall amounts in Dublin is actually quite low, ranging from 1mm to 2mm.[1] Dublin does, however, have the unenviable status of the least sunny European capital city, a mere four hours a day, and also boasts the highest number of rainy days in an average given year, some 246.[2]

Does it all have to be so overcast and civically damp? What if the city truly embraced its natural 'climatic disposition' and held an annual 'Urban Rain Festival' in the rainiest and also warmest month of August? And if it didn't actually rain, few would complain.

It's not as far-fetched as it sounds. Many other cities and cultures with similar rainy environments – Vancouver in Canada and almost all of Japan being probably the most noticeable examples – openly embrace their inclement weather through the use of creative, innovative architecture and landscape design. There are infinite watery possibilities: public space that understands rain, parks that embrace it, sculpture that plays with it, canopies and covers that magically unfold with it, views that delight in it, light and sound that dance to it. Celebrating our rain could be quirky and delightful. It could also be an unexpected and not-so-obvious economic urban driver of innovation technology. Most of all, it could be urban fun.

Flushing

If it rains too much in Dublin, the city flushes, publicly at least, too little. Dublin, a city of 500,000 people, has remarkably few public or municipal toilets. Most of the city centre's remaining public conveniences have been 'decommissioned' in the last decade. Many had become focal points for 'undesirable' urban activities and recreation – gay-cruising or drug-taking being the most inconvenient or problematic for the civic authorities.

The closure of these city facilities provided a unique opportunity to commemorate and celebrate a particular facet of Dublin urban social space. Prior to its encasement in cement, the authors of REDRAWING DUBLIN temporarily converted the men's public toilet at O'Connell Street

Motti Ruimy & Paul Kearns

Cordially invite you to visit
at your convenience

'Urban Urinal'

in the men's public toilet on the central
promenade in O'Connell Street Dublin 1.

from Wednesday 27th February to
Saturday 2nd March inclusive.

A.Y.O.R.

The public toilet at O'Connell Street will be
permanently decommissioned from March 3rd
2002 after over a century of continuous use.
This is a commemoration and celebration of
a disappearing public space.

Sponsored and supported by Dublin City Council.

R.S.V.P: urbanurinal@netscape.net

Look before you leak: art works compete for attention with more mundane concerns in the public toilets on Dublin's O'Connell Street   DECLAN SHANAHAN

Writing's on the toilet wall as Dublin city council gives art more exposure

Richard Oakley

IN Paris they have the Louvre, but for four days in Dublin, we have just had 'the Loo-vre'.

At least that's what some of the city's own might have dubbed the men's public toilets in O'Connell Street if they'd realised it had become the unlikely venue for an art exhibition.

Users of the public convenience have, during the past week, found themselves looking at photographs of the toilets they were using instead of the bare wall they would usually focus on. But who descended the toilets' dirty steps to take photos of urinals, who put those photos on the wall and for what purpose?

Israeli artist Motti Ruimy is the answer to the first question. Ruimy's work was displayed after permission was given by Dublin City Council and is the first of a series of similar art projects that have been commissioned.

The idea is to have works of art appear and disappear in parts of the city where they are least expected, but where they are likely to be seen by people as they go about their everyday business.

It's a low-cost plan, conceived to compensate for the shortage of public gallery space and will aim to celebrate ordinary buildings and public spaces.

The plan is not to give too much notice of the exhibitions, with the idea being to leave it to people to stumble upon them instead. The council is currently looking for new venues.

The O'Connell Street display was intended to explore the concept of the disappearing city. The toilets, which were known to be pick-up spots for gay men, are due to be demolished soon to make way for the millennium spike. The photographs on display feature text from a website on which gay men post messages.

An explanation of the work stated that it "looked at the physical space, not as an entity in itself but as a shell which houses layers of social activity". The toilet work, which was exhibited until yesterday, was a "a celebration of the activities or lives that engaged the space".

If you didn't see it last week, you've missed it, but keep your eyes open from now on. The next exhibition may be coming to a McDonalds, a shop or an old building near you.

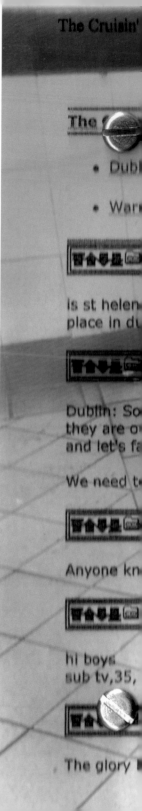

Dublin

ct

27 04:43pm

%$^%$ on Tuesday, February 19, 2002 - 09:54 am:

oing in dundalk or has it died went there last friday and it was emty as fuck whats going on.is there a new

---

okingForCock on Sunday, February 17, 2002 - 12:09 am:

ets in the Kylemore in Stephen's Green Shopping Centre are closed until further notice for refurbishment, so oilets in Dunnes in Stephen's Green are dead. There is never anyone in Royal Hibernian Way or Powerscourt - he toilets in Stephen's Green Park are just to full of Junkies. Where are you guys going now??

on a new venue or revive an old one!

---

on on Monday, February 11, 2002 - 12:27 pm:

spots around Dundalk??? Horny as hell needing relief!

---

ssylouise (Sissylouise) on Sunday, February 10, 2002 - 08:10 pm:

for real men, northside, week nites. any takers?

---

ffdub (Joffdub) on Wednesday, January 30, 2002 - 07:30 pm:

athmines shopping centre has been covered by a metal plate, alas.

into an interactive installation space. For one week, the underground Victorian urinals operated simultaneously as both a public toilet and gallery space.

Splash

If tourism is critical to the city's economy, and the unique, vibrant, Dublin pub scene a vitally important contributor to the life of the city, a particular byproduct of that vibrancy certainly is not. Yet, even the visibly challenging 'outcomes' or gut-discharge, in the very literal, wrenching sense of that word, or urination on the street, unfortunately does not seem to have shifted the issue of municipal street-hosing up the policy agenda in Dublin.

In the absence of widespread inner-urban street-hosing, we recommend 'Text Splash', a low-cost, self-policing street-cleaning solution. Whenever or wherever one encounters a 'SPLASH' (Street Personal-Liquid Action Shouldn't Happen), text its exact street location to a City Council cleansing hotline. The citizen takes the civic initiative and direct control of their own streets, the city authorities save on time and resources with discriminate and immediate cleansing of one the worst, but all-too-common Dublin street offences.

Canopies

Perhaps Dublin city's dependency on rain to clean its inner-urban streets explains a municipal equivocation as to the benefit of shop canopies in protecting its pedestrians from unwanted showers. Dublin city has a rich history of high street shop canopies, as evidenced in many photographs of the city dating from 1880s through to the 1940s. The function of these shop canopies has remained pretty much the same over the last century: they protect goods on display from the sun and shelter customers from the rain while window shopping or walking along the street. Yet, despite this aesthetic and functional legacy, the City Council today has a tendency to frown on any proposals for similar such canopies being installed, viewing them as either visual clutter or a potential source of unattractive and uncontrollable advertising.

There are exceptions, however. Certain stores are perceived as special and thus can be relied upon to behave or act responsibly – Brown Thomas and Weir's of Grafton Street being notable examples. Some premises and streets have embraced canopies without permit or permission, and are all the more engaging because of them.

Summer 2010

Somehow, when they look old, they look exhaustingly beautiful

331

H₂O view

Perhaps if we acknowledged the benefit of street canopies while looking from the outside in (window shopping), we would better understand the pleasure of viewing water while protected, sitting inside looking out. Dublin has remarkably few places where one can dine in a restaurant and simultaneously enjoy, apart from the rain, the view of water. This is somewhat odd for a city built on a river with a harbour waterfront, an extensive sweep of bay, and an built-up suburban coastline. If dining with a view of water is rare, dining from a height with a view of water is almost non-existent. This, perhaps, is explained in part by a planning policy that restricts commercial development along the coast and significant building heights almost everywhere, but particularly along both the river and the suburban coastline. This is a shame for a city and a recreational loss for its inhabitants and visitors. Dining with a view of water remains an under-exploited economic and social opportunity.

Dining alfresco in a city with fluid and changeable weather is a challenge. With a little imagination and thoughtful design, extensive glazed viewing would afford both comfort and an enormous opportunity to take advantage of the often dramatic skies and stormy coastlines. Imagining a better Dublin sometimes requires nothing more than simply opening one's eyes to present challenging realities, and creatively seeing them as exciting future possibilities.

Plughole

If Dubliners do not fully exploit the visual drama of water as a recreational opportunity, they seem equally adverse to the idea of paying for the economic cost of consuming it. Dublin is rare in a European municipal context in that it does not impose domestic charges for the use of water. The local arguments against water charges are many and well rehearsed, but none is particularly convincing. It is argued the installation costs of metering are too high. This argument is increasingly environmentally and economically unsound as the public cost of repairing leaky pipes escalates and the threat of water shortages potentially restricts the smart, spatial, sustainable growth of Dublin city.

Some predict that it would unduly negatively affect the poor. This is more a case of political laziness. International models for water-pricing provide a multiplicity of solutions in subsidising and protecting the poorest and most vulnerable in society. Others argue that water-metering would not materially affect consumption. This is simply economic illiteracy. The economic laws governing the interaction of supply, demand and price is

WE COULD HAVE BEEN SO GOOD TOGETHER

Dear Paul,

Further to your enquiry on the use of individual taps in bathrooms or similar locations.

The provision of water supplies and the development of water distribution installations in Ireland came directly from UK or British practises. This practise required that hot and cold water supplies be kept separate to avoid risk from contamination that may be presented by stored hot water that is supplied with cold water from storage cisterns that may be compromised by the ingress of various type of foreign matter.

Mixer taps have been very popular on the European continent for many years, and Churchill first encountered a wash basin mixing tap during a wartime visit to Moscow in 1942, where having sampled being able to wash his hands under mixed running water he resolved to use the new method whenever possible. Whatever about Churchill, the use of mixer taps for bathroom use did not develop in the UK or Ireland until recent years (1990s), and still has not become the preferred method in most new residential developments. The reason for this may be cost, as the price of a bath or basin mixing set could be twice that of individual hot and cold taps. In other words, builders do not wish to incur extra cost for which they will receive no additional benefit.

There are no technical reasons why mixer taps cannot be used for bathroom fittings at present; cost of materials in real terms has reduced due to the single market and there is a greater range of products available than ever before. Prices are also keener than previously and with younger persons perhaps being a little bit more aware of the aesthetic value/quality of such fittings the use of such may develop in the future.

Regards,

John   *Dublin City Council Engineering Department*

pretty much the same for all tradable goods. Water is no exception. Domestic water-supply, if supplied for free, freely and wastefully flows. Not surprisingly, Dublin ranks poorly in water sustainability. In a comparative survey of urban 'green' credentials in Europe, Dublin does not fare too well with regard to water sustainability, coming 16th out of thirty surveyed cities.[3] The study revealed that Dublin as a city consumes 128 cubic metres of water per person annually. This is more than double that of London (58 cubic m) Amsterdam (53 cubic m) Brussels (54 cubic m) and Berlin (55 cubic m), cities with similar 'rainy' climates.[4]

Taps

If Irish taps flow freely, they tend also somewhat bizarrely to flow separately. For decades, Dublin homes have been installed with independent hot and cold taps or faucets in bathrooms. This has only very recently begun to change. This deliberate, somewhat cruel separation of a natural engineering pairing inevitably leads, in the interest of personal safety, to inventive washing solutions. The explanations for this are as varied as they are amusing. The fact that few native Dubliners view the historical separation of their cold and hot tap as neither odd nor inconvenient is in itself peculiar.

Rush

Yachting, fishing, swimming and 'promenading' down windy piers are but a few of the many coastal pastimes of Dubliners. There is, however, one rapidly disappearing and little documented coastal 'pastime' – caravanning. Before it became fashionable or financially possible for middle-class Dublin families to own a second home on some relatively inaccessible windswept west of Ireland coastline, many Dublin working-class families had, in fact, already bought into the idea of owning a second seaside home of their own. These homes, often located just a few miles from the primary home on the rather more accessible but equally windswept east coast of Dublin, were usually purchased for a fraction of the price of a cottage in Dingle in or Doolin.

They basically served the same function, however. This included an escape from suburbia, fewer domestic chores and responsibilities, access to endless sandy beaches, a sense of the great outdoors, big skies (grey or not) and a general sense of wellbeing with not much to do, and all the more delighted because of it. These second homes, invariably known as mobile homes (although they rarely, if ever, moved anywhere) were – and to some extent still are – to be found in huge numbers in

never-ending rows of neatly packed plots in a patchwork of fields dotted up and down the coastline of north county Dublin from Donabate to Balbriggan.

Perhaps these mobile-home-owners were not imbued with the same sense of 'cultural' self-awakening on their annual August summer holiday as the owners of the Doolin or Dingle cottages. Perhaps it didn't matter. The smell and hissing noise of those impossibly delicate gas lights, the nightly search for undiscovered earwigs, the slight dampness, the unwanted sand, late-night fish and chips, flickering torches in the blackness of the night all added to the romance and the atmosphere. One, of course, never owned a caravan, big or small, new or old. Somebody else owned a caravan; you, instead, were the owner of a mobile home.

The high-water mark of caravan holidaying was probably the late 1970s and early '80s. The coastal village of Rush in north county Dublin, at one time the resting place for thousands of mobile homes, was the capital's retreat for caravan culture. The population of Rush in the '70s and '80s trebled in early summer as thousands of families descended on its caravan parks.

The tide has somewhat retreated on caravanning. Rush has evolved in the last twenty years into a commuter suburb of Dublin. The charm of the arrival of the annual touring carnival is a memory fast fading. Two weeks in the sun for a family of four, topped up by the odd budget-flight weekend break to a continental city, is now far more common and increasingly far less costly than the annual upkeep of the average caravan site.

Excursions in Identity
Finding the 'Real' Dublin City

There is something of an unspoken taboo about Dubliners' attitude to Dublin. It's an open secret that not an insignificant proportion of the citizens of this city have a genuinely ambivalent attitude to their home town. This is a confused and confusing relationship, a low-key, almost embarrassed affection. Dubliners are more likely to verbalise a defensive emotive pride than articulate a civic or passionate case for the virtues of their city.

Geography and class complicates the relationship. Perhaps Dublin is not particularly unique in that regard. The fact that the overwhelming majority of the citizens of this city live in suburban two-storey housing possibly affects a sense of civic urban attachment, or civic detachment to be more precise, to the capital city.

This isn't a forced or exiled detachment. Dubliners, unlike the citizens of the cities they tend to most admire, Barcelona, Copenhagen, New York or Paris, seem to 'voluntarily' choose and genuinely desire to live in suburbia. Perhaps it is a false choice. Poor-quality high-density inner-city housing choice and anti-social edginess deter many from choosing an urban life. Voluntary or otherwise, all of this suburban Dublin elasticity generates a profound sense that 'the city' is over there, or, more precisely, in there, 'in town'. It's somewhere else, but wherever it is, it's not quite here, not in our suburban cul-de-sac.

Further complicating and stretching the concept of civic urban identity is the significant number of people who live in distant outlying suburbs beyond the city boundary proper, but nevertheless live within the historic county of Dublin and continue to profess a loyalty or attachment of sorts to Dublin city. Thousands more Dublin city residents who may have lived in the city for decades but who were born in other Irish counties continue to express an equivocal attitude to their adopted county.

There is a further complication to Dublin city identity. This is the peculiar but real distinction between the inner city and the city centre. There is, of course, no line on a map, no street sign that designates where the so-called city centre ends and the inner city begins. For the uninitiated, the untrained ear or the casual foreign observer, the inner city and city centre may sound deceptively similar and interchangeable. For Dubliners, their meaning is instinctively clear, their social realities, if not their exact

geographies, acutely understood. The city centre may be an interesting place to visit; the inner city, however, continues to be perceived as an undesirable place to live. It is commonly accepted in suburban Dublin that if nobody really lives in the city centre, certainly nobody actually desires to live in the inner city. It is simply an unquestioned given for the vast majority of suburban Dubliners that those who live in the inner city do so not out of choice, but out of economic necessity.

City detachment is reinforced by the very weak political and fiscal relationship between city and citizen. The City Council doesn't raise taxes on its domestic residents. There are no domestic water charges. The Council has no responsibility for policing and little responsibility for public transport. For most Dubliners, the city cleans your street, collects your rubbish, may or may not grant you or your neighbour planning permission. Few Dubliners are capable of naming their Lord Mayor, a largely ribbon-cutting, ceremonial post. Even fewer could name the unelected City Manager, the real source of power.

Perhaps a quasi-political Dublin civic identity is not so important if other, more tangible or meaningful identities fill the void. The citizen as participant in culture may have more meaning for collective city identity. Here too, however, a contemporary shared Dublin badge of identity is missing. Dublin city is rightly acknowledged as a thriving cultural capital. It is host to many diverse music, literary, cinematic and visuals arts events. As successful as they are, do they promote or reinforce a tangible or popular broad Dublin city identity?

In recent years, 'Open House' and 'Culture Night' have greatly expanded the idea of the city as a shared living cultural space.[1] They have successfully excited a strand of middle-class suburban Dubliner, in particular, to the possibilities of urban life, however fleeting. But they have not quite managed to capture the imagination or participation of vast swathes of working-class suburban Dublin.[1] The actual largest annual cultural festival to be held in the city, and the one that truly captures the attention of most Dubliners, is the St Patrick's Day celebrations. This is, however, a national holiday and more a badge of Irishness. Dublin, the capital city, merely acts as a stage to host the country's largest parade.

Perhaps sport in Dublin can fly the flag for the city. Most major sporting occasions in the capital, however, have either a distinctly national or local flavour. The national soccer team may play in Dublin, but Dublin is not a real player at club or city football on the UEFA European stage. The UEFA Europa cup football final is scheduled to be played in the Aviva Stadium in 2011, but many Dublin soccer fans can only look on with envy at the city drama and civic excitement that the UEFA's Champion League Football brings to comparatively similarly sized but arguably less cosmopolitan cities such as Liverpool, Valencia, Porto, Turin (Juventus) or Lyon.

Rugby has either a distinctive national or regional appeal. The annual Six Nations Championship and the Rugby Union Heineken Cup are undoubtedly huge sporting occasions, and, in recent years, have been spectacularly successful for Irish participants, but neither can reasonably be described as having a particularly Dublin identity, other than the city may play host. At local or schoolboy level, rugby generates little genuine interest across Dublin beyond of a small collection of fee-paying private schools and the families involved.

Perhaps it's the architectural drama of the stadium, perhaps it's simply the resonance of the blue colours of the team and the city, but the one notable exception to this eerie lack of a Dublin sporting sense is when the GAA Dublin senior football team play at Croke Park.[2] It is somewhat ironic that one of the strongest collective badges of identity for the capital city is the GAA given the organisation's strong affinity and origins in rural Ireland.

Some of Dublin's strongest traditional badges of identity, the Guinness Brewery, its Georgian architecture or Joyce's *Dubliners*, are obviously not rural, nor indeed suburban; they are, however, historic. Their historical story is nevertheless an unashamedly modern one that remains relevant to contemporary Dublin. This is the story of progressive Georgian (and Victorian) construction techniques employed to build a residential and industrial urban city. Perversely, the drama of the 19th-century towering industrial skylines of Guinness, the 18th-century urban vision of Georgian town house building or the liberating insights into the suffocating social conservatism in Joyce's *Dubliners* have instead been smothered and reinvented to create a city of nostalgia, a city of urban restraint, a city of romanticised myth.

The industrial architecture of the Guinness Brewery, founded upon an ambition to further technological progress, has today been rewritten and employed instead as a tool for determining 21st-century building heights for the city. Guinness is in danger of becoming a historic Disneyland, a frozen urban landscape of sculptures and mausoleums.

The architecture of the Georgian era also pushed the boundaries of building technology to construct the most delightful and light-filled urban residential rooms and spaces. This was an unparalleled Dublin urban vision (and delivery) of high-density inner-city luxury homes. This 18th-century Georgian urban vision, however, has been profoundly damaged over the past hundred years. Mid-20th-century indifference that led to brutal acts of demolition has given way to a narrow revisionist 20th- and 21st-century attachment to rigid Georgian geometries. Conservation groups have increasingly conscripted these geometries as fixed benchmarks for determining rigid street parapet heights and plot widths.

The Georgians valued the drama and excitement of city-living. Looking down onto the city's street from the comfort of their living room, the *piano nobile* was, in effect, a prime seat or viewing box in the theatre of daily urban life. Only latterly did Dubliners shun the delight of urban voyeurism in favour of the hidden domestic defensiveness of the Victorian and suburban garden. With their desire for high-density living, delightful volumes, spacious dimensions, new technologies, and an eager embracement of relatively tall, mass residential housing, one can only imagine what the Georgian architects and engineers might be building today.

The literary heritage of James Joyce, including the annual Bloomsday celebrations, has also been hijacked by a form of anti-urbanism, this time by a kind of clownish annual suburban Bloomsday theatricality that bears little relationship to the acerbic urban social commentary of the author himself. There is, thus, an almost invisible but decidedly revisionist reinterpretation or muddled understanding of historical urban Dublin. This misunderstanding of Dublin city's past is a recent suburban creation grafted onto and acted out on an urban stage. It is a creation that mythologises an inner city that few have much desire to visit, let alone live in. How many of the costumed Sandycove suburban enthusiasts of Ryan's Pub on Parkgate Street actually visit Dublin's inner city outside of June 16th? It is a city of *Me Jewel and Darlin' Dublin* and *Gur Cake and Coal Blocks*.[3]

Yet, in the very midst of this city of nostalgia – an early 20th-century literary city housed in a fragmented shell of a late 18th-century built city – a new, truly urban Dublin dynamic is emerging. This new urban Dublin is cosmopolitan, confident, open and tolerant. It is a city of diversity, where foreign nationals make up just under a fifth of the population, where social and cultural interaction just happens.

Its interests are neither Georgian nor Joycean. This is a place of real, perhaps struggling, urbanism that doesn't look back but looks forward. It's comfortable in its skin, and for the most part it bubbles and excites, mixes and evolves beyond the real notice or touch of most suburban Dubliners and, critically, most of its suburban-living decision-makers. Might this new fledgling urbanism best capture the excitement and attraction of a future collective Dublin identity?

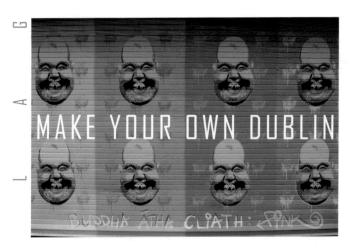

MAKE YOUR OWN DUBLIN

BUDDHA ATHA CLIATH : PINK

city / suburb

football Dublin

The Liffey

MAKE YOUR OWN DUBLIN. BUILD A.Y.O.R. NO PLANNING PERMISSION REQUIRED.

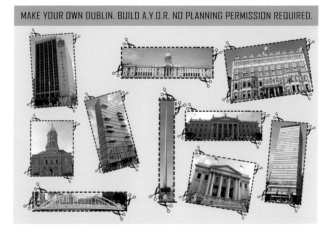

Bloom's Dublin

city I.O.

northsider / southsider

west / east

other dublins

Liffey / bay

Conclusion

Why, after a decade and a half of investment in the inner city, do so many 'Dubliners' choose a one- or two-hour commute to the alternative choice of living in the centre of Dublin? And why is it that the affluent and influential of Dublin city – unlike their counterparts in Paris, New York and London – choose not to live in the centre of their city?

In REDRAWING DUBLIN we have attempted to deconstruct the psyche of an entire city to answer those very stark, simple questions. In so doing, we have painted a particular picture of a city, debunked some urban myths, deconstructed municipal policy and created alternate city realities. We have mapped and drawn multiple statistical facts, from population densities and open-space geographies, to evolving home-sizes and rejected building-heights. Most of all we have pursued the facts and truths, often unspoken, that have shaped those realities.

Facts are important to the subject of city-making. Making sense of exponentially growing data is vital to the successful making of any city. The capacity to translate all this data, to captivate the citizen by telling interesting stories or painting urban pictures is important. It communicates knowledge and stimulates civic awareness. It democratises urbanism. Perhaps, most importantly, it separates the truth from the bunkum and frippery, and forces us to confront realities too often glossed over, misunderstood or conveniently ignored.

Understanding information opens a window to both the challenges of the present and the opportunities of the future. It also gives us valuable insight into past decision-making and, thus, our past mistakes. If an extensive, high-density and successful urbanism is to emerge in Dublin city, its civic decision-makers must learn from those past mistakes.

To learn from our mistakes, we first need to acknowledge them. In CELTIC TIGER METROPOLITAN and HOW THE EAST WAS DONE we mapped the uncontrolled suburban sprawl of housing development during the fifteen-year boom between 1991 and 2006. In CITY EXPANSION OR CITY ECLIPSE we showed how the population of the functional area of Dublin City Council has fallen, relative to its 'exurban' fringe (Fingal, Meath, Kildare and Wicklow), from a figure of exact parity to just 71% over the fifteen years of the Celtic Tiger boom.

Suburban sprawl is, of course, the outcome of push and pull factors, the relative attraction of suburban life versus city-living. Before we castigate the unsustainable commuter or ineffective regional planning, we need to reflect on the factors that have dissuaded many potential urban families from choosing Smithfield over Skerries or The Liberties over Leixlip. The diversity, quality and affordability of housing is critical in this choice. The quality of high-density urban housing built in the inner city of Dublin during the Celtic Tiger boom period has, for the most part, been very mediocre. Many homes are too small, poorly designed and badly finished. Apartments in extensive areas of Dublin city have become synonymous with short-term living, the equivalent of yellow-pack starter homes, to be discarded at the earliest opportunity. Not so much a first step on a housing ladder but rather a temporary, if lucky, transitional stop in a residential limbo.

An acknowledgment by city decision-makers of those past housing mistakes is necessary if, for no other reason, than the fact that the vast majority of Dublin's citizens continue to remain sceptical, even hostile, to embracing high-density apartment-living. Most are attached to the real benefits and comforts of a suburban two-storey house. Most, however, have been denied a real housing choice. A three-bedroom semi-detached home in a safe leafy suburb is not the equivalent of a one-bedroom single-aspect home facing onto a noisy and car-choked street littered with evidence of anti-social behaviour. Despite or maybe because of this attachment to low-density suburbia, Dublin City Council, through a mix of land-use zoning and housing policy, seeks to encourage future householders of the city to aspire to live in high-density apartment-style developments of up to a hundred homes per hectare.

Before the City Council presumes to persuade Dubliners of the environmental merits and personal benefits of high-density urban living, the city needs to offer a real choice to those who might contemplate an urban life. Until the inner city offers a proper supply of spacious, well-designed, affordable high-density homes, quality public schools, safe local parks, and clean and green streets, an extensive, quality, everyday urbanism is unlikely to emerge.

Yet despite unprecedented level of both public and private investment in Dublin city in recent years, with enormous progress made in the provision of hard infrastructure, bridges, light-rail lines and architectural set pieces, Dublin's inner city – in particular, inner-urban residential Dublin – remains fragmented and patchy. One of the primary challenges for the city over the next ten years is to consolidate this patchy and fragile embryonic urbanism. Consolidation requires a considerable shift in thinking and ambition on how to sustain and support inner-city urban living.

If urban Dublin has too few affordable quality homes, it also has too few great schools in inner-city Dublin. Few of the students who attend the better schools in the inner city live locally; instead they commute from wealthier distant suburbs. Persuading middle-income parents to choose to live close to the inner-city or city-centre school of their choice, and thus assist in building inner-urban mixed-income communities, remains a particular difficulty for Dublin.

Mixed-income communities thrive best. They attract investment and sustain a diversity of local shops and businesses. They also assist in combating social segregation, offering role models in communities blighted by poverty and low aspiration. Sustaining mixed-income communities also requires a stronger focus on the 'softer' and, in many ways, much more difficult challenges of managing inner-city urbanism. These 'softer' challenges are simple to describe but difficult to realise. They include clean and safe streets, pleasant local green spaces, greater pedestrian priority, and playgrounds that parents feel comfortable to visit with young children.

How a city sustains and manages clean, green and safe streets, how it delivers ordinary but quality public city spaces for children and teenagers, is probably the most important test of a city's commitment to inner-urban living. Most of the 'authors' of Dublin's fledgling urbanism live in the suburbs, and those lifetime suburban experiences and expectations cloud or colour the imagination and understanding of the challenges and ambition of Dublin's inner city. It is important that these 'authors' – planners, architects, city administrators – understand how to manage the real conflicts and tensions that exist between urban and suburban Dublin. Those conflicts are as numerous as they are varied. Managing this conflict effectively and fairly requires ensuring an equitable prioritisation of needs.

Dublin's inner city and city centre continue to remain in thrall to the private car. Pedestrians remain secondary. Too many radial and inner-urban roads into or in the city (Church Street, Dorset Street, Blackhall Place, North King Street, Queen Street, Cork Street, Amiens Street and the city quays), if efficient for vehicular movement, are joyless for city-living pedestrians, severing emerging fragile urban communities into isolated, fragmented city blocks of apartments. Acknowledging this vehicular slicing and dicing of city-living is not to invoke a traditional and often sterile debate of car versus pedestrian, but to rethink the balance between the urban-living pedestrian and the suburban-travelling car.

Successful urban living, despite popular perceptions to the contrary, is not hostile to either the ownership or movement of the private car. It simply endeavours to seek an appropriate balance. Many inner-city dwellers own and enjoy the benefits of a car. These are relatively environmentally friendly cars, very often remaining in 'storage', used only for recreation, supermarket trips or the occasional trip out of the city to visit family and friends in the suburbs or the countryside. It is somewhat odd, therefore, that a city council favouring high-density development

1994Q4 84,068 ▲1.4%   **1995Q1** 83,281 ▲-0.9%   **1995Q2** 87,578 ▲5.2%   **1995Q3** 87,096 ▼-0.6%   **1995Q4** 88,717 ▲1.9%

discriminates against high-density, sustainable, urban living in not allowing those who live in apartment blocks the same rights to on-street car parking as those afforded to their fellow citizens and neighbours in two-storey housing.

Taking urban living seriously requires tackling difficult issues. Sometimes it requires making politically unpopular choices and sticking to them; the minor extension of an already existing speed limit in Dublin's city centre (in the initial days it was stringently enforced) dramatically civilised the pedestrian experience of walking along parts of the city quays. Yet this modest, urban-friendly initiative was greeted with derision from suburban motorists when first announced and the city council is under enormous pressure since to abandon it. The 2007 variation in the Dublin City Development Plan to promote larger apartments constituted real and practical progress in advancing the cause of quality high-density Dublin urbanism. It is, however, a policy under constant threat of dilution as the economy and construction industry stalls. An anti-apartment prejudice has rapidly gained acceptance amongst banks and, somewhat oddly, amongst many in the architectural profession.

The successful management of high-density inner-urban residential living also requires civic assurances that people, their homes, their business and their investment decisions, will not be sacrificed to easy short-term choices. The city needs to resist the temptation of seemingly efficient but shortsighted and superficially 'low-cost' choices, such as concentrating socially challenging land-uses such as homeless hostels or methadone centres in fragile regeneration areas, areas often suffering acute social disadvantage. Poor management of the overspill impact of these facilities compounds local deprivation. Similarly, poor management of socially difficult, often psychologically vulnerable state-dependent tenants in private apartment blocks is lethal to sustaining inner-city regeneration. Devolving responsibility to management companies to manage anti-social behaviour not only abdicates the city or state of responsibility, but imposes unsustainable costs on urban living. Civic indifference to any or all of these issues is both damaging for city business and disadvantaged communities, and potentially devastating for an emerging Dublin urbanism.

These are just a sample of the urban tests of a city's commitment to real urbanism. There is no escaping the fact that some require additional public funding; most, however, simply require a new way of thinking, thinking that believes a quality, walkable and extensive city life is really a possibility for Dublin's inner city. Unfortunately. there are many unspoken barriers to imagining and delivering this urban possibility. Probably the most pernicious and reactionary is the belief – a kind of the bigotry of low

expectation of place – that inner-city Dublin can never aspire to be a genuinely attractive place to live for middle-income Dubliners. This particular view is commonly held, not just by most Dubliners, but by many of its civic decision-makers.

If the imagination of urban ambition is often constrained, the choice of language used in the making of the city is too often unrestrained. Sometimes language is as important as actions. Inappropriate euphemisms such 'gated communities', 'transients' or 'MUDs' (a legislative acronym for multiple-unit developments) communicate hostility and ignorance of the complexity of urban living. That complexity and diversity requires fresh thinking.

Existing city models of civic participation and community-engagement also require radical rethinking. There is a multiplicity of communities living in the inner city and city centre, most of whom have no desire to participate in community consultation workshops in draughty halls with well-meaning local authority officials. What is required is more observation, analysis and 24-hour understanding of city systems. We need to get out and look at what makes a street work, why some streets seem to fail, why people walk 'here' and not 'there', why certain parks are closed or empty, why some are edgy or attractive.

Just as Dublin city urbanism is diverse and complex, we should open our minds to the diversity of other cities, cities we do not ordinarily think we have much to learn from. Great urbanism doesn't begin and end in north-west Europe. How many Dublin decision-makers would dare seek urban-design metro lessons from Mexico City or high-density apartment inspiration from Tel Aviv or São Paulo? We also need to sharpen our understanding of those models we have become overly dependent upon, if not somewhat lazily addicted to. Copenhagen is regularly cited by the Irish planning and architectural establishment as an urban model for Dublin. Copenhagen is a wonderful city, regularly topping international rankings as one of the best cities to live in. Perhaps we misunderstand that the success of its quality, ordinary urbanism, its pedestrian-friendly streets and extensive cycle network is dependent less on attention to design detail than it is on high municipal tax rates which facilitate the delivery and, critically, the management of public services, or a real commitment to urban living that's reflected in the areas key city decision-makers choose to live?

Where our urban decision-makers chose to live is important. Is it not reasonable to believe that the future city planner, city manager and city architect, the sources of potentially creative ideas and real power, should, like the city's lord mayor, all live in the city, preferably in the heart of the city they profess to lead? ? It is unlikely that the civic leaders of Barcelona, Copenhagen, Paris, New York or London would choose to live in distant suburbs. It may be controversial to suggest that future Dublin inner-city regeneration should focus on the aspirations of the wealthy, but it is a incontrovertible fact that it is in the interests of the poorest residents of the inner city that the quality of their local neighbourhood should be attractive enough to entice the most affluent citizens of the city.

Why is inner-urban Dublin so important? Because after fifteen tumultuous years of an economic boom, Dublin's inner city and city centre continue to remain both the city's and, perhaps, the State's greatest economic opportunity and most significant social or civic challenge. That challenge is the realisation of a simple but powerful ambition to make Dublin, particularly inner-city Dublin, a world-class city for all its citizens. A world-class city may have become a jaded term for the cynics, the doubters, the naysayers. Ambition for some will always remain hubris for others.

REDRAWING DUBLIN believes it is possible that Dublin can one day become an economically thriving, socially inclusive and culturally dynamic walkable city that extends beyond a tiny city-centre core to include an extensive, high-density, well-connected, safe, clean and green inner city stretching from Heuston to Poolbeg, from Summerhill to Rialto. This enlarged urban space will be a well-managed, civilising, inspired and inspiring city. At its simplest and at its best, it will be a truly desirable place to live. Understanding this possibility and communicating it to others is perhaps the biggest challenge facing those responsible for designing, planning and managing urban Dublin over the next fifteen years and beyond.

References

abbreviations
Census   Census of Ireland
DoEHLG   Department of the Environment, Heritage & Local Government

I – BEYOND THE PALE

METROBUSLAND
[1] The number of Bus Éireann journeys to and from Dublin city centre every day (source: Bus Éireann timetable).

IN SEARCH OF THE METROPOLITAN REGION
[1] The Dublin Regional Authority was one of eight regional authorities established in Ireland with effect from 1st January 1994 under the provisions of the Local Government Act 1994.

CONTIGUOUS METROPOLITAN
[1] By 'areas' we mean those geographic units or electoral divisions for which small area population statistics (SAPS) data is available from the Census of Ireland. There are 3,409 electoral divisions in Ireland, 162 of them in the Dublin City Council area
[2] Census 2006. The town (electoral division) of Skerries has a population of 8,175 and a density of 3,283 people per square kilometre. The town (two urban electoral divisions) of Arklow has a population of 11,712 and a density of 1,762 people per square kilometre. Both densities are considerable higher than our 'Contiguous Metropolitan'.
[3] Census 2006. 59.6% of the total area of Fingal County Council (accommodating 86.7% of its population or 208,000 persons) forms part of our Contiguous Metropolitan region. Comparative figures for Meath are 3.1% area, 10.4% population; Kildare 4.8% area, 28.5% population; Wicklow 2.7% area, 36.8% population.
[4] Census 2006. The Dublin City Council area has a population of 506,000 and an area of 114km^2. Our Contiguous Metropolitan has a population of 1.25 million and an area of 797km^2.
[5] New York City Housing Authority.
[6] City of Los Angeles.

METROPOLIA
[1] Census 2006. The electoral division of Mountjoy B in Dublin's North Inner City had a Polish population of 373 persons or 11.3% of the total population in 2006.

HOW THE EAST WAS DONE
[1] Census 2006, Theme 6: 2(a) – Number of permanent private households by year house built, 2006.
[2] *Ibid*. The number of permanent private households accommodated in homes built prior to 1990 versus the number of permanent private households accommodated in homes built between 1991 and 2006 is as follows: Kildare – 29,442 and 28,761; Meath – 26,384 and 25,616; Fingal – 34,273 and 38,907.
[3] *Annual Housing Statistics Bulletin, 2009* (DoEHLG) and Census 2006. Dublin City Council housing typology breakdown: total 190,711; detached 9,012; semi-detached 45,826; terrace 70,519; purpose-built flat/apartment 43,140; converted flat/apartment 11,189; bedsit 4,829; not stated 6,196.
[4] *Ibid*.
[5] Census 2006, Theme 6: 1(a) – Number of private households by type of accommodation.That figure rises to 8.9% in the town of Naas (Naas Urban electoral division) – 6,506 households; and 7.2 % in the town of Navan (Navan Urban and Naval Rural electoral divisions) – 9,167 households, the largest towns in Kildare and Meath respectively.
[6] *Annual Housing Statistics Bulletin, 2009* (DoEHLG) and Census 2006. Wicklow Council housing typology breakdown: total 42,472; detached 19,232; semi-detached 12,395; terrace 6,809; purpose-built flat/apartment 2,150; converted flat/apartment 860; bedsit 154; not stated 872). Meath County Council housing typology breakdown: total 53,575; detached 29,632; semi-detached 15,306; terrace 4,857; purpose-built flat/apartment 2,277; converted flat/apartment 530; bedsit 96; not stated 877). Kildare County Council housing typology breakdown: total 60,578; detached 25,531; semi-detached 23,510; terrace 6,105; purpose-built flat/apartment 3,452; converted flat/apartment 664; bedsit 160; not stated 1,156). Fingal County Council housing typology breakdown: total 80,085; detached 16,154; semi-detached 36,791; terrace 15,119; purpose-built flat/apartment 9,397; converted flat/apartment 511; bedsit 168; not stated 1945). Dun Laoghaire-Rathdown County Council housing typology breakdown: total 68,375; detached 15,808; semi-detached 29,341; terrace 11,797; purpose-built flat/apartment 8,540; converted flat/apartment 1,493; bedsit 273; not stated 1,123).
[7] *Ibid*.

CITY EXPANSION OR CITY ECLIPSE?
[1] Census 1991. In 1991 the counties of Meath (105,370), Wicklow (97,265), Kildare (122,656), and Fingal (152,766) then had a combined population of 478,057. The population of the Dublin City Council area (then Dublin Corporation) was

1998Q3 164,076▲1.1%   **1998Q4** 169,662▲3.4%   **1999Q1** 182,295▲7.4%   **1999Q2** 186,987▲2.6%   **1999Q3** 200,022▲7.0%

478,389.

2 Census 1996.

3 Census 2002.

4 Census 2006. Fingal 239,992, Meath 162,831, Kildare 162,831, Wicklow 126,194.

5 Census 2002 and 2006. Between 2001 and 2006 the population of Dublin city increased by 10,430 or just 2.1%. The population increase within the city's Canal Ring was 10,084 or 10.8%.

6 Dublin City Council Development Plan 2011-2017, Issues, Paper 4: Population and Housing Strategy (2009).

7 Census 2006, Theme 6: 1(a) – Number of private households by type of accommodation. Dublin city 190,984; households, population 506,211.

8 In Chapter 8 – DENSITY REDISCOVERED – IN THE THICK OF IT, we explore in detail various density possibilities for Dublin city, including the potential source of these 1,200 hectares of developable land.

9 There are no exact internationally agreed definitions of what constitutes high, medium or low density of units per hectare. The DoEHLG *Guidelines on Sustainable Residential Development in Urban Areas* (Dublin, 2009), ch.5, p.49, does not state what may constitute a high density; it does, however, state that 'In general, minimum net densities of 50 dwellings per hectare, subject to appropriate design and amenity standards, should be applied within public transport corridors'.

10 ESRI projection that the Irish state population will grow from 4.24 million in 2006 to 5.1 million in 2021, *Demographic and Epidemiological Change in Ireland to 2021* (ESRI, 2009).

2 – MAPPING DIFFERENCE

THE ARC OF DISADVANTAGE OR ARC OF OPPORTUNITY?

1 Census 2006. The 'Arc of Disadvantage', as defined by the authors, covers fourteen inner-city electoral divisions. These electoral divisions are the smallest geographical unit at which small area population statistics (SAPS) data is freely available from the Census of Population of Ireland. The fourteen electoral divisions are: Arran Quay C, Inns Quay B, C, Mountjoy A, B, North City, Rotunda A, B, Merchants Quay A, B, C, F, and Ushers B, C. The population of these inner-city electoral divisions in 2006 was 43,000 people.

2 REDRAWING DUBLIN maps both Dublin's 'inner city' and 'city centre' in Mental MAPS, MUTATING GEOGRAPHIES (Chapter 3 – STREET DNA).

3 Census 2006, Theme 6: 3(a) – Number of permanent private households by type of occupancy, 2006. 7.3% of all private households in the Arc of Disadvantage own their homes outright (no outstanding mortgage), with a further 12.6% having an unfinished mortgage. This compares with an average of 26.1% and 29% respectively for the entire city.

4 Census 2006, Theme 6: 4(a) – Number of permanent private households by number of rooms in the household, 2006. 37.8% of all homes in the Arc of Disadvantage have one bedroom or less (maximum two-roomed homes). Just 11% of all homes in this area have five rooms or more. This compares with an average of 16.4% and 50.2% respectively for the entire city.

5 Dublin City Council Development Plan 2005-2011. Dublin City Council zones 2,579 hectares (25.5%) of all zoned land in the city Z9 or open space. The Council zones a total of 14.5 ha of the Arc of Disadvantage Z9 or open space. This equates to 3.5% of the total land area of the Arc of Disadvantage (413 ha).

6 NAMA (National Asset Management Agency) was set up by the Irish Government in 2009 as a direct response to State's banking crises. Its function is to manage the bad debts of Irish banks.

7 Census 2006, Theme 2: 2 – Usually resident population by nationality, 2006. The foreign-born population of the Arc of Disadvantage in 2006 was 15,556 (38.9%) of the local population. This compares with a figure of 73,989 (15.4%) for the entire city.

UNBORN STATES OF MIND AND PLACE

1 Homeless Agency and Planning & Economic Development Dept, Dublin City Council, 2010.

THE REGENERATION PARADOX

1 Economic Social Research Institute, esri.ie/irish_economy/. (GDP Growth, constant 2004 prices).

2 Census 2006, Theme 6: 2(a) – Number of private households by year built. The number of new homes built (occupied households) in the State between 1991 and 2006 was 497,303. The total number of private households in Ireland in 2006 was 1,462,296.

3 *Ibid.* The number of new homes (occupied households) built in Dublin city between 1991 and 2006 was 35,889. The total number of private households in the Dublin City Council area in 2006 was 190,711.

DESERT ISLAND RISKS OR BABY URBANISM

1 Fáilte Ireland Annual Tourism Facts: Attendances at popular visitor attractions in Ireland, 2009. The six include the Guinness Storehouse (no.1), Dublin Zoo (no.2), the Irish Museum of Art of Modern Art (no.6), St Patrick's Cathedral (no.8), the National Museum of Ireland – Decorative Arts & History at Collins Barracks (no.9) and Kilmainham Gaol (no.10).

REFUSED

1 Planning Register Reference, An Bord Pleanála PL29N.223556.

3 – STREET DNA

DUB-URBS – FINDING 'URBAN' DUBLIN

1 Census 2006. Our definition of Dublin's city centre (as opposed to Dublin's inner city) is mapped out in MENTAL MAPS, MUTATING GEOGRAPHIES in Chapter 3 – STREET DNA. Its area approximates to the electoral divisions of Royal Exchange B, a significant proportion of Mansion House B and North City, and a smaller proportion of Rotunda B, Wood Quay A, Royal Exchange A and St Kevins. We calculate the population of our 'city centre' at 8,300 people (based on a sub-analysis of each SAPS [small area population statistics]). This approximates to 1.6% of the population of the Dublin City Council area of 506,211.

2 Census 2006. For the purposes of analysis and comparison, our Greater Dublin

1999Q4 207,979▲4.0% **2000Q1** 205,753▼-1.1% **2000Q2** 225,753▲9.7% **2000Q3** 220,603▼-2.3% **2000Q4** 233,902▲6.0%

350

region is mapped out and discussed in CONTIGUOUS METROPOLITAN in Chapter 1 – BEYOND THE PALE. The population of our Contiguous Metropolitan is 1.25 million. With approx 8,300 living in Dublin city centre (as defined above), this works out at 0.66% or approx 1 in 150 people who live in the Dublin metropolitan region living in the city centre.

MENTAL MAPS, MUTATING GEOGRAPHIES

[1] The Central Area corresponds to those city-centre lands zoned Z5 in the Dublin City Council Development Plan, 2005-2011. The land-use zoning objective of Z5 is 'to consolidate and facilitate the development of the central area, and to identify, reinforce and strengthen and protect its civic design character and dignity'.

IS RANELAGH URBAN?

[1] Census 2006. 'Our Ranelagh' comprises the three local electoral divisions of Rathmines East A, Rathmines East D and Rathmines West B. The combined population is 10,252.

[2] *Ibid.* The density of population in Dublin city is 4,300 people per square kilometre. It should be noted, however, that fifteen electoral divisions in the city centre, accommodating 45,074 people, each have population densities greater than 10,000 people per square kilometre. Rotunda A has a density of 19,647 people per square kilometre.

[3] Census 2006, Theme 9: 2(b) – Households by socio-economic group of reference person. The proportion of residents of Rathmines East A, East D and West B who belong to 'Employers and Managers, Higher and Lower Professional' class is 48% compared to 30.5% for the city as whole. The proportion who belong to 'Manual Skilled, Semi-Skilled and Unskilled' is 9.5% compared to 22.8% for the rest of the city.

[4] Census 2006, Theme 11: 1 – Persons aged 5 years and over by means of travel to work, school or college. The proportion of 'our Ranelagh' residents who travel to work or school by foot is 38.7% compared to a citywide average of 27.4%.

[5] Census 2006, Theme 6: 4(a) – Number of permanent private households by number of rooms in the household. The number homes with two rooms or less is 34.8% compared to a city average of 15.2%.

[6] Census 2006, Theme 6: 1(a) – Number of private households by type of accommodation.

4 – 'TRUE DUBS' AND ADOPTED DUBLINERS

DUBLINERS

[1] Census 2006, Theme 2: 1 – Persons usually resident and present in the State on Census night, Nationalities in Dublin City and County, Nationality by usual residence in Dublin City and County. Figures for Dublin City Council area only.

DO FOREIGNERS LOVE DUBLIN MORE THAN THE IRISH?

[1] Census 2006, Theme 2: 1 – Persons usually resident and present in the State on Census Night, classified by place of birth. The population of Ireland in 2006 was 4,172,013, of which 14.7% were foreign-born. A total of 401,122 Irish-born residents of the State lived in Dublin City (out of a national population of

3,559,384), equating to 11.3%.

[2] *Ibid.* 14.1% of those who were born in the following nation states and living in Ireland reside in Dublin city. (Excluding British-born residents (266,147 persons), that figure rises to 19.8%, or 56,556 out of 285,772. Dublin city is defined as the functional area of Dublin City Council.) Australia, Austria, Belgium, Brazil, Canada, China, Cyprus, Czech Republic, Denmark, Estonia, Finland, France, Germany, Greece, Hungary, India, Italy. Latvia, Lithuania, Luxembourg, Malaysia, Malta, Netherlands, New Zealand, Nigeria, Pakistan, Philippines, Poland, Portugal, Romania, Russia, Slovakia, Slovenia, South Africa, Spain, Sweden, Ukraine, USA.

[3] *Ibid.* 5,558 of those born in China and who reside in Ireland (11,022) live in Dublin city. This equates to 50.4%.

[4] *Ibid.* 21,435 of those born in the United Kingdom and who reside in Ireland (266,147) live in Dublin city. This equates to 8.1%.

5 – ZONED OUT

ZONING UNCOVERED

[1] Dublin City Council Development Plan 2005-2011. The following are the land-use zoning categories employed by Dublin City Council:
Z1 – Residential (General)
Z2 – Residential (Conservation Areas)
Z3 – Neighbourhood Centres
Z4 – District Centres (incorporating Prime Urban Centres)
Z5 – City Centre (Mixed-Use)
Z6 – Employment/Enterprise (Light)
Z7 – Employment (Heavy)
Z7A – Employment (Heavy, excluding incinerator/waste to energy plant)
Z8 – Conservation Areas
Z9 – Amenity/Open Space Lands
Z10 – Inner Suburban (Mixed-Use)
Z11 – Waterways Protection
Z12 – Institutional Land (Future Development Potential)
Z13 – Housing Rejuvenation Areas
Z14 – Development and Regeneration Areas (including Framework Development Areas)
Z15 – Institutional Land (Long Term Institutional Use)

ZONING AND USES

[1] The total list of 'land uses' in the Dublin City Development Plan 2005-2011 are identified under each Zoning Objective, Chapter 14, 'Land-Use Zoning', pp.104-11.

Zs

[1] Dublin City Council Development Plan 2005-2011, Maps A to H. The size of each land-use zoning in hectares is as follows: Z1 – 3,829; Z2 – 663; Z3 – 50; Z4 – 186; Z5 – 231; Z6 – 695; Z7 – 308; Z7A – 3.4; Z8 – 86; Z9 – 2,579; Z10 – 40; Z11 – 120; Z12 – 183; Z13 – 57; Z14 – 301; Z15 – 767.

2001Q1 248,386▲6.2% **2001Q2** 250,268▲0.8% **2001Q3** 235,428▼-5.9% **2001Q4** 236,041▲0.3% **2002Q1** 240,402▲1.8%

351

GEORGIAN DUBLIN?

[1] Georgian architecture is traditionally understood to describe a historic period in the development of the city of Dublin, Ireland, from 1714 (the beginning of the reign of King George I of Great Britain and of Ireland) to the death in 1830 of King George IV. Our definition of 'Georgian architecture' is broad. It includes built fabric dating from as late as the 1860s. In his description of built fabric in Belgrave Square, Rathmines, Maurice Craig states 'nearly all this building, right down to the [eighteen] sixties and even later, is basically "Georgian" in character'. Maurice Craig, *Dublin 1660-1860: The Shaping of a City* (Dublin, 1952; Liberties Press, Dublin, 2006) p.325.

[2] Census 2006, Theme 1: 1 – Persons aged 18 and under by sex and single year of age and persons aged 19 and over by sex. Population of Dublin City Council area, 506,211.

[3] Census 2006, Theme 6: 2(a) – Number of permanent private households by year house built. A fifth of all homes in Dublin city were built between 1941 and 1960, 36,870 households out of a total of 190,711.

[4] Census 2006. Our definition of Dublin's city centre, as opposed to its inner city, is mapped out in MENTAL MAPS, MUTATING GEOGRAPHIES in Chapter 3 – STREET DNA. Its area approximates to the electoral divisions of Royal Exchange B, a significant proportion of Mansion House B and North City, and a smaller proportion of Rotunda B, Wood Quay A, Royal Exchange A and St Kevins. We calculate the population of our city centre at 8,300 people (based on a sub-analysis of each SAPS – small area population statistics). This approximates to 1.6% of the population of the Dublin City Council area of 506,211.

[5] Dublin City Development Plan 2005-2011, Section 14.4.8, Conservation Areas, Chapter 14. Dublin City Council zones 86 hectares (or 0.85% of all zoned land in the city) Z8. 'Lands zoned objective Z8 incorporate the main conservation areas in the city, primarily the Georgian squares. The aim is to protect the architectural design and overall setting of such areas.' Interestingly, the Dublin City Council Draft Development Plan 2011-2016 has renamed these 'Conservation Areas' 'Georgian Conservation Areas'. 88% of all land in the city is zoned. Only railways and roads are not.

[6] *Ibid.*, Section 14.4.5, Chapter 14 and Map E. Dublin City Council zones 231 hectares (or 2.3% of all zoned land in the city) Z5 or City Centre. 'The primary purpose of this use zone is to sustain life within the centre of the city through intensive mixed use development.'

[7] *Ibid.*, Section 14.4.2, Chapter 14. Dublin City Council zones 663 hectares (or 6.6% of all zoned land in the city) 'Residential Conservation Areas', zone Z2.

[8] Our overall figure of 3.8% estimate of 'Georgian Dublin' is derived from a detailed appraisal of the existing urban character of the city and incorporates the following estimated quantum of Georgian 'character' of each land-use zoning area. Our assumptions for the more relevant land-use zoning is as follows: lands zoned Z8 (Conservation Areas), 95%; lands zoned Z2 (Residential Conservation Areas), 20%. Most of the built fabric in these areas are, however, Victorian or Edwardian. Lands zoned Z5 (City Centre), 25%. A significant quantum of historic fabric in the city centre or Z5 is of Georgian origin. This figure varies enormously across Z5 lands. In Temple Bar and the Grafton Street area, the figure is significantly higher than the Smithfield, Bridgefoot or Docklands areas of the city. Lands zoned Z4 (Local Mixed-use Commercial Areas), 10%. These areas are predominantly non-Georgian suburban, but do include Camden Street, Dorset

Street and heart of Rathmines and Ranelagh. Lands zoned Z9 (Open Space) includes all four city Georgian squares. Our calculation approximates to 380 hectares or 3.8% of all zoned land within the functional territory of the Dublin City Council area. Our 380ha also include small fractions of Z1, Z6 and Z7 lands (Residential, Employment and Industrial). Note: Our calculations are based on the area percentage of zoned lands that are identifiable Georgian in 'character'. This includes a broad definition of built form and curtilage, gardens, yards and boundaries. It is not percentage site coverage of built fabric. As Z8 lands and Z5 lands are likely to have greater site coverage (built fabric as proportion of site area than most land use zonings), built Georgian fabric as a proportion of the city built fabric is likely to marginally higher. In addition, Georgian fabric is on average four-storey versus a predominantly two-storey suburban city. On the other hand, Z3- and Z4-zoned lands are overwhelming not Georgian in character, and have a relatively high built site coverage. The combined Z3 and Z4 lands at 236 ha is greater than Z5 and four times greater than Z8. Building heights in Z10, Z13, and Z14 (Regeneration Areas with little or no Georgian Fabric), with substantial site coverage, are on average higher than elsewhere in the city. Their combined zoned area is 398 ha. In addition, our zoned land calculation also deliberately excludes public roadway (14% of city land area), thus reducing 'Georgian' built fabric as a proportion of overall city land area as opposed to zoned land.

REDRAWING DUBLIN recognises the limitations of a geographic headcount of the proportion of Georgian built fabric, site curtilage and key city's Georgian squares in capturing the essence or extent of Georgian Dublin. The Liffey quays and bridges, the city's street pattern, its monuments the termination of vistas and views are all intrinsically indivisible from the historic Georgian character of the city. Our 'Georgian character' analysis is, nevertheless, a useful, thought-provoking tool to stimulate discussion, awareness and debate about what type of city Dublin truly is.

[9] Dublin City Development Plan 2005-2011. 37.9% (3,829 hectares) of all zoned land in Dublin city is zoned Z1 (Residential). These lands are almost exclusively made up of two-storey suburban housing developments. A further 6.5% (663 ha) of all zoned land is Z2 (predominantly two-storey redbrick dwellings). Excluding Z9 and Z11 (green open space and open water), Z12 and Z15 (green parkland of predominantly educational institutions), and Z7 and Z6 zoned lands (Industrial and Employment), these overwhelmingly one- and two-storey Z1 and Z2 housing areas make up 83% of all remaining built-up or developable zoned land. A total of 74.8% of all persons in the Dublin City Council area (those who stated what type of home they lived in) reside in a 'house or bungalow' as opposed to a 'flat or apartment' or 'bedsit'. Census 2006, Theme 6 – 1(b): Number of persons in private households by type of accommodation.

[10] Census 2006, Theme 1: 1 – Persons aged 18 and under by sex and single year of age and persons aged 19 and over by sex; Theme 6: 2(a) – Number of permanent private households by year house built. Dublin's South Georgian Core approximates to the ward of Mansion House B and includes St Stephen's Green, Merrion Square and Fitzwilliam Square.

HISTORICAL ARCHIPELAGO AND THE GEORGIAN ISLANDS

[1] Dublin City Council Development Plan 2005-2011. The objective of lands zoned Z8 is 'to protect the existing architectural and civic design character, to allow only for limited expansion consistent with the conservation objective'.

REPUBLIKA SUBURBIA AND MIXED-USE ENCLAVES

[1] Dublin City Council Development Plan 2005-2011. Z1-zoned land is Residential and occupies 3,829 hectares (ha) of the city. Z5-zoned lands is the city centre (Mixed-Use) zoning, and occupies 231 ha.

[2] Ibid., Z6-zoned land is mixed-use Employment / Enterprise and occupies 695 ha.

A GREEN URBAN STORY

[1] See endnote 1 under Chapter 2 – MAPPING DIFFERENCE – THE ARC OF DISADVANTAGE OR THE ARC OF OPPORTUNITY.

[2] Dublin City Council Development Plan 2005-2011. Dublin City Council zones 2,579 hectares (or 25.5% of all zoned land in the city) Z9 or open space. Dublin City Council zones 14.5 ha of the Arc of Disadvantage Z9 or open space. This equates to 3.5% of the total land area of the Arc of Disadvantage (413 ha).

[3] Census 2006. The population of the Arc of Disadvantage in 2006 was 42,997 people.

[4] The total land area of the Arc of Disadvantage is 413 hectares or 3.6% of the total functional land area of Dublin City Council (11,400 ha).

[5] Dublin City Council zones 14.5 hectares of the Arc of Disadvantage Z9 or open space. This equates to 0.5% of all Z9 Zoned land in Dublin City Council (2,579 hectares).

[6] The Canal Ring includes all electoral divisions within the Grand Canal and Royal Canal. These include in addition to those reference above in the Arc of Disadvantage the following: Arran Quay A, B, D, E, Inns Quay A, North Dock C, Mansion House A, B, Merchants Quay D, E, Royal Exchange A, B, St Kevins, South Dock, Ushers A, D, E, F, Wood Quay A, B. The population of the Canal Ring is 103,291. The total land area is 1,265 hectares. The density of population, 8,165 persons per sq kilometre. source: Census 2006.

[7] Census 2006. The 'southeast quadrant of the city (Dublin 2 and 4 inside the Canal Ring) includes the following electoral divisions: Mansion House A, B, Royal Exchange A, B, St Kevins, South Dock. The population of this area is 20,423. The total land area is 336 hectares.

[8] Dublin City Development Plan 2005-2011, Map E. Dublin City Council zones 14.5 hectares of the Arc of Disadvantage Z9 or open space. The North Inner City alone accommodates 20.7 ha of vacant or derelict land, see Why Are They Empty – A Photographic and Planning Guide to the Top 95 Underperforming, Derelict and Vacant Sites in Dublin's North Inner City (Planning and Economic Development Department, Dublin City Council, 2009).

POST-ZONISM?

[1] Dublin City Council Development Plan 2005-2011. Dublin City Council lists each land use under each zoning as either a 'permissible use' or 'open for consideration'. A 'permissible use' is defined as 'one which is generally acceptable in principle in the relevant zone, but which is subject to normal planning consideration, including policies and objectives outlined in the Plan'. An 'open for consideration' use is defined as 'one which may be permitted where the Planning Authority is satisfied that the proposed development would be compatible with the overall policies and objectives for the zone, would not have undesirable effects on the permitted uses, and would otherwise be consistent with the proper planning and sustainable development of the area'. If a land use does not appear under either, it is assumed that the specific use is not deemed acceptable in that zoning category. The Development Plan, however, states: 'Uses not listed in any of the categories in zones Z1, Z2, Z8, Z9 Z11 and Z15 are deemed not to be permissible uses in principle. Uses not specified in any of the above categories and located in the following zones will be dealt with on their merits: zones Z3, Z4 (including identified Prime Urban Centres), Z5, Z6, Z7, Z7A, Z10, Z12, Z13.'

6 – CHOKING URBANISM

INTRODUCING THE 'URBAN SUBURBAN HASSLE PARADOX' AND THE 'URBAN SUBURBAN HASSLE CALCULATOR'

[1] Tables 23 and 24, Perception survey on quality of life in European cities: analytical report, Flash Eurobarometer, European Commission, November 2009.

CREEPING GREEN

[1] Contrary to popular perceptions, more than 80% of the emissions associated with food are in the production phase. Transportation represents only 11% of food-production emissions, with delivery from producer to retailer only 4%, Steven D Levitt and Stephen J Dubner, SuperFreakonomics (Harper Collins, 2009) p.165. Christopher L Weber and H Scott Matthews, 'Food-Miles and the Relative Climate Impacts of Food Choices in the United States', Environmental Science and Technology, vol. 42, no. 10, April 2006.

[2] The study sponsored by Siemens AG and developed by The Economist Intelligence Unit ranked thirty major cities across Europe relative to one another in eight categories, with thirty underlying qualitative and quantitative indicators. Dublin was ranked 21st out of thirty European cities, with a score of 53.98. All of the other eleven north-west European capital cities surveyed were ranked higher. All eleven, in fact, made the made the top eleven rankings: Copenhagen (87.31), Stockholm (86.65), Oslo (83.98), Vienna (83.84), Amsterdam (83.03), Zurich (82.31), Helsinki (79.29), Berlin (79.01), Brussels (78.01), Paris (73.21), London (71.56). European Green City Index, Siemens, December 2009.

NOT SO GREAT? SUSTAINABLE HOUSING IN GREATER DUBLIN

[1] A Haunted Landscape: Housing and Ghost Estates in Post-Celtic Tiger Ireland, NIRSA Working Paper Series no.59 (NIRSA, NUI Maynooth, 2010) p.21. The excess housing supply for each local authority was calculated as follows: South Dublin 0.7%; Fingal 0.2%; Wicklow 1.9%; Meath 1.0%; Kildare 2.2%.

[2] Ibid., pp.23, 24, Table 2: A model of housing vacancy and potential oversupply in Ireland, column N 'potential oversupply': Dublin City Council 16,489; Dun Laoghaire-Rathdown 5,614; South Dublin 567; Fingal 205; Wicklow 914; Meath 610; Kildare 1,504. Column B 'total housing stock 2006 (Census)': Dublin City Council 223,098; Dun Laoghaire-Rathdown 77,508; South Dublin 87,484; Fingal 89,909; Wicklow 49,088; Meath 61,257; Kildare 68,840.

[3] Strategic Planning Guidelines for the Greater Dublin Area, 1999 (prepared for Dublin Corporation, Dun Laoghaire-Rathdown, Fingal, Kildare, Meath, South Dublin, Wicklow county councils and DoEHLG, in conjunction with Dublin Regional Authority Mid-East Regional Authority), p.117, Appendix 3: Population and Household Forecasts, Table A3.1: Population by County. Dublin City Council 509,655; Dun Laoghaire-Rathdown 201,648; South Dublin 235,992; Fingal

2003Q3 295,158 ▲ 2.0%   **2003Q4** 303,193 ▲ 2.7%   **2004Q1** 311,813 ▲ 2.8%   **2004Q2** 322,899 ▲ 3.6%   **2004Q3** 324,304 ▲ 0.4%

353

187,213; Wicklow 109,337; Meath 116,192; Kildare 150,772.

4 Census 2006.

5 *Strategic Planning Guidelines for the Greater Dublin Area, 1999*, op. cit. The 2006 local authority population (Census 2006) expressed as a percentage of the local authority population of the forecasted population in the Regional Planning Guidelines 1999 for the year 2006, Appendix 3, op. cit. The 2006 local authority population of Co Kildare and Co Meath expressed as a percentage of their local authority population in the Planning Guidelines strategy 'Option 1 Containment' is equally significant (Kildare 18.8%; Meath 20.4%). 'Option 1 Containment: This option seeks to confine the larger proportion of future development within an area that is relatively close to the existing built-up area of Dublin, extending from Balbriggan in the north through the Maynooth-Kilcock area in the west to Greystones in the south', Chapter 8, 'Strategic Options', p.72.

6 The relationship between housing construction, home size and statutory planning policy is clearly evident from below. The minimum floor area permissible for 1-bedroom apartments in the Dublin City Council Development Plan 1999-2004 was 38m². Critically, however, an apartment scheme (of any scale) was permissible, with 50% of all proposed residential units at this minimum size (Dublin City Council Development Plan 1999-2004). Thousands of such -bedroom units (mostly single-aspect) were built throughout the city. Prior to 1999 there were no Dublin City Council statutory minimum sizes for apartments. The City Council relied upon and interpreted Department of Environment guidelines. In the five contiguous wards of Mountjoy A, Mountjoy B, North City, Rotunda A and Rotunda B in Dublin's North Inner City, the proportion of 'Celtic Tiger homes' (the percentage of all homes built between 1991 and 2006 as a percentage of all homes, excluding not-stated) is 46.5%. This compared to a stated citywide average 20.6% (Census 2006, Theme 6: 2(a) – Number of permanent private households by year house built, 2006). A total of 2,785 (44.9%) of all the homes in this combined area have one bedroom or less. Just 8.2% of all homes in this area have five rooms or more, compared with an average of 50.2% for the entire city (Census 2006, Theme 6: 4(a) – Number of permanent private households by number of rooms in the household, 2006. The five contiguous wards of Mountjoy A, Mountjoy B, North City, Rotunda A and Rotunda B have a population of 17,882 persons.

HOW 'GREEN' IS YOUR CONSCIENCE?

1 'Carbon Footprint Calculator' (Carbon Footprint Ltd, Basingstoke, 2010). Our 'car footprint' assumes the following: a return flight to New York from Dublin generates 0.92 tonnes of carbon. All other things being equal, the difference in annual carbon output between each of the following alternative lifestyle choices is as follows: (A) A vegetarian versus those who eat red meat fish daily (0.42 carbon tonnes). (B) Those that only eat organic food only versus those who never eat organic food (0.03 carbon tonnes). (C) Those who predominantly grow all their own food versus those who are indifferent to the origins/air miles of the food they eat (0.09 carbon tonnes). (D) Those who food in season only versus those who are indifferent to eating food out of season (0.04 carbon tonnes). (E) Those who make considerable efforts at recycling waste versus those who do not (0.11 carbon tonnes). See 'Carbon Footprint Calculator', Carbon Footprint Ltd, 2010.

2 *Ibid*. Combining the difference in carbon output of the alternative spectrum of 'green' lifestyle choices of (A) to (E) above, the total annual difference is 0.69 carbon tonnes. The vehicle, assumption: Toyota Corolla 1.6 engine, year model 2005, travelling 4,000km per year would generate 0.77 tonnes of carbon annually.

3 *Ibid*. Vehicle, assumption: Toyota Corolla 1.6 engine, year model 2005, travelling 16,000km per year would generate 3.09 tonnes of carbon annually.

4 *Ibid*. All other things being equal, the difference in annual carbon output between those who predominantly grow all their own food versus those who are indifferent to the origins or air miles/kilometres of the food they eat (0.09 carbon tonnes).

5 *Ibid*. A long-distance commuter travelling on non-electrified train/light-rail system 30km daily to work (60km round trip – Dublin city to Naas) for eleven months of the year (48 weeks) would generate 0.88 tonnes of carbon annually.

7 – OPENING-UP SPACE

GARDEN CITY REVISITED

1 Our estimate of the total area of all private rear and front garden space in the Dublin city is derived from two independent methodologies. The first methodology utilises estimated average garden size and the number of private domestic houses in the city. The estimated average garden size is calculated using GIS analysis of various different housing and garden typologies (each given different weightings according to their frequency of occurrence across the city to calculate total city garden space). The census of population calculates 125,357 of all households live in detached, semi-detached and terrace houses (74.8% of all stated households live in houses as opposed to flats/apartments), Census 2006, Theme 6: 1(a) – Number of private households by type of accommodation. Utilising these two sets of data – 'proportion of zoned Z1 and Z2 devoted to garden space' and 'number of dwellings' – we estimate 3,054 hectares of private front and rear garden space in the city. The second methodology utilises land-use zoning data and calculated estimates of the average dwelling plot dedicated to the dwelling and the front and rear garden space. We estimate that on average (allowing for different housing typologies discussed above) those proportions are 20:20:60. 37.9% (3,829 ha) of all zoned land in Dublin city is zoned Z1 (Residential). These lands are almost exclusively made up of two-storey suburban housing developments. A further 6.5% (663 ha) of all zoned land is zoned Z2 (predominantly two-storey redbrick dwellings), Dublin City Development Plan 2005-2011. Deducting 15% from this figure (allowing for undeveloped Z1 lands and other lands dedicated to alternative uses on both Z1- and Z2- zoned land) generates 3,818 hectares of space occupied by private houses and gardens. Utilising these two sets of data – 'weighted garden size' and 'number of dwellings' – we estimate 3,054 hectares of private front and rear garden space in the city. This is 347 times the area of St Stephen's Green (8.8 hectares).

2 Dublin City Council Development Plan 2005-2011. Dublin City Council zones 2,579 hectares (or 25.5% of all zoned land in the city) Z9 or open space.

GARDEN REPUBLIC 'YOURS', 'THEIRS' AND 'OURS'

1 Dublin City Council Development Plan 2005-2011, Maps A to H. Our open space

2004Q4 329,447 ▲1.6% **2005Q1** 342,304 ▲3.9% **2005Q2** 346,683 ▲1.3% **2005Q3** 324,304 ▲1.3% **2005Q4** 351,263 ▲2.8%

354

calculations are as follows: 'Ours': land zoned Z9 (Green Open Space) 2,579km². 'Theirs': lands zoned Z12 (Institutional) 183 hectares and Z15, 767 ha. 'Yours', see endnote no. 1 above ('Garden City Revisited') for calculations on the estimate of private front and rear garden space in the Dublin City Council functional area.

CIÚNAS
[1] Roland Barthes, *L'empire des signes* (1970; Hill & Wang, New York, 1983)

8 – DENSITY REDISCOVERED

IN THE THICK OF IT
[1] Census 2006, Theme 1: 1 – Persons aged 18 and under by sex and single year of age and persons aged 19 and over by sex, 2006. Population of Dublin City Council area, 506,211.
[2] Department Estadistica, Adjuntament de Barcelona. Barcelona, municipal land area: 100.8km²; population (2007): 1,595,110; density of population: 15,825 persons per square kilometre. Six of Barcelona's urban districts have residential densities in excess of 20,000 people per square kilometre: Ciutat Vella, Eixample, Gràcia, Nou Barris, Sant Andreu and Sant Martí.
[3] The proportion of households living in apartments (97.4%), Urban Audit: How Cities Rank, Proportions of households living in apartments, EU27, 2001, www.urbanaudit.org.
[4] City of Copenhagen, Kobenhavns Kommune.
[5] Ville de Lyon, 'City of Lyon – Official website', www.lyon.fr/vdl/sections/en/.
[6] Dublin City Council Development Plan 2011-2017, Issues, Paper 4: Population and Housing Strategy (2009).
[7] All land in the city with the exception of roadways/pavement and railways are given a land-use zoning designation. This approximates to 88% of all land area. Canals and rivers are also zoned (Z11).
[8] Our 1,200 hectares of zoned land assumes the following additional percentage of each land-use zoning being made available for mixed-use, predominantly residential development (overall existing total zoned land area in hectares in brackets):
Z1 – 3% (3,829)
Z2 – 2% (663). These residential zonings are already built-up. The calculation excludes the possibility of extensive demolition and redevelopment of single-/two-storey housing estates.
Z3 – 5% (50)
Z4 – 20% (186). Local commercial, already built-up, limited capacity.
Z5 – 10% (231). City Centre, limited opportunity outside derelict/underperforming sites.
Z6 – 40% (695). Assumes significant opportunity in 'mixed-use' zone.
Z7 – 65% (308)
Z7A – 30% (3.4). Assumes significant proportion of industrial lands becoming available, including Guinness and Dublin Port lands.
Z8 – 2% (86). Conservation areas, severe constraints.
Z9 – 0% (2,579). Open space, no additional building capacity.
Z10 – 80% (40). Regeneration areas, extensive opportunity.

Z11 – 0% (120). Water/canal areas, no building capacity.
Z12 – 35% (183). Institutional lands, significant opportunity.
Z13 – 80% (57). Regeneration areas, extensive opportunity.
Z14 – 40% (301). Regeneration areas, significant remaining opportunity (primarily docklands).
Z15 – 35% (767). Institutional lands, significant opportunity.
[9] The 2008 estimated population of New York City was 8,363,710. The functional area of New York City is 789.4km² (New York City Dept of City Planning). The density of population, therefore, is 10,595 persons per square kilometre.
[10] The population of the Canal Ring is 103,291. The total land area is 1,265 hectares. The density of population, therefore, is 8,165 persons per square kilometre (Census 2006). The Canal Ring includes all electoral divisions within the Grand Canal and Royal Canal. These include the following: Arran Quay A, B, C, D, E, Inns Quay A, B, North Dock C, Mountjoy A, B, North City, Rotunda A, B, Mansion House A, B, Merchants Quay A, B, C, D, E, F, Royal Exchange A, B, St Kevins, South Dock, Ushers A, B, C, D, E, F, Wood Quay A, B.
[11] Population density of Manhattan.
[12] Population of Kowloon.
[13] Census 2006, Volume 3, Household Composition, Family units and fertility, 31 May 2007.
[14] Census 1991, 1996, 2006. The average household size in Dublin city has fallen from 2.99 in 1991 to 2.78 in 1996 to 2.51in 2006.
[15] Three electoral divisions in Dublin city have a density in excess of 16,000 people per square kilometre (Rotunda A, Wood Quay A and Merchants Quay). They have a combined population of 11,316 persons.
[16] The demographic projection estimates that the population will grow overall from 4.24 million in 2006 to 5.1 million in 2021, *Demographic and Epidemiological Change in Ireland to 2021* (ESRI, Dublin, 2009).
[17] Censu, 1991 and 2006. In 1991 the suburban or 'exurban' counties of Wicklow, Meath, Kildare and (the yet unborn) Fingal had a combined population 478,000 people. By 2006 the population of the 'exurb' counties had reached 713,000.
[18] Department Estadistica, Adjuntament de Barcelona. The six are Ciutat Vella, Eixample, Gràcia, Nou Barris, Sant Andreu and Sant Martí.

NEIGHBOURHOOD DENSITY
[1] Census 2006.
[2] *Ibid.*
[3] Dublin City Council Draft Development Plan 2011-2017 (July 2010), Section (17.3), Chapter 17, Development Standards, '100 units per hectare in inner city', 'outer city and suburban locations minimum densities of 50 units per hectare will generally be provided'.
[4] Dublin City Council Development Plan 2005-2011, Maps A to F.

DOES DENSITY MATTER IN STONEYBATTER?
[1] Census 2006. Our inner-urban Dublin neighbourhood is the dense housing area of Stoneybatter. It predominantly comprises the electoral division of Arran Quay E and a small area of Arran Quay D (the area bound by the North Circular Road, Manor Street, Arbour Hill and Devaney Gardens/St Bricins).
[2] Department Estadistica, Adjuntament de Barcelona. Barcelona, municipal land area: 100.8km²; population (2007): 1,595,110; density of population: 15,825

2006Q1 390,629 ▲8.1%   2006Q2 397,337 ▲1.7%   2006Q3 425,925 ▲7.2%   2006Q4 419,330 ▼-1.5%   2007Q1 417,800 ▼-0.4%

persons per square kilometre.

3 Census 2006. The density of housing units in Dublin City Council is 16.2 units per hectare. This masks considerable variations in density. Within the city's Canal Ring, the density is 31.4 units per hectare. In Arran Quay E it is 52.4 units per hectare. In Arran Quay D it is 41.6 units per hectare.

4 Census 2006, Theme 6: 3(a) – Number of permanent private households by type of occupancy, 2006. Electoral division Arran Quay E.

5 Ibid.

6 Census 2006, Theme 9: 2(b) – Households by socio-economic group of reference person, 2006. Electoral division Arran Quay E.

7 Census 2006, Theme 11: 1 – Persons aged 5 years and over by means of travel to work, school or college, 2006. Electoral division Arran Quay E.

8 Assuming an average of four bed spaces per home. The Dublin City Development Plan 2005-2011 requires 5m^2 to 8m^2 of open space per bed space.

9 The areas of Merrion Square and Fitzwilliam Square in Dublin are 4.75 and 1.3 hectares respectively.

10 The plot ratio of a development is the gross floor area of all built form divided by the total area of site. In this case, the area under study is 19.7 hecatres and the total built fabric area (including commercial) is estimated at 97,500m^2. The built area includes approx 1,300 homes with a calculated estimated average floor area of 70m^2. This generates a plot ratio of 0.5. Land zoned Z5 (City Centre) in the Dublin City Council Development Plan 2005-2011 allows for the maximum plot ratio. The indicative plot ratio on Z5 lands is (2.5-3.0). Stoneybatter is predominantly zoned Z2 (Residential). There is no indicative plot ratio on lands zoned Z2.

11 The Dublin City Council Draft Development Plan 2011-2016 aspires to densities of 135 units per hectare on inner-urban mixed-use residential sites. This is more than two-and-a-half times higher than this neighbourhood.

SIZE DOES MATTER

1 In December 2007 Dublin City Council approved to vary the Dublin City Development Plan 2005-2011, adding a new section 4.5.0 'Achieving Liveable Sustainable New Apartment Homes', 21, 22, 23, 24, 25 – and relevant site development standards (subsequently known as Variation 21). Variation 21 increased the minimum floor area of apartments from an existing 45m^2 (1-bedroom), 65m^2 (2-bedroom) and 80m^2 (3-bedroom), to 55m^2 (1-bedroom), 80-90m^2 (a range for 2-bedroom) and 100m^2 (3-bedroom).

2 The minimum floor area permissible for 1-bedroom apartments in the Dublin City Council Development Plan 1999-2004 was 38m^2. Critically, however, an apartment scheme (of any scale) was permissible with 50% of all proposed residential units at this minimum size. Thousands of such 1-bedroom units (mostly single-aspect) were built in the city centre (see no.4 below).

3 Dublin City Council Development Plan 2005-2011.

4 Census 2006, Theme 6: 4(a) – Number of permanent private households by number of rooms in the household, 2006. The five contiguous wards of Mountjoy A, Mountjoy B, North City, Rotunda A and Rotunda B have a population of 17,882 persons. A total of 2,785 (44.9%) of all homes in this combined area have one bedroom or less. Just 8.2% of all homes in this area have five rooms or more. This compares with an average of 50.2% for the entire city.

5 The demographic projection estimates that the population will grow overall from 4.24 million in 2006 to 5.1 million in 2021. Source Demographic and Epidemiological Change in Ireland to 2021 (ESRI, Dublin, 2009)

9 – BUILDING SIGHTS

A TALL STORY

1 Maximising the City's Potential – A Strategy for Intensification and Height (draft), (Dublin City Council, 2007). Maximising Intensification and Change – A Strategy for Dublin Building Height (DEGW for Dublin City Council, 2000). This study was commissioned by Dublin City Council to outline an approach to higher density and higher building in the city. It was incorporated into the Dublin City Development Plan 2005-2011.

2 The term 'high-rise' is defined by the Emporis Standards Committee as 'a multi-storey structure with at least twelve floors or 35 meters (115 feet) in height', Data Standards: High-rise building, ESN 18727 (Emporis Standards, 2009).

10 – GOING GLOBAL

WHAT'S UP WITH DUBLIN?

1 The Economist, 'The World in Figures, 2005'.

2 Mercer International Consulting, 'Quality of living global city rankings, 2005' survey.

3 The Economist, 'Pocket World in Figures, 2010'. Ireland had a score of 96.0, compared to Iceland and Norway 96.8 (joint 1st), Canada 96.7 (3rd), United States 95.0 (15th), UK 94.2 (21st). The Economist source for 2010 would appear to be derived from the 2006 United Nations Human Development Report.

4 United Nations Human Development Report, 2010. The first Human Development Report (1990) introduced a new way of measuring development by combining indicators of life expectancy, educational attainment and income into a composite human development index.

5 Mercer International Consulting, 'Quality of Living global city rankings, 2009' survey. Dublin scored 103.6 points. (New York is ranked 49th, and is the base city index with a score of 100.) Vienna tops the list with a score of 108.6. Mercer evaluates local living conditions in all the 420 cities it surveys worldwide. Living conditions are analysed according to 39 factors, grouped in ten categories:
- Political and social environment (political stability, crime, law enforcement, etc)
- Economic environment (currency exchange regulations, banking services, etc)
- Socio-cultural environment (censorship, limitations on personal freedom, etc)
- Health and sanitation (medical supplies and services, infectious diseases, sewage, waste disposal, air pollution, etc)
- Schools and education (standard and availability of international schools, etc)
- Public services and transportation (electricity, water, public transport, traffic congestion, etc)
- Recreation (restaurants, theatres, cinemas, sports and leisure, etc)
- Consumer goods (availability of food/daily consumption items, cars, etc)
- Housing (housing, household appliances, furniture, maintenance services, etc)
- Natural environment (climate, record of natural disasters)

2007Q2 426,900▲2.2% **2007Q3** 412,324▼-3.4% **2007Q4** 402,346▼-2.4% **2008Q1** 397,697▼-1.2% **2008Q2** 390,544▼-1.8%

[6] *The Economist*, 'Pocket World in Figures, 2010'. It would appear *The Economist* figures for city ranking are directly sourced from Mercer Consulting. The data are identical.

WHAT'S THE WEATHER LIKE?

[1] European Union, Urban Audit, *How Cities Rank*, Environment – 2001: Number of days it rains per year, Capital Cities).

[2] *Ibid.*, Environment – 2001: Average number of hours of sunshine per day, Capital Cities. (London 4.7 hours, Amsterdam 4.4 hours)

SUPERCITY

[1] 'Biggest City', *CIA World Fact Book*, www.cia.gov/library/publications/theworld-factbook/geos/br.html.

[2] 'Best City', Mercer Consulting, www.mercer.com/qualityofliving

[3] 'Richest City', *The world's richest cities by personal net earnings in 2009* (UBS Survey, 2009)

[4] 'Connected City', GaWC (Globalization and World Cities) Research Network, Loughborough University, UK, www.lboro.ac.uk/gawc/.

II – DELUSIONAL DUBLIN

DOMESTIC SPACE OF CITY DECISION-MAKERS

[1] In 2007, as part of the international collaborative project with the Fundación Metropoli (Madrid), Dublin City Council identified and invited 85 'key decision-makers' (those most likely to influence the future of Dublin city from fields as diverse as public service, law, business, the arts, media) to participate in research on 'Clusters of Excellence' in Dublin. A total of 59 of the 85 people identified agreed to participate. *Capital D, Proyecto Cities – Dublin City, 2008* (Fundación Metropoli, Madrid / Dublin City Council, 2008). We subsequently wrote to those 59 people and asked them three further simple questions: Where do you live? (Dublin postal code or town/townland); What type of home you live in? (apartment, detached house, semi-detached, terraced, mews, bedsit); and finally, How do you travel to work? (walk, cycle, motorbike, bus, Luas, DART, car). Of those 59 contacted, 45 replied (76%).

[2] Of those 45 who replied, fourteen (31%) live in a detached house; sixteen (36%) live in a semi-detached house; seven (16%) live in a Georgian, Victorian or Edwardian terrace; four (9%) live in other terrace; two (4%) live in a mews; and two (4%) live in apartments.

[3] *Annual Housing Statistics Bulletin, 2009* (DoEHLG) and Census 2006.

[4] Over 30% of Dubliners live in apartments or flats compared to just 4% of its decision-makers. Less than 5%, or just one in twenty, of all Dublin city homes is detached. Dublin City Council housing typology breakdown: total 190,711; detached 9,012; semi-detached 45,826; terrace 70,519; purpose-built flat/apartment 43,140; converted flat/apartment 11,189; bedsit 4,829; not stated 6,196.

[5] *Annual Housing Statistics Bulletin, 2009* (DoEHLG) and Census 2006.

TAPS AND THINGS IN DUBH LINN

[1] Met Éireann, the Irish Meteorological Service.

[2] European Union, Urban Audit – How Cities Rank, Environment, 2001: Number of days it rains per year, Capital Cities and Average number of hours of sunshine per day, Capital Cities.

[3] Siemens European Green City Index, December 2009. The study, sponsored by Siemens AG and developed by the Economist Intelligence Unit, ranked thirty major cities across Europe relative to one another in eight categories, with thirty underlying qualitative and quantitative indicators. Dublin was ranked sixteenth out of thirty European cities in terms of water sustainability. Amsterdam, a city of canals which obviously has a very special relationship to water, was ranked first. The 'green' criteria employed included total annual water consumption in cubic metres per head and the percentage of water lost in the water distribution system.

[4] The average annual consumption for Helsinki, Amsterdam, Berlin, Brussels, Paris, Vienna, Zürich and London was 74.8m³ compared to 128m³ for Dublin. Apparently only Scandinavian cities consume as much water per person as Dublin.

EXCURSIONS IN IDENTITY

[1] 'Open House' is an Irish Architectural Foundation-organised access tour of private and public buildings in Dublin city held over a weekend. 'Culture Night' is a Temple Bar Cultural Trust initiative facilitating free access to museums, cultural venues and events for one evening. Both 'Culture Night' and 'Open House' are annual events, usually held in late September or early October. The greater middle-class turnout on 'Culture Night' in Dublin is clearly evident in the following facts. Residents of postal code Dublin 10 (the overwhelmingly working-class neighbourhood of Ballyfermot) accounted for 1.6% of all 'Culture Night 2009 venue visitors' who are resident in the functional area of Dublin City Council. Ballyfermot residents make up 3.6% of Dublin City Council residents (population 18,414, small area statistics: Cherry Orchard A Carna, Cherry Orchard C, Decies, Drumfinn, Kylemore). Residents of postal codes Dublin 4, 6 and 6W (the predominately middle-class neighbourhoods of Ballsbridge, Sandymount, Rathgar, Ranelagh and Terenure) accounted for 30.6% of all 'Culture Night 2009 venue visitors' who are resident in the functional area of Dublin City Council. These residents make up 15.7% of Dublin City Council residents (population 79,347, small area statistics: Pembroke East B, C, D, E, Pembroke West A, B, C, Rathfarnham, Rathmines East A, B, C, D, Rathmines West A, B, C, D, E, F). Allowing for the population difference and assuming an equal interest or turnout between working-class Dublin 10 and middle-class Dublin 4, 6 and 6W, one would have expected to bump into one resident of D10 for every four residents of D4, 6 and 6W on Culture Night, whereas the reality was one resident of D10 for every nineteen residents of D4, 6 and 6W. (D4, 6, 6W and 10 can all reasonably be described as inner suburbs). See Temple Bar Cultural Trust, Dublin, Culture Night Survey 2009, Postcodes in Dublin.

[2] The GAA (Gaelic Athletic Association) is an 'amateur' Irish and international cultural and sporting organisation focused primarily on promoting Gaelic games, which include the traditional Irish sports of hurling, camogie, Gaelic football, handball and rounders. The GAA was founded in 1884.

[3] Nostalgic autobiographical Dublin novels by Éamonn Mac Thomáis, *Me Jewel and Darlin' Dublin* (O'Brien Press, Dublin, 1974) and *Gur Cake and Coal Blocks* (O'Brien Press, Dublin, 1976).

2008Q3 347,23 ▼ -11.1% **2008Q4** 329,62 ▼ -5.1%   **2009Q1** 290,402 ▼ -11.9% **2009Q2** 256,749 ▼ -11.6% **2009Q3** 250,081 ▼ -2.6%

Definitions

Urban 'Urban' is commonly defined as an area relating to or located in a city, displaying characteristics of city life. Urban areas are usually characterised by higher densities, higher building heights, and a greater diversity of land uses than found elsewhere in the wider city. Urban is a somewhat elastic term. Our urban Dublin is mapped out in Chapter 3 – STREET DNA. What we do not define spatially or functionally as urban is, by default – within the context of the boundaries of the Dublin City Council area – suburban.

Suburban A suburban area commonly refers to low and medium-density development patterns that surround the urban areas of a city. The suburbs are predominantly residential in character, with single-family detached, semi-detached and terraced houses being the primary use of land. Our suburban Dublin lies beyond our urban Dublin, and extends beyond the artificial administrative Dublin City Council boundary into the adjoining local authorities of Fingal, South Dublin and Dun Laoghaire-Rathdown.

'Exurban' 'Exurban' is a term used to describe those areas that are semi-rural, extending just beyond the fringes of the outer-city suburbs. It is a region made up of small towns and newly built housing estates, often separated by agricultural fields. Exurban areas have a strong functional relationship with the city core.

City Centre Our city centre is mapped out in Chapter 3 – STREET DNA. While the exact boundaries of our city centre are potentially fluid and necessarily subjective, our city centre is inherently urban. The density of both built form and pedestrian activity, the centrality of location, the diversity of uses, services and city attractions define the urbanity of the city centre.

Our city centre is what is commonly referred to in North America as the downtown or central business district. Dublin city centre is characterised by buildings predominantly four or five storeys in height. This is a mixed-use area, with retail, recreational, office and civic uses accounting for most of the existing land uses.

Despite the dynamism of daily pedestrian life, relative to the overall size of Dublin city's population, few people actually reside in the city centre. Dublin's city centre is generally a quality urban environment. Whist not without its challenges, this is a city centre that is visually engaging, socially dynamic, economically vibrant and, in places, exceptionally charming and beautiful.

Inner City Our inner city is mapped out in Chapter 3 – STREET DNA. Like the city centre, our inner-city boundaries are somewhat flexible; it is, however, a much more problematic place. Simultaneously revered by some as the authentic voice of Dublin, this is an urban space avoided, if at all possible, by most Dubliners.

Dublin's inner city is a peculiar place of contradictions. It is characterised by buildings predominantly four or five storeys in height, peppered by many two-storey and occasionally single-storey residential buildings. While retail, recreational, office and civic uses are not uncommon, residential development predominates. The inner city, despite fifteen years of a property and development boom, is also pocked with derelict sites and vacant buildings.

Whilst there is less dense pedestrian activity in the inner city than the city centre, the density of built form and centrality of location, the diversity of uses, services and significant tourist attractions combine to qualify the inner city as inherently urban.

Dublin's inner city is generally a poor-quality urban environment. Whist not without its attractions, many quite exceptional, it is visually and physically fractured, architecturally challenged, socially deprived, economically fragile and, in places, derelict, forlorn and edgy.

In Town 'In town' is a colloquial expression in Dublin. We interpret this space as including all of our city centre and parts of our inner city. 'In town', by our definition, is an exclusively urban place.

Metropolitan Region The Metropolitan Region includes the inner city and city centre, the inner and outer suburbs, extending to outlying exurban areas. Our Dublin Metropolitan Region (CONTIGUOUS METROPOLITAN, p24) has a population of 1.2 million and extends as far south as Kilcoole in Co Wicklow and as far west as Kilcock in Co Kildare.

Proto-Urban or Embryonic Urban 'Proto-urban' or 'embryonic urban' are used interchangeably and refer to an emerging quality residential urban way of life in parts of Dublin's inner city and city centre.

The City 'The city' is a broader term, and, depending on context of discussion, can refer to an area as small as Dublin's city centre or as large as the Dublin Metropolitan Region. It is a term usually employed in REDRAWING DUBLIN to refer to the inner city or city-centre core.

Dublin City 'Dublin city' is another broad term, and, depending on context, can refer to an area as small as Dublin's city centre or as large as the Dublin Metropolitan Region. It is a term usually employed in REDRAWING DUBLIN to refer to the functional area of Dublin City Council.

Dublin City Council Dublin City Council refers to the geographic functional municipal area of the local authority of Dublin City Council, home to 506,000 people.